CONFLICT
AND
TERRORISM
IN
SOUTHERN
THAILAND

Edited by Rohan Gunaratna,
Arabinda Acharya
and Sabrina Chua

Marshall Cavendish
Academic

© 2005 Marshall Cavendish International (Singapore) Private Limited
Published 2005 by Marshall Cavendish Academic
An imprint of Marshall Cavendish International (Singapore) Private Limited
A member of Times Publishing Limited

Times Centre, 1 New Industrial Road,
Singapore 536196
Tel:(65) 6213   9300
Fax: (65) 6288 9254
E-mail: mca@sg.marshallcavendish.com
Website: http://www.marshallcavendish.com/academic

First Printed 2005
Reprinted 2005(twice), 2006

ISBN-13: 978-981-210-444-1
ISBN-10: 981-210-444-5

A CIP catalogue record for this book is available from the National Library Board (Singapore).

Printed by Times Graphics Pte Ltd, Singapore
on non-acidic paper

London • New York • Beijing • Bangkok • Kuala Lumpur • Singapore

Contents

Acknowledgements   iv

Preface   v

Abbreviations   vii

Introduction   x

Chapter 1
History and Genealogy of the Conflict
A.   A Short History of the Conflict   1
B.   The Nature of the Southern Thai Insurgency   7
C.   Factors Catalytic to the Surging Violence in Southern Thailand   10

Chapter 2
Understanding the Threat
A.   Analysis of Major Incidents   22
B.   The Actors   32
C.   Religious Schools   46
D.   The Complex Interplay of Militancy and Religion   53
E.   Global Insurgent Links   59

Chapter 3
Strategy, Targets, and Tactics
A.   Strategies   77
B.   Targets   79
C.   Tactics and Weapons   80
D.   Government Response   83
E.   Escalation Potential   91

Conclusion
Responding to the Threat
A.   Key to Threat Management   102
B.   Key to Ending the Threat   110
C.   International and Regional Implications of a Domestic Insurgency   112

Appendixes   117-204

About the Editors   205

Index

Acknowledgements

We wish to express our gratitude to Mr. Barry Desker, Director, Institute of Defence and Strategic Studies in Singapore for his steadfast support to examining regional conflicts. His foresight in initiating a study to assess the threat and trajectory of regional conflicts in Singapore's immediate neighbourhood enabled us to visit and observe the conflict in southern Thailand in its formative phase.

We thank our colleagues Mr. Nicholas Seow, Mr. Amir Rana, Ms. Faizah Samat, *Ustaz* Muhammad Haniff bin Hassan, and *Ustaz* Hassan Abdoun Mohamed Ahmed for their assistance. We wish to thank two field researchers, Ms. Amporn Marddent of Mahidol University, as well as her assistant, who risked their lives to make this project a success. We are grateful to Dr. Andrew T. H. Tan, Dr. Joseph C. Y. Liow, and Mr. S. P. Harish for reading the manuscript and having made invaluable suggestions.

The views expressed in this book are that of the authors and do not reflect the official views of the Institute of Defence and Strategic Studies in Singapore.

Preface

Ethno-nationalist and politico-religious conflicts are the predominant forms of armed violence in many parts of the contemporary world. Human rights violations, internal displacements, flow of refugees, and formation of terrorists are rampant in these regional hot spots. Like Kashmir, Chechnya, Palestine, Mindanao in the Philippines, Algeria and Sri Lanka, the conflict in southern Thailand is not be an exception to this trend.

Unlike the Cold War era, regional conflicts today have profound international implications. Enhanced communication—flow of ideas, inexpensive travel, greater mobility of people, unregulated flow of finance, and a saturated arms market—have dramatically increased the globalisation of violence. With internal displacement and refugee flows, most armed conflicts assume regional and international dimensions. With time, most become intractable. Therefore, it is imperative to resolve conflict in its formative phase. The violence in southern Thailand is escalating rapidly. Unless the situation is stabilised early and normalcy restored, it will affect the entire region. For instance, Southeast Asian nationals (Singaporeans, Filipinos), Arabs (Saudis, Jordanians), and Westerners (Australians, Spaniards) participated in the conflicts in Ambon and Poso in Indonesia. Similarly, more than two dozen nationalities—including Muslims from southern Thailand—trained in the Moro Islamic Liberation Front (MILF)-run guerrilla and terrorist training camps in Mindanao, in the southern Philippines.

Managing cross-border conflicts are particularly difficult. The resolution of the conflict in Thailand rests neither in counter-terrorism nor in counter-insurgency. The right combination of measures—ranging from developing intelligence dominance, carrying out intelligence-led operations, forging a special relationship with Malaysia, co-opting the Muslim elites, and instituting good governance, particularly, farsighted leadership—is critical to manage and terminate the threat.

Our study on Thailand is not an exhaustive work on the country's south. It should be viewed as an initial attempt to survey the situation and propose measures to manage the threat. As the violence is escalating rapidly, we decided to make our preliminary findings known without further loss of time. Some of the recent government policies and practices developed to address the conflict in the south are contrary to the long-term national and strategic interests of Thailand. We have briefed the appropriate authorities in Thailand from time to time on the conflict trajectory.

Bangkok will have to invest substantially to stabilise the current and emerging situation in southern Thailand, before the threat escalates and affects the rest of the kingdom. The situation will not improve unless there is appreciable commitment at multiple levels of government to change the status quo. It is also necessary for the Thai elite and the informed public to understand the erosion of security in one part of the country and play a more proactive role in helping the government restore stability and peace in southern Thailand.

Although the government has the biggest responsibility to resolve the conflict in the south, the Muslim leaders throughout the country have significant leverage to contain the threat. A few power hungry Muslim political leaders in Thailand's south and Malaysia's north should not be allowed to mislead the Muslims of southern Thailand. It would be instructive to mention that "The Fight for the Liberation of Pattani" (*Berjihad di Pattani*), the blueprint for combat in southern Thailand, was authored not by a Muslim from southern Thailand but a Muslim from northern Malaysia. A group of Muslims in southern Thailand paid 2,000 ringgit to Issamul Yameena (alias Isamail Jaffar alias Pohsu) in Kelantan, Malaysia to write the manual. Issamul Yameena expressed his surprise to the Malaysian police when he was told that the insurgents that undertook no surrender missions on 28 April 2004 had pages from his manual strapped to their bodies. He requested the authorities for a copy of his own work as it had created such a momentum. He is neither a trained religious scholar nor a man of letters. Furthermore, Issamul Yameena earned his income by selling stones that he claimed were blessed. Our analyses of the manual authored by Issamul Yameena together with Abdul Wahab Data alias *Babor* Wahab of Thailand suggest that it had no religious foundation. It is essential for the true guardians of Islam in Thailand and Malaysia to ensure that their religion be preserved and protected, and not be hijacked by a few deviant groups. Without waiting and watching for the government to act, Muslim leaders particularly those living in the south should take on the grave challenge of fighting the ideologues and preachers of hate.

Abbreviations

ABIM	Islamic Youth Movement of Malaysia
ABREP	Angkatan Bersenjata Revolusi Patani
APEC	Asia-Pacific Economic Cooperation
ASEAN	Association of Southeast Asian Nations
ASG	Abu Sayyaf Group
BBMP	United Mujahideen Front of Pattani
BIPP	Islamic Liberation Front of Pattani
BNP	Mujahideen Pattani Movement
BNPP	Pattani National Liberation Front
BRN	Barisan Revolusi Nasional
CEO	Chief Operating Officer
COIN	Counter-insurgency
CPM 43	Civilian-Police-Military Task Force 43
CSOC	Communist Suppression Operations Command
CT	Counter-terrorism
CTIC	Counter Terrorism Intelligence Centre
FAA	Federally Administered Areas
FLN	Algerian National Liberation Front
FPI	Front Pembela Islam
GAM	Free Aceh Movement
GMIP	Gerakan Mujahideen Islam Pattani
HRCP	Human Rights Commission of Pakistan
HUJI	Harkat-ul-Jihad-al Islami
HUM	Harkat-ul-Mujahideen
ICC	Islamic Central Committee
ICPVTR	International Centre for Political Violence and Terrorism Research
IDB	Islamic Development Bank
IDSS	Institute of Defence and Strategic Studies
ISA	Internal Security Act
ISOC	Internal Suppression Operations Command
JD	Jamaatud Daawa
JEM	Jaish-e-Mohammad
JI	Jemaah Islamiyah
JUI	Jamiat Ulema-e-Islam
KMM	Kumpulan Mujahideen Malaysia

LEJ	Lashkar-e-Jhangvi
LET	Lashkar-e-Toiba
LTTE	Liberation Tigers of Tamil Eelam
MILF	Moro Islamic Liberation Front
MITGT	Malaysia-Indonesia-Thailand Growth Triangle
MMA	Mutahidda Majlis-e-Amal
NAMY	National Association of Muslim Youth
NESDB	National Economic and Social Development Board
NWFP	North-West Frontier Province
PAS	Parti Islam seMalaysia
Perkim	Malaysian Islamic Welfare Organisation
PLO	Palestinian Liberation Organisation
PRNS	National Revolutionary Party of South Thailand
PULA	Pattani United Liberation Army
PULO	Pattani United Liberation Organisation
PUSAKA	Pusat Persatuan Tadika Narathiwat
RF	Radio Frequency
RM	Rabitatul Mujahidin
SBPAC	Southern Border Provincial Administration Committee
SBPCC	Southern Border Provinces Coordination Centre
TJ	Tablighi Jamaat
TOT	Telephone Organisation of Thailand
TRT	Thai Rak Thai
UAQ	Umm al-Qura
UGB	Urban Guerrilla Brigade

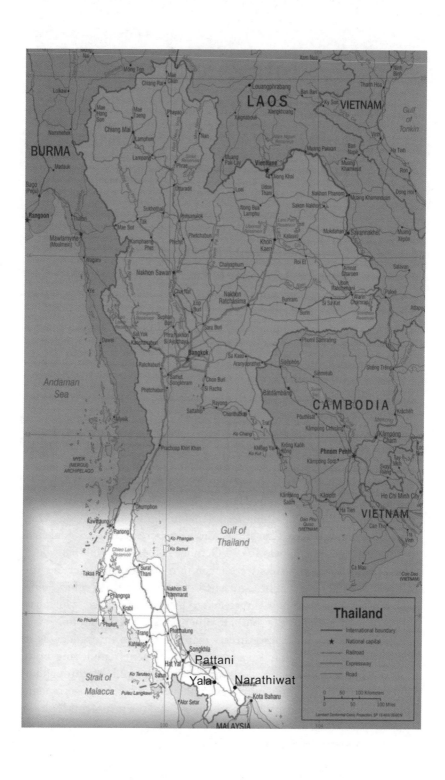

Introduction

Maybe in the near future and within the coming few seconds, we will start attacking the enemy lines. Are all your weapons prepared? ... If you have not prepared them, then seek for them. Prepare yourself also ... May the warrior blood continue to flow in our veins and strengthen our muscles to carry weapons into battlefields.

Our struggle is also for the liberation of our beloved country, one which is continuously under the occupation of heretic imperialists and their alliances. That is why we need the support and sacrifices from the believers.[1]

4 January 2004 marked the watershed in the continuing violence and counter-violence in southern Thailand. On that day, the relative calm in Thailand's southern provinces of Narathiwat, Pattani and Yala was rudely broken when in near simultaneous attacks, Muslim insurgents stormed a military camp and armoury in Narathiwat. The insurgents killed four guards and made off with 364 weapons. At the same time another group set fire to eighteen schools—sixteen in Narathiwat and two in Yala. The attacks were clearly well planned and coordinated. They were also the most daring that southern Thailand had seen in recent months.

Since then, the southern provinces have been in a cauldron. From January 2004 to the end of the year, more than 550 people have been killed in the simmering violence. Attacks have been carried out against almost everyone, but it is the security forces and government officials that are the insurgent's favoured targets. Thailand's security agencies have also responded in kind, killing insurgents in significant numbers. One notable instance where Thai authorities were perceived to have taken a particularly heavy hand was the 25 October 2004 riot in Tak Bai where about 78 Muslim protesters were taken into custody and later died of suffocation. That incident brought a new dimension to the conflict. Some separatist groups have now threatened to bring the violence, which has so far been localised to the south, to other parts of the kingdom.

Whether or not these threats materialise, the insurgency as it currently stands is a domestic one, with insurgents employing both guerrilla and terrorist tactics. This threat remains significant throughout 2005, despite the counter-measures implemented by the government. The existing terrorist capabilities are robust, and the insurgents look set to develop new skills. They have learned that to survive and succeed, they need to adapt to the government's security measures. Thus, despite intermittent government successes, the overall terrorist threat in southern Thailand looks set to grow and the violence is likely to escalate.

Contrary to other assessments, the insurgency in southern Thailand is at the formative phase. Although the insurgency dates from the late 1960s, it declined in the 1990s, due to lack of public support. The Thai authorities however did not take advantage of this opportunity to nip the problem in the bud, and the violence began to rear its ugly head again. The contemporary wave of violence began in 2001, but only escalated in the year 2004. The current Thai strategy of using the military to restore security and stability in the south is flawed and counter-productive. The government response throughout 2004 favoured the insurgents as it merely drove up ground support for the separatist cause and hence gravely damaged the long-term national security interests of Thailand. Not all is lost, however, as long as the Thai military refrains from overreacting to incidents such as Krue Se (28 April 2004) and Tak Bai (25 October 2004), the insurgency will remain manageable. If the basic principles of counter-terrorism (CT) and counter-insurgency (COIN) are applied, the government will be able to restore security in the immediate term (one to two years) and stability in the mid term (five years).

This book gives an assessment of the conflict in southern Thailand from the following perspectives: a short history of the conflict, an overview of the major groups operating in the south and their intra-regional and international connections, the role of religious schools, an analysis of the incidents as well as the strategies, tactics and targets employed, the probable escalation scenario, and recommendations for the management of the crisis. This analysis not only makes a prognosis of the conflict in the south, but also provides a series of policy prescriptions, which would be useful for security agencies and policy-makers in understanding the threat better and responding to it more effectively.

METHODOLOGY

This study is based on literature survey, interviews, and extensive field research in southern Thailand. We had access to key religious leaders and students in Islamic institutions as well as to the police, military, and intelligence agencies. The method of analysis used here employs the 'adversarial analysis matrix' used for threat assessments, especially in the context of asymmetric conflicts. This involves consideration of issues such as the *intention* and the *capabilities* of the adversary as well as the *opportunities* available to the insurgent to carry out attacks.

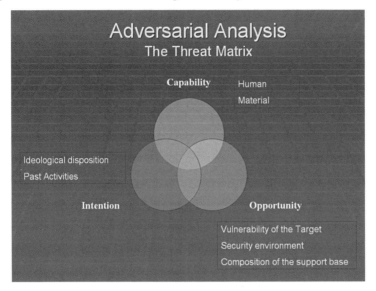

Intention is derived from the ideological disposition of the adversary and its past activities, while capability is a factor of human and material resources—trained personnel, the nature and the quality of armaments. etc.—at its disposal. The opportunity to conduct successful terrorist attacks depends upon the vulnerability of the target, the support base of the adversary as well as the overall security environment. This model is being used throughout the analysis to assess the potential of what is currently a predominantly localised conflict confined to three provinces of southern Thailand, to escalate into an international Islamic *jihad* with reverberations elsewhere in the kingdom including especially in Bangkok, and more worryingly, throughout the region.

NOTE

1   Taken from *Berjihad di Pattani* (The Fight for the Liberation of Pattani), a Yawi manual found on the bodies of some insurgents killed on the significant attack of 28 April 2004. A translation of the manual—done by the International Centre for Political Violence and Terrorism Research at the Institute of Defence and Strategic Studies—can be found in Appendix 1.

1

History and Genealogy of the Conflict

A SHORT HISTORY OF THE CONFLICT

Thailand is a Buddhist country with a strong central government functioning as a constitutional monarchy. It is the only country in Southeast Asia and one of the few in the third world that has never been colonised.[1] Known as Siam until 1939, a unified Thai kingdom was established in the mid-fourteenth century. The Thai population is predominantly Buddhist (95 per cent), with Muslims comprising 4.6 per cent of the population. The majority of the Muslim population is *Sunni* with a miniscule *Shi'a* minority. Geographically, the Muslim population has been concentrated in southern Thailand, particularly in Narathiwat, Yala, and Pattani, collectively known as the Southern Border Provinces.[2]

The three Southern Border Provinces now constitute the restive segments in southern Thailand. These provinces, together with Songkhla, Satun, and the northern Malay states of Kelantan, Terengganu, and northern Kedah, were all part of what was known as Patani Raya (Greater Patani[3]), a domain of the earlier Sultanate of Pattani, which was itself derived from the ancient kingdom of Langkasuka.[4] The population in the south consisted of settlers of Malay ethnicity, "with their own culture, their own religion, their own language and their own kingdom."[5] According to some sources, it was in the mid-thirteenth century that the kingdom adopted the name "Pattani" under the rule of Sultan Ismail Shah. After the fall of Malacca in 1511, the kingdom's stature as a major trading centre grew with Indian-Muslim traders competing vigorously with the kingdom of Sumatra in Aceh. In 1786, the forces of Rama I, the founder of the Chakri Dynasty in Siam (which continues to the present), invaded Pattani. Its ruler Sultan Muhammad was killed and the city was destroyed. Many Malays were taken to Bangkok as slaves. In 1791 and 1808, there were several rebellions against the central Thai rule which led to short periods of nominal independence in the southern provinces. The Thai Provincial Administration Act of May 1897 (Phraratchabanyat Laksana Pakkhrong Thongthi) was later enacted and effectively destroyed whatever remained of the southern states provincial independent existence. In 1902, Siam formally annexed Pattani. The seven provinces of Pattani—Pattani, Nong Chik, Saiburi, Yala, Yaring, Ra-ngae and Reman—came under the Boriween Chet Huamuang (Area of the Seven Provinces), which was placed under a centralised administrative structure governed by Siamese-appointed bureaucrats.[6] In 1906, the seven Malay provinces were brought even closer together under a single administrative unit called Monthon Pattani. Following the Anglo-Siamese Treaty of 1909, which recognised Siam's absolute suzerainty over Pattani, there have been systematic attempts to develop a mono-ethnic Buddhist Thai character, which was seen to be at odds with the Islamic identity in the provinces of the Pattani.[7] Thus even as the Malay Muslims in Pattani became a part of the Thai nation, they remained a self-conscious ethnic minority that is still culturally distinctive today.[8]

Islam in Pattani

In Thailand, the majority of the Muslims are ethnically Malay. Others are Thai Muslims (who are either hereditary Muslims, Muslims by marriage, or converts); Cham Muslims of Cambodian origin; West Asians; South Asians (including Tamils, Punjabis, and Bengalis); Indonesians (especially Javanese and Minangkabau); and Chinese Muslims.[9]

Southeast Asia's initial contact with Islam was through Arab traders in the region as early as eighth century CE.[10] Between the twelfth and fifteenth centuries, Islam spread extensively, with large numbers of people converting, including the king of Pattani, who declared an "Islamic kingdom" in 1457.[11] The Islamisation of Pattani replaced many elements of the Hindu-Buddhist culture, with Muslim religious elite dominating the kingdom's socio-political system. Islam in Thailand has been largely inclusive. Like Buddhism, it has become integrated with many beliefs and practices, which are not central to the Islamic faith.[12]

The Pattani Kingdom in south Thailand was known to be a major centre for Islamic learning, comparable to the prestigious Sultanate of Aceh itself.[13] It was then considered as the 'cradle of Islam' in Southeast Asia.[14] The Islamic teachings affirmed the traditional virtues and greatness of the kingdom of Pattani (*Patani Darussalam*), the identification with the Malay race and a religious orientation towards Islam.[15] The centralisation of the Thai state since the eighteenth century had brought the Pattani Kingdom under Buddhist influence, with controls exerted in taxation, education and through Thai-icising the local culture, language, and religion, with a reform orientation that sought to abolish backward customs and dialects and to enforce uniformity in social behaviour. The Education Act of 1921 forced Muslims to attend Siamese schools to receive a secular education. Muslim scholars were greatly undermined as Islamic schools were forced to close down. The act also saw the promotion of the Koran in the Thai language, an insult to Muslims, as it is not permissible in Islam to reproduce the Koran in any other language without its original Arabic text. There were also attempts at the integration of the southern Muslims into mainstream Thai Buddhist society.

Geographical Location

One of the primary reasons why Bangkok attempted to integrate the southern provinces into Thai culture has been a sense of vulnerability. As a result of the demographic surge of the Malay-Muslim population in the south, and the larger Indonesian Muslim population, the Thai state felt the grave need to integrate the north and the south of the country. This mentality is similar to the Sinhalese Buddhists in Sri Lanka, and their perceived siege complex. The Sinhalese, demographically overwhelmed by the Hindu-Tamils in Sri Lanka and India, suffered from a similar minority-majority complex.

Secondly, the proximity of the southern Muslims to the porous Malay border and the Malay-Thai dual citizenship has made cross-border movement extremely easy and hence difficult for authorities to monitor. The proximity of the northern Malay border states of Kelantan, Trengganu, and Kedah reinforces the ethnic affinity of the Malay Muslims with their Muslim brethren in southern Thailand.[16] Despite administrative separation, people on both sides share the same language, political culture, social structures, customs, and values, with a very high level of cross-border contact.[17] This explains how many southern insurgents get sanctuary and support from the population across the border.

The physical geographical delimitation between Thailand and Malaysia is overridden by prevailing historical, cultural, and ethnic

3

affinity of the Malayan Islamic civilisation of the region. The Malayan-Muslim civilisation is historically deep and has been fostered by the learning of Islam with its conservative and traditional leanings.[18] There is a dimension of nationality and geography in this equation. The Malay-Muslim population of southern Thailand has been integrated with the Thai state politically and in administrative terms, but their ethno-cultural and ethno-religious identity is with the Malay world and Malay civilisation and Islamic faith. Language is a point of contention as it is a symbol and identification of religion.[19] This inextricable linkage is one of the reasons why the southern Muslims are refusing to be integrated with the Thai mainstream.

Thai Political Dynamics and Muslim Separatism

One of the earliest manifestations of discontent against what the southern Muslims call 'Thai imperial dominance' was in 1903, when Pattani Malay aristocrat Tengku Abdul Kadir Qamaruddin revolted against Bangkok. However he was defeated and imprisoned. After another failed attempt in 1915, Tengku Abdul Kadir fled to Kelantan and attempted to regroup his forces with the help of its ruler, Sultan Muhammad IV. In response to the educational reforms imposed under the Education Act of 1921, Tengku Abdul Kadir launched one of the biggest campaigns against Bangkok. The education reform was seen as a deliberate and calculated attempt to erase Pattani-Malay identity and to convert the Pattani Malays to Buddhism.[20] However, the rebellion failed and many key leaders were either captured or killed.

In 1932, the military under General Phibun Songkhram, a right-wing nationalist, seized power in Thailand. This marked the beginning of the manifestation of the concept of popular sovereignty in Thai political space and Thai nationalism. In 1939, General Phibun's government introduced the *Thai Ratthaniyom* (Thai Customs Decree), which forced all Thai citizens including the minority groups to conform to a set of common cultural norms.[21] Muslims were prevented from adopting Muslim names or using the Malay dialect. The *Shari'ah* was replaced by Thai Buddhist laws of marriage and inheritance.[22] In some cases, Muslims were even forced to participate in the public worship of Buddhist idols, and men were required to wear western-style trousers.[23] This process challenged the ethno-cultural identity of the Muslims and led them to rebel against the central government. The community not only offered resistance but also 'threw up a new cadre of religious leaders'.[24] However the rebellion was harshly quelled. Many Pattani leaders were either killed or arrested and many of them fled to Malaysia.

During the Second World War, the Malay Muslims were on the side of the British while the Thais were supportive of the Japanese. Under the leadership of Tun Mahmud Mahyuddin and Haji Sulong Tohmeena, the president of the Islamic Religious Council, the Malay Muslims fought alongside the British, believing they had an agreement that the latter would grant independence to Pattani. The goals of Tun Mahmud and Haji Sulong however differed. The former favoured the re-establishment of the Pattani Sultanate, while Haji Sulong was for an Islamic republic in Pattani. In 1945, the Malay leaders under Tengku Abdul Jalal, petitioned the British to grant independence to four southern provinces from Thailand. However, the British reneged on their 'gentlemen's agreement', as for them, a unified Thai state was a strategic counterweight to the communist insurgency in China, Indochina, and Malaya. This marked the beginning of militant separatism in 1946.

Following the Second World War, Malay nationalism experienced a resurgence when the British granted equal citizenship status to non-Malays in British Malaya, leading to political independence.[25] Pattani Malays demanded integration with the Malay-dominated Malaysia, which was however not accepted by Britain and the United States, due to their concerns about the territorial integrity of Thailand. Though there was an attempt by the central Thai administration to be more conciliatory in the post-war period, centuries of marginalisation, suppression, state penetration of Muslim civil society, and the absence of political participation stood in the way of any meaningful cultural assimilation of the southern provinces with the rest of Thailand. A manifestation of virulent antagonism was the Dusun Nyiur incident of April 1948, in which an estimated 1,100 Muslims and 30 policemen were killed in violent clashes between Thai police and Pattani Muslims.[26] Haji Sulong, who led the rebellion was arrested and purportedly executed by the Phibun Songkhram administration. Insurgency, violence, and repression increased after the arrests.[27] In the 1960s, there was a massive transmigration of Thai-Buddhists from other parts of Thailand to the south. This relocation policy was meant to 'balance up' the racial and religious demography of the southern provinces. Under this policy, each migrating Thai-Buddhist family was to be granted landed property which was scarce in southern Thailand. By 1969, about 160,000 Buddhists had moved into the area.

The process of social and cultural assimilation was very much resented by ethnic Malays. Malaya Muslims decried this 'territorial invasion' as cultural colonisation by the central government.[28]

This led to the development of radical Muslim movements in southern Thailand with a number of groups such as the Barisan Revolusi Nasional (BRN) or the National Revolutionary Front, the Pattani United Liberation Front (PULO) and the New PULO at the forefront. The objectives of these groups were to establish an independent Islamic state in the three provinces of Pattani, Yala and Narathiwat. These groups were however different in their ideological orientation and did not foster any unity among themselves.[29] Their methods have been similar to the communist groups, indulging in political violence that included assassinations, abductions, terror attacks against the government, and extortion. According to some scholars, the Pattani resistance movements developed a more radical Islamist character following the Islamic revolution in Iran in 1979, with groups like the Pattani National Liberation Front (BNPP), moving closer to the global current of Islamist radicalism.[30] A few examples bear this out. In 1979, the BNPP upgraded its military training programme. In 1985, the more radical and insurgent elements of the BNPP broke away and formed the Barisan Bersatu Mujahideen Pattani (BBMP, United Mujahideen Front of Pattani) under the leadership of Wahyuddin Muhammad. In 1986, the BNPP renamed itself the Barisan Islam Pembebasan Pattani (BIPP, Islamic Liberation Front of Pattani) with a view to 'underline its stronger commitment to Islamist politics.'[31]

The successive Thai governments were able to contain the violence from the separatists using various methods. Between 1968 and 1975, Bangkok launched a series of military operations in the south codenamed 'Operation Ramkamhaeng' and the 'Special Anti-Terrorist Campaign' to destroy the networks of the Pattani liberation movements.[32] During the seven-year period there were 385 violent armed clashes between Thai security forces and Pattani insurgent groups resulting in the death of about 329 insurgents. A total of 1,208 persons were arrested and about 250 insurgent camps were destroyed.[33] The December 1975 killing of five Pattani youths by the Thai security forces sparked off anti-government rallies which spilled over to the neighbouring state of Kelantan, prompting the Parti Islam Se-Malaysia (PAS) to raise the issue in the Malaysian Parliament in favour of their co-religionists.[34] This was the beginning of cooperation between Muslims on both sides of the

6

border in which Thai Muslim activists found refuge and safe haven in Kelantan. The Thai-Malay dual citizenship also enables the insurgents to flee southern Thailand to escape the counter-terror efforts of the Thai security forces. However, there has also been cooperation between the authorities on both sides of the border. Thailand and Malaysia are both concerned about the rising incidence of Muslim terror and are keen on combating the threat. The bilateral security cooperation between Thailand and Malaysia envisaged the border monitoring of the two states.

The Thai government has also initiated a number of administrative and political initiatives for the socio-economic development of the provinces in southern Thailand. In 1981, the Prem Tinsulanond administration constituted the Southern Border Provincial Administration Committee (SBPAC, *sau-aor-bau-tau*), a special unit of the army, police, and Interior Ministry and the Civilian-Police-Military Task Force 43 (CPM 43), to oversee security in the region and to work as an advisory body to the policy-making establishment in Bangkok.[35] Economic and industrial development packages were also implemented to develop the south so as to eradicate poverty and backwardness. At the political level, democratisation was used as a means to allow the Malay-Muslim community to enter parliamentary democratic politics. It was hoped that this would in some way release the radical steam in their political agenda. The Democratic Party and the New Aspiration Party reinforced their presence in the south, incorporating several Malay-Muslim politicians and providing them with new public space in national politics.[36]

One of the thrusts of the economic development packages that the Thai government vigorously pushed was the tourism and entertainment industry that would attract foreign tourists and much needed revenue. Bangkok perceived that tourism would be the major catalyst in the economic transformation of the region. This would create new job opportunities and consequently lessen the deprivation and induce equality. However, the southern Muslims shunned the tourism and entertainment sector, considering them to be infidel and against Koranic precepts.[37]

THE NATURE OF THE SOUTHERN THAI INSURGENCY

Following the September 11 attacks on the World Trade Center and the Pentagon, which triggered an extraordinary response against

7

terrorism from the international community led by the United States, it has now become almost axiomatic to put all separatist/nationalist violence in any part of the world in one basket. Sweeping generalisations such as 'Al Qaeda spearheaded universal jihad',[38] 'Islam's inherent incompatibility with modernity',[39] 'moral and ideological crisis' that has beset 'the collective Muslim mind'[40] seek to explain conflicts that may have to do something more with the sociological, historical, and political contexts rather than abstract philosophies and radical ideologies. This has created debate among academics and analysts alike in placing conflicts in different parts of the world in proper contexts. According to Farish A. Noor, bracketing the separatist struggle in southern Thailand as fanaticism or terrorism is reflective of the Cold War era mindset 'when legitimate autonomy and freedom movements were criminalised and pathologised'. Noor insisted that the 'talk of "insurgent Islamist groups" and "war on terror"' should be exposed for what it is: a shallow and facile disguise for a divisive form of politics that has thus far torn apart Thai society, at the cost of the country and its neighbours.'[41] On the other hand, *Chularajamontri* Sawas Sumalayasak, the Muslim spiritual leader of Thailand does not concede the southern unrest a separatist status. 'Our nation has more than 63 million people with different languages and different cultures,' Sawas Sumalayasak contends. 'There is no need to talk about separatism just because of these differences.'[42] Both the arguments are on extreme ends and need to be put in the proper context.

In the Asia-Pacific, two aspects are particularly noteworthy in respect to the evolving Islamist threat. These are the increased cultural conservatism—focusing on the form rather than the substance of religious belief—and greater awareness of Islam's global identity. However, this does not explain the emergence of trans-national terrorist networks, nor the desire to establish exclusionist Islamic states in the region.[43] Furthermore, because of the heterogeneity of culture and religious traditions, Islam in Southeast Asia has adapted to modernity more easily than the orthodox Islam of the Middle East and of North Africa.[44] What is important here are the global linkages that homegrown groups have developed under the influence of the pan-Islamist ideology of the type being propagated by groups like Al Qaeda. The transfer of Al Qaeda's ideology and the Afghan combat experience to local insurgent organisations has raised the level of sophistication and the capacity for violence of these groups.[45] This has also led to the re-orientation and upgrading of local military training camps—Mindanao in the Philippines, Indonesia, Pakistan Occupied Kashmir, and Myanmar—and the increasing radicalisation of education in the religious schools, with radical readings of the *Koran* and with attempts to cloak political issues in extremist terminology.[46]

In Thailand, the Muslim separatist movement has so far not been driven by abstract or ideological rejection of modernity or 'the West', but rather developed as an opposition to Bangkok's attempts at assimilation.[47] It is not merely religious ideas per se, but the 'local, institutional, spatial and historical contexts of religious expression and interaction, conflict and reconciliation' that is driving the insurgents in southern Thailand.[48] Violence in southern Thailand predates Islamist revivalism in Iraq and the conflict in Afghanistan which, according to the predominant viewpoint, radicalised Islamist discourse in the later part of the twentieth century. This is evidenced in the December 1975 protests in Narathiwat which were the largest anti-government rallies in the history of the region.[49] Moreover, during the 1980s, separatist groups such as Pattani United Liberation Organisation (PULO) were largely secular. Many Muslim leaders from the south also assimilated successfully into the political mainstream through democratic processes, occupying key political positions such as Deputy Prime Minister, Speaker of the Thai Parliament, and ministers in the Ministry of the Interior and Foreign Affairs. The most distinguished of the high government officials was Surin Pitsuwan, who served as Foreign Minister from 1992 to 2001.[50]

The most recent example that the southern Thai insurgency does not fall into the global jihad phenomenon can be found in the booklet found on the bodies of some of the insurgents killed on 28 April 2004 entitled *Berjihad Di Pattani* (or, *The Fight for the Liberation of Pattani*). In it, the author sought to employ Islam primarily for the preservation of material possessions—wealth, freedom, peace, and security—and then religion.

> ... [E]very possession that belongs to an individual legally belongs to that individual. These include housing estates, material possessions, financial wealth, children and wives, country, and cultural traditions and the most important thing of all, is the religion. Thus, let us work together to protect all these, even if it costs us our life.[51]

This is quite unlike the rhetoric used by leaders of global jihadi movements such as Al Qaeda or even the Southeast Asian Jemaah

Islamiyah (JI). As can be ascertained by an analysis of this text, the movement is still largely separatist, devoid of the international jihadist ideology that is propagated by Al Qaeda.

FACTORS CATALYTIC TO THE SURGING VIOLENCE IN SOUTHERN THAILAND

Against this backdrop of assimilation and suppression, several factors have inflamed the conflict and hence led to a surge in the violence. These factors are the result of the Thai government's initiatives and policies that have directly or indirectly impacted the Muslims in the south.

National Assimilation and Communal Backlash

The roots of ethno-religious unrest in Thailand is much the same as with the rest of Southeast Asia. They are founded in the perceived insensitivity to local concerns, regional neglect, military repression, and forcible attempts to impose uniformity of language and social behaviour on entire communities.[52] Moreover, there has always been a clash between the cultural values of the dominant group and the religio-cultural identity of the subordinate one. In Southeast Asia, national identity is invariably defined in terms of 'the dominant group's values and culture, with other groups on the periphery tending to be left out.'[53] Domination, as Jack Snyder puts it, works if the power of the dominant group is so overwhelming as to preclude rational resistance or when it is tolerated by those who are deprived of power yet decide that being second-class citizens is better than being first-class rebels.[54] In an ethno-nationalist context, identity conflict and strife is the outcome if domination fails or is not tolerated by the minority community. According to Ernie Regehr, 'Identity conflicts emerge with intensity when a community, in response to unmet basic need for social and economic security, resolves to strengthen its collective influence and to struggle for political recognition.'[55]

In Thailand, attempts to evolve an integrated Thai polity with the unitary systems of Buddhist religion, Thai language and a uniform assimilative education that would nevertheless accommodate Islamic values, have become a measure of the reconstruction of national identity. Thai citizenship was unitary, revolving around the symbols of Buddhism and the monarchy. In Thai nationalist discourse, ethnicity is seen as a 'potential threat to national sovereignty',[56] which has been at the root of a historical sense of vulnerability among Siamese rulers.[57] This explains why the central political dispensation had been relentlessly attempting to assimilate the ethnic minorities in the south in a centralised power structure with Bangkok. Though this has never been directed at Muslims in southern Thailand exclusively, the Malay Muslims have perceived such policies as direct threats to the region's particular ethno-religious identity.[58] An example of the government's policy of forced assimilation and integration was the Patronage of Islam Act of May 1945. The Act envisaged the integration of the *ulama*, or religious scholars and leaders, into the government bureaucracy. The Act institutionalised the position of *Chularajamontri* as the spiritual leader of all Thai-Muslims and as the 'chief functionary of the Islamic religious system.' Appointed by the king, the *Chularajamontri* was adviser to the government in all Muslim affairs and head of the Central Islamic Committee, under the Ministry of the Interior. Subsequent legislations in 1947 and 1949 required each mosque to have a Mosque Council as the basic organisational unit of the Muslim community and to voluntarily register with the government. The Mosque Councils were placed under the *Chularajamontri*.[59] The system however was doomed to failure from the beginning as the Muslims perceived this centralisation as government interference in religious affairs. This also reflected a misunderstanding of the nature of Islam. For Muslims, 'Islam is not merely a religion but an entire identity—both religious and secular.'[60]

The methods employed by successive Thai governments in their zeal to modernise the south and evolve a market economy have involved the threat of force and violence, though financial inducements have also been offered. The administration has been pursuing what some analysts call the policy of 'check and rule' that entailed the crushing of dissent, even if it was moderate, and the reinforcement of the Buddhist unitary system on a predominantly Muslim populace in the south. Even though there had been occasional shifts towards a policy of 'rule by the local people', such attempts had ended more as rhetoric than as any long-lasting policy.[61] Consequently, the Thai-icisation process has been perceived to be hasty and brutal, stamping out local sentiments. The limited measures to evolve democratic means of articulation have been choked, leaving the southern Muslim insurgent groups with only the means of violence. The problem was also aggravated because the sensitivities of the Muslims were not met. In the field of education and language policies, there was a very deliberate attempt to dilute the ethnic salience of the Malay consciousness. The assimilation into the mainstream has not been voluntary and based on ownership of Thai nationhood, but one that was enforced. [62]

Counter-Productive Administrative Measures

The central government in Bangkok has been allocating large and regular resources for combating secessionism, as well as for development projects (a key plank of Thai administrations since 1975) in the south. However, the corruption of several local government officials and the mismanagement of resources earmarked for development projects have led to discontentment. The south has always been seen as a dumping ground for corrupt and/or incompetent civilian and military officials.[63] Added to that are the criminal elements present in the south, especially in urban areas, which are plagued by high levels of banditry and lawlessness. There have been illegal businesses and local mafia indulging in the narcotics trade competing for development project grants. Several local government officials have also connived with local mafia and criminals and have regularly resorted to murders, assassinations, abductions, and the like to suppress dissent. The result has been an incidence and increase of personal conflicts and crimes that have inflamed the volatile communal situation. In most cases, government officials, including personnel from security agencies, are intensely distrusted. As Thai Deputy Prime Minister Chaturon Chaisang himself admitted, 'People don't trust state officials. They aren't confident that they can be safely protected by state officers.'[64] Furthermore, Bangkok's failure to deliver the reforms and to deal with issues like local corruption, nepotism, brutality, and violence by its security forces has alienated vast segments in the south and turned them back to radical religio-politics as they did in the 1980s.[65]

Between March to April 2002, Prime Minister Thaksin Shinawatra overhauled the Southern Border Provinces Administrative Committee (SBPAC) and replaced it with the Southern Border Provinces Coordination Centre (SBPCC). This step marked the beginning of the end of good governance in the southern provinces. This was seen as another manifestation of the centralisation of power, police misadministration, and corruption.[66] Officials associated with the SBPAC claim that the committee was able to calm the southern unrest significantly by being responsive to and accommodating the region's unique security and social needs.[67] SBPAC served as an 'interface between Bangkok and local provincial administrations while acting as a watchdog on errant officialdom and liaising with local communities.'[68] It was successful in integrating the local Muslim population into the Thai mainstream. Similarly, the Civilian-Police-Military Taskforce 43 (CPM 43), under the Internal Suppression Operations Command (ISOC), coordinated different elements of the government and the military. '(It) maintained several very large and effective agent networks, which were tied into many of the Muslim and criminal communities located throughout the region.'[69] Dismantling of the SBPAC infrastructure, according to Panitan Wattanayagorn of Chulalongkorn University, 'created a conducive environment for the rise of a power struggle among many groups in the southern provinces.' It enabled organised crime gangs in connivance with corrupt local politicians to proliferate.[70] This has been further exacerbated by a centralised administration and the policies of exclusion as reflected in Bangkok's reluctance to engage Muslim leaders from the south.[71] This, as well as the lack of established and institutionalised outlets of expression, has made violence an appealing avenue of 'symbolic empowerment.'[72] Referring to the Thaksin administration, Islamic scholar Chaiwat Satha-Anand said, 'Thailand has never lived with a central power so strong, and this has created defiance' among the Muslims in the south.[73]

Ignorance and Insensitivity

The cardinal principle in the operations of counter-terrorism is sensitivity to the issues of discontent. It is a dismal fact that the events and incidents that have happened in the south and its recurrence reflect the absolute lack of sensitivity and understanding of local Muslim sentiment. Some analysts believe that the resurgence of violence is the result of government policies that have not only been insensitive to Muslim values, but also repressive and frequently irrelevant.[74] The prevalent attitude of the Thai local government officials and the security personnel has been one of ignorance of the southern Thai Muslim culture. In most instances, there have been manifestations of inherent bias and prejudice against the Muslims.[75] This has been complicated by the fact that the deployed officials and personnel are not properly trained to handle sensitive situations. The government's 'eye-for-eye' policy in responding to the violence and its lack of sensitivity towards Muslims has turned the traditional mistrust among the Muslims into hatred. For example, the Islamic Central Committee (ICC) of Thailand and three of its provincial affiliates distanced themselves from the administration, protesting against what they termed 'disgraceful' and 'un-Islamic raids' on schools, houses and mosques looking for suspects. As Ismail Abdureman, a member of a group of Thai businessmen living in Malaysia reflected, 'They have violated the sanctity of mosques and have searched schools as if the students were real criminals.'[76]

Relative Deprivation

One of the factors contributing to the simmering discontent in southern Thailand as well as other terror and conflict-prone regions has been economic deprivation. Most of the ethno-nationalist conflicts are rooted in 'the failure of governing structures to address fundamental needs, provide space for participation in decisions, and ensure an equitable distribution of resources and benefits.'[77] Thailand has been described by several economists as having experienced an uneven pattern of economic growth that has featured lopsided pockets of affluence and vast areas of deprivation.[78] The southern region is the least economically developed and ethnic Malays feel that they are discriminated against in terms of educational opportunities and government jobs.[79]

The Muslim provinces account for only 1.5 per cent of Thailand's gross domestic product. Nearly one-third of the southern population live under the poverty line. The south has virtually no industry.[80] The southern provinces are marked by fundamental aberrations like poverty, unemployment, lack of public infrastructure, lack of capital, uneven land ownership, low levels of living standards, lack of markets for agricultural products, environmental disasters, and flooding of the low-lying regions in nine districts of the three southern provinces.[81] There is a high income disparity between the centre and the southern provinces. For example, as in 2002, average monthly household income per capita was 28,239 baht (US$735) for Bangkok in contrast to 2,224 baht (US$58) in the Narathiwat. Unemployment has increased from 1.9 per cent in 1998 to 2.3 per cent in 2003 in the three provinces.[82] The southern provinces boast popular tourist spots, but the government controls a major share of the tourism sector and most of the revenues and job opportunities available in the sector are in the hands of non-Muslims.[83] There is now a fear that continued violence and the government's reactive policies could drive away future tourism and foreign investment opportunities to the area.[84] The thriving criminal-narcotics networks have preyed especially upon the unemployed, leading to the proliferation of drugs and drug-related crimes.[85] The financial assistance programmes offered by the government have been largely rejected by the locals due to inherent complexities and religious bias. For example, the educational support programmes for the Muslim students created a lot of resentment in the south when it was discovered that funds came from the Government Lottery Agency.[86]

Thai Foreign Policy

An interesting correlation to the surging violence is Thailand's foreign policy and its alignment with the United States and the West in the War on Terror. There are vital strategic reasons for Bangkok's US orientation. As Thai Prime Minister Thaksin Shinawatra puts it, the US is important to the kingdom not only in terms of security cooperation but also for trade. The US is the largest market for Thai products and the kingdom enjoys a trade surplus of 400 billion baht (about US$10 billion) with the superpower.[87] Thailand has hence been very supportive of America's efforts in the War on Terror, especially in Afghanistan, and has joined the other US allies in sending about 420 troops to Iraq. Moreover, in March 2003, ahead of the US invasion of Iraq, Bangkok expelled three Iraqi diplomats citing them as threats to its national security interests.[88] Justifying the support to the US on Iraq, the Thai Prime Minister said, 'Thailand and the US are allies. When the United States requests help from us, we respond. It is a gesture of hospitality.'[89]

The US has reciprocated Thailand's support by declaring the kingdom as a non-NATO ally, along with Pakistan and the Philippines. However, many Muslims in the south are not supportive of Bangkok's alliance with Washington in the War on Terror, especially its stand on Iraq. The handover of Riduan Isamuddin (alias Hambali), who was captured in Thailand in August 2003, to the US has also inflamed Muslim sensitivity. This is particularly so as many Muslims are sceptical about the Prime Minister's claim that Hambali used Thailand not only for safe haven but also to commit acts of terrorism.[90] Moreover, measures adopted by Thailand to combat terrorism especially after the September 11 incidents—People's Protection and Internal Security Act 2002 and the Executive Decree amending the Anti-Money Laundering Act 2003 to name a few—have been regarded not only as draconian and repressive, but also unnecessary. Many analysts contend that Bangkok adopted these measures under pressure from the Bush administration.[91]

Similarly, in June 2003, Bangkok signed an impunity agreement with the US, which is against its obligations as a signatory to the Rome Statute of the International Criminal Court. The latter purports to impose obligations to punish the perpetrators of human rights abuses, genocides, war crimes, and crimes against humanity. The impunity agreement provides that 'Thailand will refuse to surrender US nationals accused of genocide, crimes against humanity and war crimes to the International Criminal Court if requested to do so.'[92] Critics of the government argue that Bangkok joined Washington's initiative to undermine the International Criminal Court as its provisions could expose its police and security forces to prosecution. According to some, this is another instance of Bangkok's Washington courtship and the Thai government's support and encouragement of tough measures, which is a trademark of its security forces.[93]

NOTES

1   While the entire Southeast Asian region has been colonised by the British, French, Dutch, and Portuguese colonial empires, Thailand has remained a strong monarchical state. It withstood the turbulence of the events of the neighbourhood and has not been subject to the imperial intervention of the colonial powers.

2   See the analysis of Clive Christie, *A Modern History of Southeast Asia: Decolonization, Nationalism and Separatism* (London: Tauris Academic Studies, 1996).

3   'Pattani' is the anglicised spelling whereas 'Patani' is how it is written in Malay. This book will use 'Pattani' except when referring to the ancient kingdom of Patani Darrussalam.

4   Jan M Pluvier, *Historical Atlas of Southeast Asia* (Leiden, New York and Koln: E. J. Brill, 1995), 11.

5   Grandson of Haji Sulong, 'Colonisation reason for southern Thai conflict', *Malaysiakini*, 9 November 2004, available at http://www.malaysiakini.com/letters/31339.

6   Ibid.

7   Syed Serajul Islam, 'The Islamic Independence Movements in Pattani of Thailand and Mindanao of the Philippines', *Asian Survey* vol. 38 (May 1982): 441–56.

8   Geoffrey M. White and Chavivun Prachubmah, 'The Cognitive Organization of Ethnic Images', *Ethos* vol. 11, no. 1/2 (Spring–Summer 1983): 9.

9   'Thailand Islamic Insurgency', GlobalSecurity.org, available at http://www.globalsecurity.org/military/world/war/thailand2.htm.

10   Islam, 'The Islamic Independence Movements'.

11   Ibid.

12   'Thailand Islamic Insurgency', GlobalSecurity.org.

13   Christie, 'A Modern History of Southeast Asia', 174.

14   Carlo Bonura Jr., 'Location and the Dilemmas of Muslim Political Community in Southern Thailand' (paper presented at the First Inter-Dialogue Conference on Southern Thailand, University of Washington, Seattle, 13–15 June 2002), 15, available at http://mis-pattani.pn.psu.ac.th/registra/grade/temp/speech/Bonura/Bonura's%20paper%20(panel%2016).html.

15   Connor Bailey and John Miksic, 'The Country of Patani in the Period of Re-Awakening: A Chapter from Ibrahim Syukri's Serjarah Kerajaan Melayu Patani', in *The Muslims in Thailand, Volume II: Politics of the Malay-Speaking South*, ed. Andrew Forbes (Bihar: Centre for South East Asian Studies, 1989), 151.

16   Peter Chalk, 'Separatism and Southeast Asia: The Islamic Factor in Southern Thailand, Mindanao, and Aceh', *Studies in Conflict and Terrorism* vol. 24 (July 2001): 241–269.

17   W. K. Che Man, *Muslim Separatism: The Moros of Southern Philippines and the Malays of Southern Thailand* (Ateneo de Manila University Press: Manila, 1990).

18   Peter Chalk, 'Insurgent Separatism in Southern Thailand', in *Islam in Asia: Changing Political Realities*, eds. Jason F. Isaacson and Colin Rubenstien (New Brunswick (US) and London (UK): Transaction Publishers, 2002), 166.

19   Moshe Yegar, *Between Integration and Secession: The Muslim Communities of the Southern Philippines, Southern Thailand, and Western Burma/Myanmar* (Lanham, Maryland: Lexington Books, 2003), 131.

20   Che Man, *Muslim Separatism*, 63–64.

21   Ibid.

22   Andrew D. W. Forbes, 'Thailand's Muslim Minorities: Assimilation, Secession, or Coexistence?', *Asian Survey* vol. 22 (November 1982): 1056–73

23   Che Man, *Muslim Separatism*, 65.

24   Pasuk Phongpaichit and Chris Baker, *Thailand: Economy and Politics* (Kuala Lumpur: Oxford University Press, 1995), 271. For more information on the Muslim leaders and organisations, see Areepen Uttrasin, *The Local Administration of the Special Area of the Five Provinces in the South of Thailand* (in Thai, unpublished, the Partial Fulfilment Report for the High Certificate, King Prajadhipok's Institute, 2002), 3–4.

25   See Omar Farouk Bajunid, 'The Historical and Transnational Dimensions of Malay-Muslim Separatism in Southern Thailand', in *Armed Separati*

in Southern Thailand, eds. Lim Joo Jock and Vani S. Aldershot (Singapore: Institute of Southeast Asian Studies, 1984), 234–60.

26 Islam, 'The Islamic Independence Movements'.

27 Pasuk and Baker, *Thailand: Economy and Politics*, 270–71.

28 Yegar, *Between Integration and Secession*, 125.

29 See the analysis of R. J. May, 'The Religious Factors in Three Minority Movements', *Contemporary South East Asia* vol.13, no. 4 (1992): 403–4; Chalk, 'Separatism and Southeast Asia'; and Dan Bristow, 'Porous Borders Aids Muslim Insurgency', *Jane's Intelligence Review Pointer* 005/003 (March 1998).

30 Farish A. Noor, 'The Killings in Southern Thailand: A Long History of Persecution Unrecorded', *Just International*, 15 May 2004, available http://www.just-international.org/article_print.cfm?newsid=20000634.

31 Ibid.

32 Ibid.

33 Ibid.

34 Ibid.

35 See Surat Horachaikul, 'The Far South of Thailand in the Era of the American Empire, 9/11 Version, and Thaksin's "Cash and Gung-ho" Premiership' (paper presented at MSRC-KAF Intercultural Discourse Series, Dealing with Terrorism Today: Lessons from the Malaysian Experience, Kuala Lumpur, 23 July 2004).

36 Ibrahim Syukri, 'Sejarah Kerajaan Melayu Patani', in *The Muslims in Thailand, Volume II: Politics of the Malay Speaking South*, ed. Andrew Forbes (Bihar: Centre for Southeast Asian Studies, 1989), 151

37 See the analysis of Joseph Liow, 'Bangkok's Southern Discomfort: Violence and Response in Southern Thailand', *IDSS Commentaries* 14/2004 (May 2004).

38 Peter Chalk, 'Al Qaeda and Its Links to Terrorist Groups in Asia', in (eds) *The New Terrorism: Anatomy, Trends and Counter-Strategies*, eds. Andrew Tan and Kumar Ramakrishna (Singapore: Eastern Universities Press, 2002), 109.

39 See Fareed Zakaria, 'The Return of History: What September 11 Hath Wrought' in *How Did This Happen?*, eds. James F. Hoge and Giden Rose (New York: Public Affairs, 2001); Timur Kuran, 'The Religious Undercurrents of Muslim Economic Grievances', *Social Science Research Council*, available at http://www.ssrc.org/sept11/essays/kuran.htm; and Karim Raslan, 'Now a Historic Chance to Welcome Muslims into the System', *International Herald Tribune*, 27 November 2001, available at http://www.asiasource.org/asip/raslan.cfm.

40 See Farish A. Noor, *New Voices of Islam* (Leiden: Institute for the Study of Islam in the Modern World, 2002).

41 Noor, 'The Killings in Southern Thailand'.

42 'Unrest in the South; Muslims pledge loyalty to King', *Nation*, 16 February 2004.

43 Barry Desker, 'Islam and Society in South-East Asia After 11 September', *Australian Journal of International Affairs*, vol. 56, no.3 (2002): 385.

44   Alfonso T. Yuchengco, "Southeast Asia Awakens to the Terrorist Threat", *Issues and Insights – Pacific Forum CSIS*, no. 1-03 (January 2003):, 1, available at http://www.csis.org/pacfor/issues/v03n01_pdf.pdf.

45   Barry Desker, 'The Jemaah Islamiyah Phenomenon in Singapore', *Contemporary Southeast Asia* 25:3 (2003): 495.

46   Ibid.

47   Joseph C. Y. Liow, 'Violence and the Long Road to Reconciliation in Southern Thailand' (paper presented at the Conference on Religion and Conflict in Asia: Disrupting Violence, Arizona State University, 14–15 October 2004).

48   Thomas Scheffler, introduction to *Religion between Violence and Reconciliation*, ed. Thomas Scheffler (Beirut: Orient-Institut der Deutschen Morgenländischen Gesellschaft, 2002), 13–14.

49   Noor, 'The Killings in Southern Thailand'.

50   Peter Searle, 'Ethno-Religious Conflicts: Rise or Decline? Recent Developments in Southeast Asia', *Contemporary Southeast Asia* vol. 24, no. 1 (April 2004): 78.

51   ICPVTR, IDSS, trans., *Berjihad di Pattani* (The Fight for the Liberation of Pattani), 2004.

52   Chalk, 'Separatism and Southeast Asia'.

53   See Andrew Tan, 'Armed Muslim Separatist Rebellion in Southeast Asia: Persistence, Prospects, and Implications', *Studies in Conflict and Terrorism* vol. 23 (October–December 2000): 267—88.

54   Jack Snyder, *From Voting to Violence: Democratization and Nationalist Conflict*, (New York: W. W. Norton & Company, 2000), 322–3.

55   Cited in Linda J. True, 'Balancing Minorities: A Study of Southern Thailand' (*SAIS Working Paper Series*, Working Paper No. WP/02/04, May 2004).

56   Saroja Dorairajoo, 'Violence in the South of Thailand', *Inter-Asia Cultural Studies* vol. 5, issue 3 (December 2004): 465–72

57   See Thongchai Winichakul, *Siam Mapped: A History of the Geo-Body of a Nation*, (Chiang Mai: Silkworm Books, 1994).

58   Thailand Ministry of Foreign Affairs, 'Thai Muslims' (Bangkok, 1979) 5–6; Muthiah Alagappa, *The National Security of Developing States: Lessons from Thailand* (Massachusetts: AcornHouse, 1987), 204–07.

59   Yegar, *Between Integration and Secession*, 95–96.

60   Ibid., 130.

61   Arong Suthasasna, 'Muslim Minority in the Context of Thai Politics', *Warasan Sangkhomsat* (Journal of Social Science), vol. 31, issue 1, (July–December 2000): 82.

62   See the analysis of Uttrasin, *The Local Administration of the Special Area*.

63   'Thailand Islamic Insurgency', GlobalSecurity.org.

64   'Southern plan needs more local participation: Chaturon', *Business Day Newspaper*, 30 March 2004.

65   Noor, 'The Killings in Southern Thailand'.

66   'Thai Opposition Leader Slams Government's Scrapping of Previous Mechanisms in South', *Nation*, 18 July 2002.

67   See Horachaikul, 'The Far South of Thailand in the Era of the American Empire'.

68   Anthony Davis, 'Thailand Confronts Separatist Violence in Its Muslim South', *Jane's Intelligence Review*, 1 March 2004.

69   'Primer: Muslim Separatism in Southern Thailand', Virtual Information Center, 22 July 2002, available at www.vic-info.org/Regionstop.nsf/0/ e42514a843d9a3260a256c05006c2d84?

70   'Latest Violence Highlights Tense Relations between Bangkok, Muslim South', channelnewsasia.com, 11 January 2004, available at http:// www.channelnewsasia.com/stories/afp_asiapacific/view/65764/1/.html.

71   'PM Brushes Off Muslim Leaders' Call', *Nation*, 10 February 2004.

72   Mark Juergensmeyer, 'Holy Orders: Religious Opposition to Modern States', *Harvard International Review* vol. XXV, no. 4 (Winter 2004): 36.

73   'Latest Violence Highlights Tense Relations between Bangkok, Muslim South', channelnewsasia.com.

74   Ibid.

75   Uttrasin, *The Local Administration of the Special Area*, 6.

76   Kazi Mahmood, 'Poverty Grips Muslims in Southern Thailand', *Islam Online*, 12 February 2004, available at http://www.islamonline.net/English/ News/2004-02/12/article04.shtml.

77   John Paul Lederach, *Building Peace – Sustainable Reconciliation in Divided Societies*, (Washington DC: United States Institute of Peace Press, 1997), 8.

78   A comprehensive analysis of Thai economic development and its social and ethnic tensions can be found in Michael Parnwell, *Uneven Development in Thailand* (Sydney: Aldershot, 1996).

79   Dana R. Dillon, 'Insurgency in Thailand: The U.S. Should Support the Government', *The Heritage Foundation, Executive Memorandum* #936 (10 June 2004), available at http://www.heritage.org/Research/ AsiaandthePacific/em936.cfm.

80   Daniel Lovering, 'Bloodshed in Thailand's Restive Muslim South Follows Decades-Old Struggle', *Associated Press*, 28 April 2004.

81   See Prinya Udomsap et al., *The Findings to Understand Fundamental Problems in Pattani, Yala and Narathiwat* (in Thai) (Bangkok: National Research Council of Thailand, 2002), 62–66.

82   NSO (National Statistics Office), 'Statistics of Household Income and Expenditure and Their Distribution' (2002), available at www.nso.go.th/ eng/pub/keystat/key03/key.pdf.

83   Mahmood, 'Poverty Grips Muslims In Southern Thailand'.

84   'Thailand Islamic Insurgency', GlobalSecurity.org.

85   Uttrasin, *The Local Administration of the Special Area*, 5–6.

86   Surin Pitsuwan, 'Abode of Peace', *Worldview Magazine* vol. 17, no. 2 (Jun–Aug 2004): 3.

87   'Legality of the Thai-US initiatives questioned', *Nation*, 26 October 2003, available at http://www.nationmultimedia.com/specials/THAIinIraq/index_oct26.php.

88   'Thailand expels Iraqi diplomats', *Reuters*, 19 March 2003, available at http://www.iol.co.za/index.php?sf=2813&art_id=qw10480546838B262&click_id=2813&set_id=1.

89   Richard S. Ehrlich, 'Thailand takes "hospitable" action on Iraq', *Asia Times*, 1 October 2003, available at http://www.atimes.com/atimes/Southeast_Asia/EJ01Ae06.html.

90   'Thailand PM: Hambali Was Plotting', *CBS News*, 16 August 2003, available at http://www.cbsnews.com/stories/2003/08/17/attack/main568735.shtml.

91   Marwaan Macan-Markar, 'Thai Gov't Faces Political Storm over Anti-Terrorism Law', *One World US*, 13 August 2003, available at http://us.oneworld.net/article/view/65553/1.

92   'Thailand: US impunity agreement should not have been signed', *Amnesty International Press Release*, 12 June 2003, available at http://web.amnesty.org/library/Index/ENGASA390062003?open&of=ENG-THA.

93   Horachaikul, 'The Far South of Thailand in the Era of the American Empire'.

2

Understanding the Threat

> Today, in the name of God who commands us to go to war ... I release all of you to enter the battlefield either alone or in groups.

> O ye who believe! Take your precautions, and either go forth in parties or go forth all together.
> **An-Nisaa [4:71]**[1]

In order to accurately assess the situation in the south, a detailed look at the incidents that have occurred thus far is required. This chapter will first analyse the significant attacks and incidents that have occurred since the beginning of 2004. It will then give a broad overview of the separatist groups still active in southern Thailand, as well as the links these groups have with other organisations on the international stage. Another dimension of the threat which has recently received much attention—religious schools—will also be examined. This chapter will round off with a possible scenario of the situation in southern Thailand if effective measures are not taken to quell the insurgency.

ANALYSIS OF MAJOR INCIDENTS

4 January 2004
In what appears to be a coordinated simultaneous operation, groups of Muslim insurgents moved against targets in nine districts in two of the southern provinces, Narathiwat and Yala. In Narathiwat, insurgents numbering about 30 raided a military camp and armoury, killed four guards, and made off with 364 weapons, including 330 M-16 rifles, two M-60 grenade launchers, and seven rocket-propelled grenades. The soldiers who were killed were Buddhists and it was reported that the raiders lined up the troops and asked each for his religion. After the four Buddhists were identified, they were dragged in front of the assembled men and executed. Two had their throats slashed while the other two were shot in the head. One of the attackers reportedly shouted

'Pattani has returned!' in *Kelantanese*, a dialect widely spoken among Muslims in the south. At the same time, 18 schools—16 in Narathiwat and 2 in Yala—were set on fire by miscreants using mosquito coils put on petrol-soaked sacks. Though there were no injuries in the arson attacks, nails were placed on the roads to prevent fire engines from getting near the burning schools.

7 January 2004
Insurgents opened fire using grenade launchers and machine guns on Ayer Weng police station in Betong, Yala, near the Malaysian border. Two policemen were injured. It was believed that this was the same group that attacked the army camp in Narathiwat and that some of the rifles stolen on 4 January were used. The attackers set fire to a bridge in the area to lure police out of the station.

22 January 2004
A monk was hacked to death with a machete in Narathiwat by two men who fled the scene on a motorbike. The monk was begging for alms at the time.

24 January 2004
Three monks were attacked, two fatally. A 13-year-old novice in Pattani was slashed to death by youths on motorcycles. A 65-year-old monk in Yala died and another aged 25 was critically injured when they were attacked while seeking alms. These attacks on monks were seen as attempts to fuel a religious divide between Buddhists and Muslims.

5 March 2004
Arsonists set fire to five schools (four in Yala and one in Narathiwat) and an unused police checkpoint in Pattani, causing minor damage.

23 March 2004
A 4-kilogramme remote-controlled bomb hidden in a toilet exploded across Narathiwat town hall, where Interior Minister Bhokin Bhalakula and Defence Minister Chetta Thanajaro were having a meeting. The attack was meant to be a challenge to government authority and intended to stir up chaos and panic.

27 March 2004

A Powergel bomb attached to a motorcycle exploded at a strip of bars in the tourist spot of Sungai Kolok, Narathiwat. The area is especially popular with Malaysian tourists. 30 people were injured, seven of them Malaysians.

30 March 2004

A group of about ten armed masked men broke into the Manoon Rock Grinding factory. They made off with at least 1.4 tonnes of ammonium nitrate, 56 sticks of dynamite, and 176 detonators. The material stolen has yet to be found.

4 April 2004

A bomb exploded outside the residence of Preecha Damkerngkiart, chief of Bannang Sata district. Though no one was injured, the incident followed the search of an abandoned cave called Tham Sua in Ban Bannangluwa in Muang district the previous day. The cave was believed to have served as a hideout for separatists and a training site for new recruits. The 500-metre long cave was suspected of being used for bomb preparation and terrorist training. During the raid, security forces found many articles, including PVC pipes, batteries, electric wires, and books in Yawi.

22 April 2004

In near-simultaneous attacks, assailants set fire to about 50 public buildings in all 13 districts of Narathiwat and killed two firefighters who were rushing to put out the blazes. Among the targets were 11 schools, 24 phone booths, government offices, living accommodations for railway officials, a highway rest area, and some Buddhist monasteries.

28 April 2004

Security forces shot and killed 108 insurgents in Yala, Pattani, and Songkhla provinces when they attempted to attack security establishments in various locations. The insurgents launched simultaneous pre-dawn raids on 10 police outposts and a police station in military-style operations. In Yala province, 10 persons, aged between 19 and 42, mostly from the Yaha district, were killed at Ban Niang checkpoint in Muang district. In the same district, two more were killed at an army base. Security forces seized a pickup truck, a shotgun, three large knives, and bullets from the assailants. 16 persons were killed when they attempted to attack the Krong Pinang police station. The attackers were aged between 18 and 43 and came from a village in the Krong Pinang sub-district. The police seized eight M-16 assault rifles, seven shotguns, three rifles, 16 knives, and a motorcycle. Eight Yala residents aged between 18 and 30 were killed at a Border Patrol Police base in Bannang Sata district. Four motorcycles, eight knives, and petrol were seized. At an army camp in Than To district, five persons were killed and three were injured. The attackers, who were from the Muang district, were aged between 20 and 32.

In Pattani, the major incident first took place at the Krue Se checkpoint in Muang district. The attackers however, retreated to a nearby mosque and began to incite the public using mosque's loud speaker to urge all Muslims in the area to take up arms against security forces and 'fight to the death'. In the ensuing raid by security forces, 32 persons were killed. Most of those killed were aged between 17 and 63 and were residents of Yala while few others came from Pattani, Songkhla, and Narathiwat. Also in Pattani, two persons from Yala, who came on a motorcycle wielding machetes were killed at Mo Kaeng checkpoint in Nong Chik district. Similarly, 12 machete wielding persons, aged between 18 and 41 were shot dead when they attempted to attack the Mae Lan police station.

In Songkhla, 19 persons were killed at Saba Yoi market. All except one who came from Pattani were local residents. Authorities seized one M-16 assault rifle, four shotguns, three hand grenades, seven machetes, and nine motorcycles.

Of all the above, the incident at the historic Krue Se Mosque on the outskirts of Pattani was the most unusual. According to Andrew Forbes, a Chiang Mai-based Islamic scholar, the attack bore the trademark of jihad.[2] Some reports go even further, saying it appeared as if the attackers wanted to die in the ancient mosque in order to send fellow religionists a message about their beliefs. They were like suicide insurgents willing to die near their God. As Richard C. Paddock summed up in a report carried in the Los Angeles Times,

> The smell of blood hung over the Krue Se mosque ... Its historic brick walls were marred by hundreds of bullet holes. Its marble floors were gouged where rocket-propelled grenades exploded. A torn, bloodstained Koran lay salvaged in the courtyard ... Muslim rebels

chose to die Wednesday in a hail of lead and shrapnel rather than surrender to police ... To many, the dead were heroes.[3]

However, Dr. Ismael Lutfi Jatika, rector of Yala Islamic College, said he believed the Muslim teenagers who attacked Thai security forces were brainwashed.[4] Interviews with those arrested revealed that the attackers had been told that they would be protected by their faith, and that by using 'cursed sand', roads would look like the sea. Protective incantations and chanting certain words would also make them invisible and hence impervious to bullets.[5] These teachings were later found in the *Berjihad di Pattani*, found on the bodies of some insurgents killed on 28 April.

Whether or not the attackers intended to die or were brainwashed into giving up their lives, the incident left a lasting impact. Weera Somkwamkid, head of the Confederation for Democracy, believes that the masterminds of the unrest achieved their goal—to awaken millions of others with the sacrifice of a few.[6] Chidchanok Rahimullah of the Prince of Songkhla University suggested that one of the insurgents' objectives could be further polarisation of the community.[7]

The incident is also seen as the beginning of a jihad by fanatical Muslims. Abdulloh Abru, Islamic economics lecturer at the Prince of Songkhla University, has expressed concern that the killings would most probably provoke greater aggression, including the possibility of suicide attacks.[8] Interestingly, Bersatu, the umbrella body for several secessionist groups, posted a statement on the PULO website, praising the dead raiders as 'freedom fighters' and stating that their killing by the army would be paid for 'with sweat and tears'.[9] The statement praised the dead for their bravery and warned foreign tourists not to travel to the southern provinces of Pattani, Narathiwat, Satun, Songkhla, Yala, Phuket, Phangnga, Krabi, and Phattalung.

It is also important to note that the choice of April 28 as the date for the attacks probably could have been more than just a coincidence. The clashes in Ra-ngae district in Narathiwat on the same date in 1948 between Malay-speaking Muslim villagers and police were the climax of a revolt that left 400 villagers and 30 police dead.[10] Known as the Duson Nyor Revolt, the uprising was led by Hajji Abdul Rahman, a religious leader. 28 April 2004 also marked the first anniversary of the raids in Narathiwat and Yala provinces in which groups of men armed with automatic rifles stormed military outposts, spraying bullets at the installations and killing five marines who were asleep. Moreover, the

Krue Se Mosque itself is seen as a symbol of Islamist resilience in Malay-Muslim folklore.[11]

On the whole, 28 April 2004 appears to be a scenario in which local disaffected youth have been exploited by an underground movement with perhaps a core of trained leaders who could have links to local separatist groups. With the deaths of so many who are now revered as martyrs, the ground is now exceptionally fertile for groups willing to exploit it for recruiting members into their ranks.

16 May 2004
Three bombs exploded almost simultaneously at Buddhist temples in Narathiwat province's Takbai, Ruesoh, and Rangae districts. Two people were injured and the temples' sanctuaries were damaged. Police had earlier warned of possible attacks and sabotage by about 300 insurgents from the Gerakan Mujahideen Islam Pattani (GMIP).

29 May 2004
Suspected Muslim insurgents decapitated a rubber-tapper and threatened to carry out more killings if security forces continued to arrest 'innocent Muslims'. The beheading has raised concerns that the southern insurgents may have developed links with Al Qaeda terrorists. However, this may simply be an example of the insurgents copying the tactics of the insurgents in Iraq.

22 August 2004
Three bombs exploded in the capital of Yala province, wounding 13 people and damaging more than 30 vehicles. The bombs, hidden in cars and motorcycles, blew up almost simultaneously outside karaoke bars and in hotel parking lots shortly before midnight. The attack occurred five days ahead of a five-day visit to Yala, Pattani, and Narathiwat by Thaksin. The attack was seemingly directed at undermining the tourist industry.

26 August 2004
A bomb exploded at the busy Mamong market in the Sukhirin district of Narathiwat province at around 7:30 a.m. It triggered a powerful explosion that damaged four shops, three pickup trucks and several motorcycles as far as 40 metres away. One person was killed in the blast, while at least 27

others were injured. The attack was seen as aimed at damaging public confidence in the government's moves to stem out violence in the region.

17 September 2004
Rapin Ruangkeow, 37, a Pattani provincial court judge, was shot seven times in the head, torso, and chest by three gunmen on a motorcycle while his car was stopped at an intersection in Muang district's Tambon Sa-barang. Judge Rapin sped away but rammed into a pick-up truck. The gunmen followed and shot him again. He died in hospital. The killing of the first and highest-level Justice official in the south had intensified the anxiety of other judges in the area.

Police arrested Abdullah Bali, 20, a student at the private Islamic Pattana Suksa Wittaya School, who confessed that he and two friends killed Judge Rapin. Abdullah said he committed the crime in hopes of going to heaven after his death.

25 October 2004
A 2,000-strong crowd assembled outside the Tak Bai district police station in Narathiwat, demanding the release of six defence volunteers taken into custody. The crowd which initially comprised the relatives of those detained had wanted to see the suspects. The police however told them that the men, accused of giving their guns to insurgents, had earlier been transferred to Narathiwat central prison. Despite this, the crowd did not disperse. Instead, more and more locals joined in the protest.

As the situation became volatile and chaotic, soldiers fired into the air to warn the protesters to back off. However, the crowd grew larger as more people, some from neighbouring Yala and Pattani, joined the rally. About 50 core protesters wore hoods and were armed. Religious leaders and locals later confirmed they were not from the neighbourhood. Fire engines were brought in to spray water at the protesters but security officers were unable to contain the crowd. When security forces used tear gas at the protesters, pandemonium ensued in which at least six protesters were killed.

Security forces arrested more than 1,300 people, laid them face down in rows on the pavement with their hands tied with rope before taking them to different locations to be questioned. All were packed tightly into trucks for a journey to Pattani province that took five hours. Unfortunately, about 78 of them died due to suffocation. The men were already weakened from fasting as the incident took place during the

Ramadan month, and when they were piled on top of each other, the likelihood is that the detainees were not able to breathe. Some were also crushed to death. Dr. Pornthip Rojanasunan, a forensic expert for the Justice Ministry, told news agencies that 80 per cent of the victims died from smothering or suffocation and 20 per cent from stress or convulsions. 'Some may have been injured to begin with; others may have been lying on top of each other, or squashed in the front of the trucks and suffered from dehydration.'[12] With three more bodies recovered from the Tak Bai River close to Tak Bai district police station, the death toll in the carnage rose to 87. Authorities reportedly seized from the riot scene four M-16 assault rifles, three AK-47 assault rifles, one .38 pistol, 14 machetes and a handful of cartridges. Four hand grenades were also retrieved from the Tak Bai River.

Fourth Army deputy commander Sinchai Boonsathit said that the soldiers had handled the protesters humanely and did not toss them into the trucks or pile them on top of one another as alleged. To add insult to injury, Prime Minister Thaksin, who flew to the south after the clashes, praised the security force's response. 'They have done a great job,' he told reporters. 'They (the protesters) really set out to cause trouble so we had to take drastic action against them.' He also said that the government had run out of patience and would take drastic action against elements instigating violence.[13] 'If we're soft, they'll think we're caving in. I won't have it.'[14] According to southern Police Chief Lieutenant-General Manote Kraiwongse, the rally was planned by the same leadership that masterminded the April 28 attacks at Krue Se mosque.[15] General Sirichai Tunyasiri, chief of the Southern Border Provinces Peacekeeping Command, believed that a 'third hand' had plotted the unrest and had fired pistols into the air during the scuffle. According to the Interior ministry, if road blocks had not been set up on various highways, there could have been 10,000 people at the riot.[16]

With this incident, the situation in southern Thailand has now reached volcanic pitch. Abdullahman Abdulsomat, chairman of Narathiwat provincial Islamic committee, fears that the incident could spark a violent reaction. 'Certainly, this will escalate further and who knows what will happen next,' and some groups may try to do something about taking revenge.[17] Nideh Waba, chairman of a private religious schools association, said, 'Those insurgents ... will fight back harshly with suicide attacks.'

As condemnations for the gross abuses by the Thai security forces were coming in, on 28 October, PULO, which has been dormant since the 1980s, came out with threats to set Bangkok ablaze in 'revenge suicide attacks in the wake of the riot in Narathiwat's Tak Bai district.' According to a message posted on the insurgent group's website, 'their Phra Nakhon (capital) will be burned to the ground like the capital of Pattani', by a suicide squad.[18] 'We pledge before Allah that from now on, the infidel will suffer sleepless nights, the property they have robbed from us will be totally destroyed and their lives will face consequences for the sins they have committed. Their blood will be shed on the soil and flow into water. Our weapon is fire and oil, fire and oil, fire and oil.'[19] However, the group also maintained that the coming operations would be targeting Thai policemen and soldiers only.[20]

In the meantime, the Fourth Army's intelligence reports suggested that a group of people in the three provinces had signed a pact to retaliate against the government, urging followers to kill 40 people, including civilians and informants, and to sabotage government buildings.

Since then, there has been no pause in the violence. A string of bombings took place in the immediate aftermath of the Tak Bai debacle. On 28 October 2004, a bomb exploded at a beer bar in Narathiwat's Sungai Kolok district, killing a Malaysian tourist and injuring about 20 others, half of them Malaysian tourists. Two locals later succumbed to their injuries. This is believed to be the first attack that involved the killing of a tourist. On the same day, the police bomb disposal squad also defused a 10-kilogramme time bomb at a food shop near a school and a Buddhist temple on Wosbian road in Narathiwat's Muang district. The bomb was set to explode at 7:15 a.m., when there would be many buying food at the shop. On 29 October, two bomb explosions killed a police sergeant and injured eight other policemen and six civilians in Yala. The first bomb went off at 8:10 a.m. at a food shop on Siroros road, injuring three policemen having breakfast at the shop and six other people. A 12-member police bomb squad was sent to the scene. While they were working, another bomb exploded at 9:25 a.m. All the bomb squad members and a local reporter were injured. A police officer later died of his wounds.

There were also numerous revenge killings on a smaller scale, most of them drive-by shootings by gunmen riding pillion on motorcycles. One notable killing was the beheading of a senior village official in Narathiwat province on 2 November 2004. The head of Jaran Tulae was found in a plastic bag on the roadside near Ai Yari village in Tambon Sukhirin. Attached to the bag was a handwritten letter stating: 'This is revenge for the innocent Muslim youths who were massacred at the Tak Bai protest.' The man's body was found later beside a cottage in a rubber plantation one kilometre from where the head was discovered. However, police believe that the victim was shot in the chest and his head was only cut off after he died.

Revenge attacks were also sparked off by the arrest of four Islamic school teachers in the south. Waeyusoh Waedeuramae (alias Loh Supeh), Abdulrohseh Haji Doloh, and Ahama Bula from Thamma Witthaya School in Yala, and Muhamad Kanafi Doloh from a sister school, Satri Islamic Witthaya Foundation School, were accused of being behind the recent spate of violence in the region and charged with treason and terrorism-related offences. Sapaeing Basor, the headmaster of Thamma Witthaya School, was also a suspect. However, he managed to evade arrest and is still at large. The arrests have sparked widespread outrage among the Muslim community in the south as they perceive this to be another initiative by the government to clamp down on religious schools and to undermine the south's Muslim identity.

Anniversary of January 4 attacks

Nearing the end of 2004, Thai authorities warned that militants were planning major attacks in the southern provinces as well as the capital Bangkok around 4 January 2005. This was meant to commemorate the first anniversary of the raid on the Narathiwat armoury, which also marked the beginning of a resurgence of violence in the southern provinces. As a result, security forces were on high alert and the anniversary came and went without major incident. However, the violence did continue on an almost daily basis. The bulk of the attacks consisted of arson and drive-by shootings, but bombings occurred quite frequently as well. The most serious attack took place on 16 January 2005 when a bomb triggered by a mobile phone exploded at a noodle shop in Yala, killing one and injuring at least 47. Eight were seriously wounded, including two policemen. The 4.5-kilogramme improvised bomb was hidden in a briefcase. Police believe the bomb was targeted at police and officials who were regular customers at the shop. The attack followed reports that separatists had planned 20 bomb attacks on government offices, shops, railway stations, and bus terminals in

31

the three southern border provinces, to take revenge for the arrest of Muslim religious teachers in Pattani and Yala.[21]

THE ACTORS

At the beginning of the crisis, the Thai government maintained that the violence and unrest in the south were the handiwork of criminal elements engaged in illegal trades including drugs rather than ideologically motivated extremists.[22] According to local political sources, 70–80 per cent of the incidents were caused by personal conflicts, which the media projected as 'acts of terrorism'.[23] Many analysts even maintained that some of the attacks were 'due to political rivalry'. 'Some cases were actually due to the rivalry among candidates in the provincial administrative organisation election.'[24] It is significant to note that some of the suspects held in connection with the 4 January 2004 raid on the army camp have identified two Thai Rak Thai (TRT) Members of Parliament—Najmuddin Umar and Areepen Uttarasin— and Pattani Senator Den Tohmena as co-conspirators.[25] Incidentally, the three are believed to be leaders of PUSAKA, a foundation of schools that Thai authorities believe is the public face of an underground separatist movement. Thaksin believes that reactionary politicians and security officials who are resisting efforts to end government corruption and professionalise the police and military may have contributed by provoking the radicals.[26] On another occasion, he insisted that the violence was the work of 'well-trained militants crossing from Malaysia to Thailand to stir up chaos in exchange for financial reward from some Middle East countries.'[27]

Thus the problem was projected variously to be due to political conflict and rivalry among local mafia gangs and corrupt officials or by the criminals themselves for financial gains. Some local religious leaders have also suggested that local mafia who ran underground businesses might have masterminded the incidents.

This stand has now been substantially reversed and there is no doubt that the government has a serious Muslim insurgency at hand. However, as Sirichai Thanyasiri, the Deputy Supreme Commander of the Southern Border Province Peace-Building Command puts it, 'I admit that I don't know who the enemy is.'[28] There are indications that Muslim insurgents had been conducting 'training and recruitment' programmes in the south with plans to seize Narathiwat province 'within 1,000 days,' and 'plant their flag pole at Thaksin Rajanivej Palace,' King Bhumibol Adulyadej's southern retreat.[29]

Thai authorities initially speculated that three separatist groups—PULO, BRN, and the Gerakan Mujahideen Islam Pattani (GMIP)—coordinated the 4 January attacks. They believe that members of at least one separatist group, GMIP, with links to Al Qaeda and the JI, may be trying to stir up trouble. Malaysian authorities have arrested Jaekumae Kutae, whom Thailand alleges is GMIP's leader. Jaekumae is also suspected to be the mastermind of many attacks in the south, including the 4 January attack. He is said to be a Malaysian national but Thailand alleges he also has Thai citizenship. At the time of writing, Bangkok is working on negotiating Jaekumae's extradition despite there not being an extradition treaty between the two states. Another group which has attracted attention is PUSAKA, a group focused on ideological indoctrination. The consensus in the Thai intelligence community is that the BRN Coordinate is responsible for the 4 January 2004 attacks.

Major Groups[30]

Barisan Revolusi Nasional (BRN)

BRN, also known as the Pattani Malay National Revolutionary Front, was founded by Dr. Haji Harun Sulong, Abdul Karim Hassan (previously known as *Ustaz* Karim, former Youth Chief of the Islamic Party of Malaysia), Tengku Jalal Nasir, Yusof Chapakiya, and Amin Tohmeena (BRN's current president, now residing in Sweden), among others.[31] The current chairman of BRN is Yalan Abdulroman, who is believed to be hiding in northern Malaysia.[32] The commander of the military arm ABRIP is Pak Yeh.[33] BRN also has a paramilitary wing, the Pattani People's Revolutionary Commando Brigade (PKRRP) with Lukman Iskandar as its chairman.[34] Lukman is also BRN's Secretary of Foreign Affairs.[35] He recruited, trained and commanded more than 600 urban guerrillas from 1974–77.[36] The deputy commander of PKRRP, Ahmad Matnor, more popularly known as Mat Jabat, is the most destructive guerrilla chief of BRN in Pattani history.[37]

A new name under the BRN banner that has emerged after January 2004 incident is that of Masae Useng. Also believed to be a member of the GMIP as well as the new group PUSAKA, Masae is alleged to have been involved in a series of weapon heists, including the raid on 4 January 2004.[38]

Through its high profile leaders, BRN formed a network outside of Thailand. Masari Savari, who served as Deputy Chairman of BRN, established links with the Algerian National Liberation Front (FLN) when he studied in Algeria in 1974. In 1975, his brother, Sofian, was the BRN representative in Algeria. In 1976, at least 10 batches of students have gone to Algeria.[39] BRN also maintains links with the Palestinian Liberation Organisation (PLO). *Ustaz* Karim, one of the founding members of BRN, met Yasser Arafat in Beirut in 1976.[40]

Many believe that BRN was a recipient of Malaysian official patronage, especially for its services against Malaysian communist guerrilla groups. According to the BRN, Malaysia requisitioned BRN for military operations with its armed forces against communist groups operating along the Thai-Malaysia border, at the peak of the communist threat from 1976–77. In return, Malaysia agreed to support BRN logistically and financially.[41] BRN Secretary of Foreign Affairs Lukman Iskandar allegedly maintained a close friendship with Malaysia's former Deputy Prime Minister Anwar Ibrahim, dating back to their student days when they worked in ABIM (Islamic Youth Movement of Malaysia).[42]

BRN's initial objective was the establishment of an Islamic Republic of Pattani, comprising the southern provinces of Pattani, Yala, Narathiwat, Satun, and Songkhla. BRN aimed to achieve this by staging a revolution to overthrow the Thai government. However, BRN has since done away with the objective of an independent Pattani state, preferring now to opt for autonomy. A 22-point demand list set out by the group includes the appointment of a Malay Muslim to be the governor-general of the Southern Border Provinces of Thailand, the recognition of Malay Language as a Second Official Language and Islam as the Official Religion, and the establishment of a Shari'ah Court in the Southern Border Provinces.[43] BRN wants to be recognised as a legal political party in southern Thailand.[44]

BRN has been plagued by a series of dissentions and divisions. In 1970, dissatisfactions with the leadership of BRN led Yusof Chapakiya to quit from BRN and set up his own group, the National Revolutionary Party of South Thailand (PRNS).[45] In 1972, Tengku Jalal Nasir also quit from the BRN and declared his own Patani National Liberation Front (BNPP). He took Pak Yeh and more than half of the 600-strong Angkatan Bersenjata Revolusi Patani (ABREP), the first military wing of BRN, with him.[46] PRNS and BNPP are no longer active in southern Thailand.

In 1972, an urban unit known as Black 1902 was formed by Cikgu Ding. Black 1902 (named so after the year Patani was absorbed as a Thai territory) was known for urban sabotage. Ding Jerman and Lukman Iskandar were among its leaders. One of its most noted operations was the kidnapping of three Christian missionaries in Saiburi in 1975. Black 1902 was dissolved in 1975 after Ding Jerman joined Tengku Jalal's BNPP.[47]

In April 1974, a new Urban Guerrilla Brigade (UGB) was formed with Lukman Iskandar as its Commander-in-Chief. In 1977, Lukman was involved in a conspiracy to overthrow the Malaysian government for which he was sacked by BRN's Supreme Command Council. However, supported by the Armed Forces, the Urban Guerrillas, and the Constabulary Guards, Lukman led a rebellion against the Supreme Council in which three Supreme Council members were shot dead. Other council members fled the country and remained in self-imposed exile in Malaysia. Lukman was arrested under Malaysia's Internal Security Act (ISA) and was jailed for 4 years.[48]

Recent reports suggest that BRN has now split into four major factions, due to a conflict of interest. They are: BRN Congress, BRN Coordinate, BRN Asli, and BRN Progressive. BRN Congress led by Rosa Burako was thought to be the most active.[49] However, recent reports indicate that BRN Coordinate, which initially dealt with political matters, has emerged as one of the leading groups involved in the violence in the south. As mentioned previously, four Islamic school teachers were arrested in December 2004. They were thought to be members of BRN Coordinate. Waeyusoh Waedeuramae (alias Loh Supeh) was said to be responsible for BRN Coordinate's military affairs and allegedly ordered the January 4 raid in Narathiwat as well as the torching of 36 southern schools in 1993. Waeyusoh was slated to become defence minister in liberated Pattani. Another teacher—Abdulrohseh Haji Doloh—was responsible for economic affairs, controlling finances sent by overseas donors. He deposited millions of baht in Thamma Witthaya School, which he taught in. Authorities were also on the hunt for

Sapaeing Basor, headmaster of Thamma Witthaya. However he managed to escape the dragnet and is thought to have fled to Malaysia. Sapaeing is said to be the leader of the political arm of BRN Coordinate and is slated to become Prime Minister in the liberated Pattani.

BRN receives its funding through criminal activities like extortion, ransom, kidnapping and the imposition of revolution taxes on the Muslim masses and other types of protection funds.[50] Finances are also channelled through legitimate businesses. Some Islamic businessmen and Malaysian political parties provide it with logistical and financial support.[51]

The group is not known to have conducted any large-scale attacks. Since the 1990s, BRN has been conducting surprise, small-scale attacks against the Thai military and police. BRN has also attacked civilians and soft targets as evidenced in the bombing of a railway station in Hat Yai in 1993. As few Muslims use this train station, the attack was meant to have been against non-Muslim civilians.

The strength of its military cadre has deteriorated gradually and according to a 2002 estimate by Thai authorities, the number stands at just about 30.[52] BRN has resorted to grass-root militancy, targeting symbols of Thai authority and attempting to infiltrate private Islamic schools to spread the separatist cause and to train Muslim youths in insurgent activities.[53] However, it has reportedly been recruiting new members, acquiring new weapons, and sourcing for logistical and financial support in order to boost its military capability.[54]

BRN is allegedly part of a coalition called Bersatu with PULO and New PULO (NPULO). Some however believe that it is a breakaway faction of BRN, and not the core of BRN, that has joined Bersatu.[55] Under the banner of Bersatu, BRN has sent volunteers to train in Afghanistan.[56] On its own, BRN also sent 10 members to Syria to train in explosives and sabotage in the late 1990s or early 2000.[57]

BRN's capabilities are as yet unclear since the group seems to have lost its focus. However, they continue to launch regular skirmishes in the south, enough to set Thai authorities on alert. Though the support for Pattani armed groups dwindled to insignificant levels, the attacks in January 2004 show that the Pattani struggle has not been abandoned.

Pattani United Liberation Organisation (PULO)
The Pattani United Liberation Front (PULO) or Pertubuhan Pembebasan Pattani Bersatu is the largest of the Malay-Muslim groups in Thailand. PULO was founded by Tungku Bira Kotoniro on 22 March 1968, although some reports put the year of establishment as 1967.[58] Tungku was the political leader and has remained chairman of the group ever since. Before founding PULO, Tungku went into exile in 1962 following unrest in southern Thailand. He hails from a well-respected, aristocratic family and has lived in Saudi Arabia and more recently in

Syria.[59] Haji Kabir Abdulrahman is another of PULO's founders[60] and is also the organisation's president. According to the PULO website[61], he was later replaced by Dr. Haji Harun Moleng (Mohammad Bin Mohammad), who was elected president at the First National Conference (Congress I) in June 1988.

The group split in 1992, with Hayihadi Mindosali at the helm. Breakaway faction New PULO was later established in 1995 by Dr. A-rong Muleng. Hajji Samaae Thanam was the military commander and regional leader of PULO. Of all PULO leaders, Samaae Thanam held popular sway. He set up the PULO Army Command Council or MPTP to give support to Tuanku Abdul Kade, the pioneer of the south's terrorist movement in the 1940s. Samaae Thanam was based in Malaysia and was arrested by the Malaysian authorities in February 1998. He was later deported to Thailand.[62]

PULO was established on the principles of 'UBANGTAPEKEMA', an acronym for religion, race, national identity, homeland, and humanitarianism.[63] PULO believes that the former Pattani state was unlawfully annexed by Thailand in 1902.[64] PULO Deputy President Lukman B. Lima charged that Bangkok 'illegally incorporated' the far south into Thailand 100 years ago and now rules it with 'colonial' repression while 'committing crimes against humanity in the area.'[65] It thus wants secession from Thailand for the five southern states of Yala, Narathiwat, Songkhla, Satun, and Pattani and wants to form an independent Muslim or Malay state or sultanate called the 'Patani Malay Republic' with Pattani as the centre, pursuing development of language, culture, economy, and the management of its own affairs.[66]

PULO has close links with some elements of the fundamentalist Parti Islam seMalaysia (PAS), whose stronghold is in the northern Malaysian state of Kelantan. Bangkok has repeatedly alleged that PULO has benefited from the provision of safe-haven in Kelantan and that this support has come with the sanction of PAS, as well as the official indifference of the central Kuala Lumpur government. There have also been charges that the radicals in Kelantan have facilitated the trans-shipment of weapons from Cambodia to help in terrorist operations in southern Thailand.[67]

External Malaysian support, though not from the Malaysian government, assumed increased prominence in late 1997 following the initiation of 'Operation Falling Leaves'. The operation was characterised by the killing of state workers and officials in southern Thailand, an exercise that Thai intelligence maintain could not have taken place in the absence of PAS support.[68] Some sources also claim links between PULO and Malaysian terrorist group Al Maunah, which has a following in southern Thailand and is believed to include a number of former PULO members.[69]

Links have also been discovered with the Free Aceh Movement (GAM) in Indonesia, the Moro Islamic Liberation Front (MILF) and the Abu Sayyaf Group (ASG) in the southern Philippines, as well as groups fighting for the independence of Kashmir in South Asia.[70] Repeated accusations have been made by intelligence sources that PULO operatives facilitated the entry of foreign nationals into Thailand, both for operational and logistical purposes. PULO also featured in the foiled Hizbollah truck bombing of Israel's Bangkok embassy in 1994.[71] Many members were reportedly trained in the Middle East especially in Libya and Syria where they had received specialised training in bomb-making and assassination techniques in the 1970s.[72] Some cadres have trained in camps in Malaysia under trainers from Chechnya and Afghanistan.[73]

Funding for the separatist group comes mostly from criminal activity including extortion rackets (targeting local businesses particularly in the construction industry), illegal 'protection' rackets, and smuggling (contraband products, narcotics, weapons and people).[74] It has also raised funds in Europe and the Middle East from sympathetic charities and from groups and charities based in Malaysia.[75] The Lebanese Hizbollah is also said to have supplied funds to PULO in exchange for the group's logistical support for Hizbollah operations in Thailand.[76]

In the 1970s, at the peak of its popularity, PULO had 1,000 members. That number is now reduced to about 30–50 active armed cadres.[77] The group mainly uses assault rifles (AK-47, M-16, and HK-33), 9-milimeter calibre pistols, and bomb making equipment and materials, which it gets mostly from raids on Thai army and government offices and from illegal arms trades operating in Cambodia, Myanmar, the Philippines, Indonesia, and even South Asia.[78] The armed wing of the group—Pattani United Liberation Army (PULA)—has carried out insurgent insurgency attacks. Its traditional forms of attack have been bombing, arson, and drive-by shootings from motorbikes.[79]

PULO targets symbols of the Thai government, especially the military. Perceived symbols of Thai cultural dominance have also been periodically targeted, including schools and Buddhist temples. Soft targets, such as shopping areas, railway stations, and infrastructure sites have also been attacked. There is little evidence however to indicate that PULO could mount any significant operations outside its territory. Nevertheless, the group once claimed it would conduct aircraft hijacking operations and threatened to launch a campaign of kidnapping.[80]

The years from 1970 to the late 1990s saw the crest of the PULO terror wave. It undermined the stability of the region by instigating unrest and civil disturbances in the south of Thailand. In June 1980, PULO operatives carried out four bomb attacks in Bangkok, resulting in injuries to 47 people.[81] In 1981, the group claimed responsibility for another three bombings in busy shopping areas, leaving 50 people injured.[82] The group suffered setbacks when the Thai government announced general amnesties, once in 1984 and again in 1991, which many PULO cadres took advantage of. PULO was thrown into disarray in 1998, when some of its leaders were arrested. Morale plunged and some of its members who lost faith in the group gave themselves up to the Thai government. Military campaigns have since reduced the rebel movement to a shadow of its former self. However, there was a resurgence in violence in 2002.

In operational terms, PULO seems to be somewhat resilient, with some PULO factions opting to continue the struggle. However, the group has never posed a sophisticated terrorist or guerrilla threat. Sources on the ground say that PULO is now focusing on propaganda instead of militant activity. It continues to issue threats and warnings of attacks from its website, although these are taken by security forces to be of little credibility. Despite this, PULO represents a continual challenge to the general peace and stability in the region as it may provide inspiration to other groups in southern Thailand.

New Pattani United Liberation Organisation (New PULO)

New PULO emerged in 1995 as the dissident faction of PULO, three years after the mother organisation splintered. It was originally established by A-rong Muleng and Hayi Abdul Rohman Bazo, with the intent of achieving Pattani autonomy by way of a focused terror strategy against the Thai authorities. New PULO was not for dramatic attacks but preferred minor attacks that were more of harassment tactics. The idea was to conserve the limited operational resources with the aim of developing legitimacy for a separatist Islamic agenda.[83]

New PULO insurgent activities have been integrated under the overall direction of a supreme Armed Force Council that coordinates, directs, and controls the three separate sabotage wings—the Sali Ta-loh

Bueyor Group, the Maso Dayeh Group and the Ma-ae Tophien Group—with specific geographic concentration.[84]

Like PULO, New PULO obtains funds by extorting protection fees from wealthy landowners and businessmen in the southern states of Thailand and even Kelantan, Malaysia. Its armed wing, the Caddan Army would usually threaten to injure or kill the victim and steal the family's valuables if they failed to pay 'taxes'.[85] New PULO also gets funds through criminal activities such as kidnappings.[86]

New PULO does not have the capability to carry out large-scale insurgent attacks. It generally carries out small-scale attacks like arson and drive-by shootings. The group also conducted bombings of a hotel and a theatre in Muang Yala district in the 1990s.[87] New PULO generally carries out sabotage missions and bombings, arson, extortion, and kidnappings. These are usually undertaken by young members most of whom are also drug addicts.[88]

PULO and New PULO did not agree much for a coordinated strategy, due to their differences in strategy and doctrine. However in 1997–98, they set their differences aside and worked out a solidarity alliance codenamed 'Operation Falling Leaves', aiming to attack and kill law enforcement personnel, state officials, and schoolteachers.[89] They were able to conduct 33 separate attacks resulting in nine deaths and several dozens injured, besides causing enormous economic damage.

Gerakan Mujahideen Islam Pattani (GMIP)

GMIP was one of the first groups bandied about by Thai leaders as the culprits behind the January 4 raid.[90] Unlike the other insurgent groups in southern Thailand, GMIP is the organisation most influenced by events in Afghanistan and the global jihad phenomenon. It was established in 1995 by Nasori Saesaeng (alias Awae Keleh) after returning from fighting in Afghanistan.[91] While in Afghanistan, Nasori, who is GMIP's operational chief, reportedly befriended Nik Adli Nik Aziz, the son of PAS spiritual leader Nik Aziz Nik Mat.[92] Nasori managed to slip through the hands of both the Thai and Malaysian authorities twice. In 2001, Nasori fled from a gun battle with Thai soldiers in Narathiwat's Bacho district in 2001.[93] Nasori also managed to escape in August 2002 when Malaysian security forces raided a prestigious hotel in Kuala Lumpur often used by GMIP as a meeting place. Three GMIP members were arrested in that raid.[94] An arrest warrant is out for Nasori for his alleged involvement in the January 4 raid on the arms depot in Narathiwat.[95]

Other significant members of GMIP believed to be involved in the January 4 incident include Jaekumae[96] and Masae Useng.[97] Jaekumae was thought to be residing in Trengganu, Malaysia, and has been arrested by Malaysian authorities in early 2005. He is believed to have connections in Malaysia as well as Indonesia.[98] As discussed above, Masae is also a BRN member.[99] Masae's role in the southern Thai insurgency will be elaborated on later in the section on PUSAKA.

GMIP's objective is similar to the other groups in that it aims to establish an Islamic state in southern Thailand. The deadline set for achieving this goal is reportedly the year 2008.[100] However, GMIP is also thought to have wider regional Islamist aspirations. Some of its members are said to support Al Qaeda and its vision of a worldwide Islamic caliphate.[101] In fact, in late 2001, GMIP leaflets were found scattered in districts of Yala urging holy war and support for Osama bin Laden in the service of the separatist cause.[102] Apart from fighting in the Afghan jihad, the leaning towards Al Qaeda is thought to stem from members who were educated in the Middle East, particularly Saudi Arabia and Pakistan, as well as at Wahabi institutions in Southeast Asia.[103]

A considerable amount of funding for GMIP comes from charitable or religious foundations from countries such as Saudi Arabia.[104] GMIP also reportedly owns the Seafood Tomyam restaurant in Kuala Trengganu, Malaysia.[105] Apart from legitimate sources, GMIP also receives funds from criminal activities such as sabotage and hired killings. The group reportedly has an annual turnover of 10 million baht (US$254,478).[106] As a result of this criminal element, GMIP is often dismissed as little more than a criminal cash cow, possibly raising funds for allied groups operating in other parts of the region.[107] This has some parallels with ASG in the southern Philippines and has led authorities to fear that GMIP could provide Al Qaeda or its associated groups with similar help to that provided to the ASG.[108] This concern is heightened in the light of GMIP's network that was formed during the Afghan jihad.

Apart from links with Al Qaeda, GMIP is also said to have close links with the Kumpulan Mujahideen Malaysia (KMM), the Malaysian branch of the regional JI. KMM was founded in 1995 by GMIP founder Nasori's close associate in Afghanistan, Zainol Ismael. This cross-border link is said to still remain.[109] In fact, KMM's support to the southern Thai insurgent groups is thought to have transformed GMIP and BRN into insurgents with a regional agenda.[110]

GMIP and BRN appear to have a good working relationship. Apart from joining hands with other separatist groups to form Bersatu, it has also collaborated on other ad-hoc projects. Of note was an operation in 2002, which offered cash rewards of 100,000 baht for the murder of police officers or informers. Leaflets bearing the name of both groups were found in Ra-ngae district, which is one of GMIP's strongholds.[111] GMIP also operates in Rue-Sor district in Narathiwat and Mayo as well as Yaring districts in Pattani.[112] According to the Thai Internal Security Operations Command, GMIP is a front for BRN.[113]

GMIP has an estimated strength of between 30–70 members, of which 30 are thought to form the core of its fighters.[114] Its members are reportedly hiding in dense jungle between the Thai-Malaysian border. Near the border in Kuala Berang is where a GMIP training camp is believed to be located.[115]

A number of GMIP's organisational leaders are in exile but continue to use propaganda measures rather than resort to armed struggle to achieve their objectives.[116] Analysts are mixed as to the capability of the group. Some reports say GMIP is the only significant armed Muslim separatist group operating in southern Thailand.[117] However, others cite the capture of its members as a loss in the group's operational effectiveness.[118] The group is not believed to enjoy a high level of support from the Malay Muslims in the south, perhaps because of its Wahabi leanings.

Bersatu

On 31 August 1989, the core leaders of all the separatist groups in southern Thailand—Barisan Islam Pembebasan Patani (BIPP, Islamic Liberation Front of Patani)[119], Mujahideen Pattani Movement (BNP)[120], BRN Congress, and New PULO—in a joint meeting called 'the gathering of the fighters for Pattani', decided to set up the 'Payong Organisation'[121] to unify all the groups in order to move as one force to secede from the Thai Kingdom.[122] PULO and GMIP were also reportedly part of this meeting. It was only in 1991 that the organisation came to be known as the United Front for the Independence of Pattani or Bersatu, as it is still called today.[123]

Bersatu reportedly has international ambitions; it wants to launch more serious operations to bring the separatist cause to the world's attention. Samsuding Khan heads Bersatu and is currently residing in Sweden.[124] Mahadey Da-or is Bersatu's Chairman and is said to be in hiding in Narathiwat after crossing back from Malaysia.[125] Dr. Wan Kadir Che Man has also been named as a Bersatu leader. However, the man who is living in exile in Malaysia is thought to be largely a symbolic figure with no real power.[126] Lusalan Paluka Peloh is said to be the leader of Bersatu's armed wing.[127]

Bersatu is currently made up of renegade members of the various groups, namely PULO and BRN, and apparently no longer functions as an umbrella organisation but as an independent group with its own capabilities. It is named as one of the groups behind the string of violence that has plagued southern Thailand since January 2004, especially the bombing at the provincial headquarters of TOT Corp on 23 March 2004.[128] According to military intelligence, 12 Bersatu rebels, one of them a woman, apparently arrived in Pattani province from Malaysia on 22 March 2004 and split into two groups of six. The group with the woman went to bomb the TOT Corp branch office. A witness said he saw a woman leave a black briefcase with the second bomb inside the Government Savings Bank.[129]

Bersatu has no permanent bases on Thai soil. Its cadres are on the move all the time and avoid engaging in armed clashes with Thai security. If a clash occurs, the terrorists would see to it that they withdraw from the scene promptly. Bersatu has tried to create rifts among the Thai Buddhists and Thai Muslims and tried to disrupt the government's education programme by attacking schools, harming and threatening the life and property of school teachers, coercing parents to stop sending their children to those schools.[130] It is mainly known for sabotage activities against public facilities in towns or in rural areas.[131]

Thai authorities feel that Bersatu is no longer a threat as it has seemingly degenerated to that of a bandit group, with kidnappings and extortions as their main activities in recent years. However with the upsurge in violence in Southern Thailand since January 2004, Bersatu has come under the spotlight again. It has perhaps used this period of relative inactivity to regroup and re-strategise. The latest attacks that have been attributed to Bersatu signal a more violent leaning.

PUSAKA
Pusat Persatuan Tadika Narathiwat (PUSAKA) or the Centre of Tadika Narathiwat Foundation is the latest group to emerge in the southern Thai insurgency. Established in Tanyong Mat, Narathiwat on 22 September 1994[132] by Thai Rak Thai MP Najmuddin Umar, PUSAKA

was formed as a foundation to teach Muslim children about Islam during weekends. It has a branch in Yi-ngo District, Narathiwat which it is now hoping to turn into its headquarters. PUSAKA aims to support Muslim ethics schools, to help them draft standard curricula for Muslim ethical teachings and the spread of Islamic knowledge.[133] It also offers free education to orphans, promotes health, tradition and culture, and engages in public charities.

Najmuddin is allegedly a staunch advocate of southern Muslim separatism and had reportedly urged his followers to carry out activities, which would undermine the credibility of the Thai government.[134] Najmuddin is now suspected to be one of the masterminds behind the 4 January 2004 attacks on the army camp.[135] According to Anupong Panthachayangkoon, one of the suspects detained in this connection, the group of attackers conducted several meetings at Najmuddin's residence before the attack. The meetings were chaired by Najmuddin who offered a high position to everyone involved if an independent Pattani state could be set up.[136] Najmuddin is allegedly the head of PUSAKA in Narathiwat. Fellow TRT MP Areepin Uttarasin is the head of the chapter in Yala, while Pattani Senator Den Tohmena heads the Pattani chapter. The two are also suspected of involvement in the raid.

As a result of these connections, PUSAKA is now being blamed as one of the possible perpetrators behind the January 4 raid. It is also being held responsible for about 50 per cent of the attacks in southern Thailand since.[137] Security officials claim that PUSAKA was brainwashing children in their schools to rebel against the Thai motherland and to reject Thai nationality and that these schools have radicalised Thai Muslims and have fomented unrest.[138] Thai authorities also believe that PUSAKA was the underground movement that instigated the 28 April attacks.[139] The movement has been building its ranks for almost a decade by inciting people and training militias at religious schools in the south.

PUSAKA has been subjected to intense scrutiny by the government for the role Masae Useng plays in the foundation. Masae Useng, a known separatist activist also linked to BRN and Bersatu, is believed to be the Secretary of the foundation. It was during a raid in 2002–3 on Masae's home that Thai authorities found out about the group from some documents.[140] Masae is also believed to be running training camps for PUSAKA and is wanted by Thai security forces in connection with various incidents in the south, including the 4 January 2004 raid.[141]

According to security analyst Panitan Watanayagorn, an estimated 20,000 students have studied in schools under the PUSAKA foundation. Of this number, about 500 to 1,000 radicals have emerged. These radicals have divided themselves into various groups in the south and are now conducting or coordinating attacks at various places.[142] PUSAKA is said to provide military training through its schools under the guise of sports[143] and indeed 'sports' figures very highly in its list of activities.[144] PUSAKA also preys on young, unemployed, people who do not have access to education. Some of its recruits are also said to be drug addicts.[145]

As part of its responsibilities, PUSAKA visits *tadikas*, organises training sessions and seminars for *tadika* teachers and *tadika* committees who are working under the foundation. It also arranges meetings with other private organisations of Narathiwat, as well as observes *tadika* activities in Pattani. As such, PUSAKA can be said to have wide-ranging influence in the education sector in Narathiwat, and to a lesser extent, Pattani and Yala. It is highly plausible that PUSAKA may have used its reach to spread separatist ideology among its students and teachers. This concern is heightened as it is said to receive considerable funding. As it is a public institution, PUSAKA receives donations from the community in the south, private and government sectors, as well as the Office of Public Welfare in Narathiwat, Ministry of Welfare and Human Security.[146]

From the type of attacks for which PUSAKA members are being held responsible, it can be said that the group has significant capabilities compared to other separatist groups in southern Thailand. This may be because it has pooled resources with other groups such as BRN Coordinate, and is acting as a tactical alliance for specific missions. Being a clandestine organisation, it is also dangerous, as like the JI, PUSAKA was functioning for about a decade before its dubious role came to the attention of the government. Having been recently discovered, very little is known about PUSAKA. It seems to have a ready pool of recruits in the form of students of their schools. Although the separatist ideology in southern Thailand has somewhat waned since the 1980s, PUSAKA has managed to revive it through incitement and indoctrination under the guise of Muslim educational programmes in its schools.

The Situation Today

Apart from the major incidents such as the January 4 raids, it is difficult to determine the groups responsible for each particular attack. While some analysts suggest the reason for the resurgence in violence is that some groups may be working together, there is no real coordination among the groups as in the heydays of Bersatu. A very disturbing development could be found in the overlapping nature of the group membership. For example, the membership of Masae Useng, one of the key masterminds behind the southern unrest cuts across many groups. He was primarily a member of BRN. However, reports also suggest that he is also a member of the GMIP as well as new group PUSAKA. Thus the insurgency could very well be the handiwork of a group of free-floating cadres actually owing allegiance to none of the groups. This makes them more amorphous and more difficult to apprehend.

Emerging reports also indicate that BRN (more specifically BRN Coordinate) is working with PUSAKA and that this alliance is now the vanguard for the separatist movement in the south of Thailand. BRN Coordinate provides the military strength and firepower while PUSAKA deals with training and indoctrination. The movement is said to have a 1,000 day plan to take over the three southern provinces of Pattani, Yala and Narathiwat and establish an independent Pattani Darussalam.

RELIGIOUS SCHOOLS

The only one clear frontline that has emerged from this disturbingly opaque conflict in southern Thailand is the region's educational system. Here the educational system has become an arena of suspicion, fear and violence. In the provinces of Pattani, Yala and Narathiwat, schools have been repeatedly burnt. Teachers—both Muslim and Buddhist—have become prime targets for assassination. Security forces have raided Islamic schools in search of insurgents, which further angered the Muslims. The Thai prime minister has accused the *pondoks* of being a breeding ground for Muslim insurgents bent on causing disturbances in the south.[147] The government has repeatedly asserted that 'distorted' Islamic teaching has now become an ideological catalyst for unrest. It asserts that some young Islamic teachers (*ustaz*) are now recruiting volunteers for jihad and training them.[148]

Thailand's primary education is compulsory. The Ministry of Education has been following the national curriculum prescribed by the Education Act of 1921.[149] This provides children from the Malay-speaking Muslim minority with a solid grounding in the national language, and acts as a point of entry into the national mainstream.[150] In predominantly Muslim communities, students receive dual education—one in accordance with the prescribed curriculum and the other on Islamic studies.[151] The basic religious education is tutored in community-based tadika schools. *Tadika* (a contraction of the Malay *taman didikan kanak-kanak or kindergarten*)—informal schools attached to local mosques and funded by the community—provide instruction in Koranic teachings as well as lessons on Arabic and Malay. This is supplemented by senior students or teachers from higher-level Islamic giving weekend classes.[152]

Secondary education is compulsory for the first three years. At this stage, the education is provided by state-run schools as well as by private institutions. State schools (*rongrian rat*) account for an estimated 25–30 per cent of Muslim youth in the three border provinces. The system follows the standard national curriculum with instruction in Thai. There is also provision for Islamic studies for a few hours each week. The system that is more popular among Muslim parents however is the so-called 'private Islamic schools' (*rongrian ekachon sorn saatsanaa Islam*).[153] Muslims in the south view state-run schools with suspicion and believe that this is an attempt by Bangkok, to assimilate the region's distinct Malay-Muslim culture into the Thai mainstream. Furthermore, according to the local Muslims, the national curriculum is not able to meet all their needs, for example linguistic differences, and is not in sync with their belief systems and culture. As a result, there is an estimated enrolment of some 70-75 percent of Muslim youth in the three provinces in private Islamic schools. These institutions teach an integrated curriculum—general subjects and Islamic studies. General subjects are usually taught by both Muslim and Buddhist teachers in Thai. Instruction on Islam, taught in Arabic and Malay language in the afternoon, include Koranic and theological studies. The teachers are called *Ustaz* (Arabic), *Babo* (Malay) and *Acharn* (Thai). Upon completion of their studies, the students receive academic qualifications based on a centralised evaluation standard, which permit them to continue studies, general or religious, in the national tertiary system.[154]

Registered with the Ministry of Education, these private schools receive financial assistance from the government. The extent of financial assistance depends on the size of the enrolment (which varies from a few hundred pupils to more than 5,000 in larger institutions) and the point of entry into the educational system. Bigger schools operating under Clause 15 (1) of the Private School Act 1982 get 100 per cent support. Smaller institutions operating under Clause 15 (2) of the same Act, get

60 per cent support from the government. Nonetheless, the schools are free to receive donations from non-government benefactors, both from inside and outside of the country. For example, the Darun Sasna Wittaya School (*Pondok Babo Tar/Pondok Saphan Ma*) in the village of Saphan Ma in Pattani receives funding from the government, the Islamic Development Bank (IDB), the Islamic Bank of Thailand, its alumni, the local population, as well as donors and institutions in Malaysia and the Middle East.

Outside the mainstream education, there is another category of schools known as *pondoks* (locally known as *ponoh*, a corruption of the Malay word *pondok*). The reforms of the 1960s and international Islamic revivalism have led to the opening of many new *pondoks*, mostly unregistered. *Pondoks* are traditional village-based and conservative institutions that teach only Islamic studies. The language of instruction in these institutions is Malay. Islamic education includes teachings on *Nahu* and *Saraf* (Arabic grammar, learnt by rote memory), *Tafsir* (interpretation of the Koran), *Fiqh* (Islamic jurisprudence), *Hadith* (Prophet's Tradition), *Auzuluddeeen* or *Usool Addeen* (principles of religion or Islamic theology), *Balaghah* (eloquence) and Tasawuf (Islamic mysticism). The specific aspects of the curriculum are formulated by a respected Islamic scholar (or *doh-kru*). Also known as *Babo*, he is generally the owner of the school. If the enrolment in the school is large, *Babo* is assisted by *Ketua Mutalalaah* (assistant teachers). These are usually disciples or former students of *Babo*. There are usually no regular classes, the pattern of learning is loosely structured and study periods are elastic, often extending to seven or eight years at the end of which no formal diplomas or qualifications are issued.[155]

Pondok education prizes the virtues of simplicity and frugality as a way of life that stands in increasingly stark contrast to the financially driven materialism of Thailand's urban centres.[156] The teachers receive little or no payment and most, including the *Babo*, may also work in agriculture for sustenance. Students, usually from neighbouring communities, are mostly self-supporting, often building themselves simple palm-thatched huts as accommodation.[157] The simple lifestyle and focus on Islamic discourse in the *pondoks* have attracted pupils and teachers from neighbouring countries, notably from Malaysia, Indonesia, Cambodia and Myanmar. By law, foreign students and teachers are required to have study visas or work permits to gain entry into Thailand. However, education and immigration officials concede that the use of tourist visas and local border-passes is common. Added to the porous nature of the Thai-Malaysian border, this makes evading passport controls altogether a simple matter.[158]

Various Thai administrations since the 1960s have made efforts to assert control over the *pondoks*. Bangkok's first intervention was launched in 1960 under military strongman Sarit Thanarat, who viewed the schools as breeding grounds for separatist tendencies that were championed by dispossessed scions of Pattani's former sultanate.[159] Several of the traditional *pondoks* were then integrated by administrative fiat into the mainstream education system under Ministry of Education guidelines and 'upgraded' to private Islamic schools. Others closed down in protest. In some cases, teachers turned to armed revolt in what was seen as a defence of Islam. The most famous was the case of *Ustaz* Abdul Karim of Narathiwat, who took to the jungle and co-founded the National Revolutionary Front (Barisan Revolusi Nasional, or BRN).

Pondoks have long been set up as symbols of resistance against the centralised educational system imposed by the government.[160] It bears mention again that one of the biggest resistance movements against Bangkok was in response to the educational reforms imposed under the Education Act of 1921. This explains why many *pondoks* shun government funding, as this would expose them to national regulation and control. However, in June 2003, Thai police arrested Maisuri Haji Abdulloh and his son, both teachers at Islam Burana Tohnor School (Islamic Private School) in Narathiwat, and Waemahadi Wae-dao, a medical doctor. They were allegedly involved in a plot with JI to target foreign embassies in Bangkok and tourists resorts elsewhere in the kingdom. As our research suggests, this led to self-reflection among the *pondok* administration. 237 *pondoks* grouped themselves, registered and established the Association of *Pondok* Institutions on 19 August 2003.[161]

As part of its economic and social development packages, Bangkok has also been promoting greater investment in the southern provinces. In 2001, the government established the country's first Islamic Bank with its headquarters in Bangkok and branches in the south. This was an initiative to attract investment from the Gulf countries. However, there are concerns that this would increase radical Islamic influence, particularly from Saudi Arabia and Iran. Indeed, radical influence from outside Thailand has come under the spotlight especially after the 11 September 2001 terrorist attacks on the US. That incident alerted Thai authorities to the possibility that schools could emerge as breeding grounds for future insurgents with jihadist education. This triggered close scrutiny of the schools by security officials. However, subjects taught in the *pondoks* do not necessarily preach jihad. The Darun Sasna Wittaya School, known for both its secular and Islamic curriculum, is a good example. The school also provides vocational education, so as to prepare students for their traditional vocations such as in rubber plantations, orchards and fishery when they graduate. The curriculum also includes, ethical education (related to Islamic ethical principles), community relations, cross-cultural studies including the Thai way of life, environmental studies, social issues such as drug abuse, as well as sports. Despite this, there is still a concern that *Tasawuf* which deals with spirituality, could be misused to preach radicalism. *Tasawuf* deals with mysticism, which is a hallmark of *Shafi'ee* tradition. Use of religious mysticism to indoctrinate believers was very much evident during the 28 April 2004 uprising. Many of the suspects taken to custody told the interrogators that, before the attack, religious teachers gave them holy water to drink. This, they were told would make them invisible to the security forces. The manner in which groups of fanatics holding machetes and sticks challenged and attacked the highly trained and armed security forces demonstrates the level of indoctrination that the religious teachers have instilled using simple tenets of the religion.

Most of the *pondoks* are however non-radical. In a research interview, a teacher in Chongraksat Wittaya School (*Pondok Jor Ro Wor*) in Muang district of Pattani, said that the benefit of traditional *pondoks* is that they provide *Ilmu* (knowledge) to students free of charge. In his view, *pondoks* also 'develop the human heart, and he insisted that these religious schools have never engaged in military training.' The problem really lies with some of the teachers, especially those that have received religious education abroad—in Saudi Arabia, Pakistan, Bangladesh, to name a few. It is no secret that local teachers returning from studies in the Middle East, in particular Egypt and Pakistan staff these *pondoks*. Many teachers in Darun Sasna Wittaya School for example have studied in Egypt, Saudi Arabia, India, Indonesia, and Malaysia. Hayee Nima Waba, one of the earlier administrators of the school graduated in Islamic Education from Darul Ulum at Mecca, Saudi Arabia. Abdul Kadir, the *Babo* of Sasna Samakkee School (*Ponoh Keudae*, which means 'growth and development') in Nong Chik District, Pattani, graduated from Darul Ulum Institute at Mecca, Saudi Arabia. The founder of Sakun Sasna School (*Pondok Tuyong*) in the Nong Chik District of Pattani, Baba

Mayeh, studied Halqah (traditional form of teaching) at Al Haram Mosque, Saudi Arabia. The current chief of the school and also its manager, Baba Makorseng, and Abdulkarim Madiyu, an *ustaz* in the school, studied at the King Saud University in Saudi Arabia. Many religious scholars who studied abroad have established *pondoks* after their education and managed to sustain them because of their social standing or theological expertise. Others have turned to these private institutions for employment.[162] According to a recent report, the Thai police are in lookout for 21 religious teachers, mostly from Thamwittaya and Islamic Witthaya schools in Yala's Muang district, for instigating violence in the south. The Department of Special Investigation is also investigating about 100 foreign religious teachers who taught Islam in the southern provinces. Reportedly, about 20 of the teachers hailing from Indonesia, Jordan, Syria and Libya, are thought to have instigated young Muslim students to indulge in violence.[163]

The fact that some of the *pondoks* might have been used by the radicals with cross-border linkages is evident from the debriefing of one of the members of KMM. The KMM detainee told his interrogators that in 1999 he attended a religious indoctrination session at a retreat in Malaysia where 'at least one representative from the *madrasahs* in southern Thailand was present.' (In Malaysia, Islamic religious schools are called *madrasahs* while they are called *pondoks* in Thailand). Later they were 'also introduced to representatives from the Jemaah Islamiyah (JI).' Afterwards he was contacted to go for a retreat in southern Thailand. 'We were taken to a *madrasah* and I met other people from different groups like the JI, Hamas, Hizbullah. We were preached about armed conflict and discussed how to undertake suicide bombings.' Some of them were taught how to handle C4 explosives and weapons like M-16 assault rifles and how to network with other militant groups. They were also given instructions about covert work, jungle training, and the importance of secrecy. According to him, the *madrasahs* are run by Thai Muslims and Malaysians. From the outside, they look like ordinary religious schools. Even the students are not aware that the schools are used by the radicals to meet and conduct discussions. According to him, these *madrasahs* can be found all over southern Thailand. However, he was not sure if the radicals were responsible for the bombings in southern Thailand.[164]

However, as the teacher in Chongraksat Wittaya School puts it, '*Ustazs* in the traditional *pondoks* are not terrorists.' Many teachers do not accept violence as a means and do not agree with the claims of the radical groups that these are being done in the name of Islam. Similarly, Abdul Kadir of the Sasna Samakkee School said that the school's main concern is the educational empowerment of Muslims and not the establishment of a state based on *shari'ah*. He tells his students to be good citizens and integrate with the Thai mainstream. According to the Babo of Bakong Pittaya School in Nong Chik District, Pattani, 'Muslims have to be united and move into the future in the right path of Islam.' He maintains that 'there are some bad persons in every society, including the *pondoks*, but the authorities should not conclude that they all are terrorists.' According to Imtiaz Yusuf, head of the religious department at Bangkok's Assumption University, these institutions generate 'a very impressive amount of Islamic literature and religious scholars.'[165] Similarly, Surin Pitsuwan, former Thai foreign minister argues that the *pondoks* do not produce extremists or separatists.[166] This view is even echoed by the Thai security forces. Sirichai Thanyasiri, the head of the Southern Border Province Peace-Building Command said that *pondoks* are important Islamic institutions that teach morals and ethics to Muslims. However, he added that it was necessary to remove some 'bad elements' and 'distorted teaching'.[167]

Another area of concern that is closely linked to the *pondoks* is the mosques. As many of the *pondoks* operate in mosques, (the Darun Sasna Wittaya School operates in the Darul Nasi Een Mosque) students are liable to be exposed to radical preaching in the mosques, which often dabble in political issues. In many *pondoks*, religious education is imparted in the mosques themselves. For instance, in the Sakun Sasna School, every religious subject is taught at the mosque after the five praying times, using traditional *Kitab Melayu* (Malay books). The school also permits its male students to preach in the local mosques.

Educating students at a higher level is the Yala Islamic College. The south's first privately run Islamic college is the most obvious manifestation of what some may consider an extremist Wahabi intrusion into the traditionally moderate and tolerant Islamic traditions of southern Thailand (and the wider Southeast Asian region). The college has more than a dozen Arab teachers from across the Middle East. Most of the native staff are also educated in institutions in the Middle East, such as Al-Azhar University in Cairo, Egypt. The president, Dr. Ismael Lutfi, is himself a graduate of a hardline Wahabi institution, Riyadh's Imam Muhammad bin Saud Islamic University.[168]

The Wahabi connection is also evident in the funds the school receives. The college receives no support from the Thai government, relying on large donations from foreign organisations in the Middle East and construction capital from Saudi Arabia's Islamic Development Bank and International Islamic Relief Organisation. It also receives additional backing from Kuwait and Qatar, which have poured over 300 million baht into facilities and operations in the school. This heavy dependence on the Middle East has raised suspicion among authorities that groups with radical ideologies may be using money to influence Islamic educational institutions.[169]

Established in 1998, Yala Islamic College started with 200 local and foreign Muslim students and two majors in Islamic subjects, *shari'ah* law and theology, taught in the Arabic language. Today, it boasts more than 1,200students, some from as far north as China. Most of the students are togged in Arab-style dress. The school offers five majors, including public administration and foreign languages. Two more Islamic subjects on economics and information technology are expected to be offered in the in the coming years, in preparation for the promotion to a university within four years.[170]

Local intelligence and foreign observers have kept a close eye on Ismael Lutfi's movements and the development of his institution for any links with terrorist networks. It has been documented that Dr. Lutfi attended the Rabitatul Mujahidin (an umbrella organisation of Southeast Asian groups including the JI) meeting in Malaysia in 2000. In fact, Dr. Lutfi has been named by Ahmad Sajuli bin Adbul Rahman, a JI suspect held in Malaysian custody, as head of a group in Thailand linked to the JI, the Jemaah Salafiyah (JS).[171] However, Dr. Lutfi and his school have not been linked to the recent violence. The man himself has also dismissed the terrorist connection, saying he is against violence. Furthermore, the college's books are reported to the authorities regularly, and the curriculum is under the supervision of the Education Ministry, his staff says.[172] Still, the school is regarded as a dangerous influence, not just for its Wahabi leanings, but also Dr. Lutfi's supposed links to some militant groups.

THE COMPLEX INTERPLAY OF MILITANCY AND RELIGION

The schools may have tried to distance themselves from violence, but looking at how BRN was established, one cannot deny that religious education is inextricably linked to the southern Thai insurgency. Since the 1990s, many separatist groups have systematically targeted the education system. BRN has been particularly active in targeting schools and recruiting both teachers and students into their network. Documents seized in 2003 from the house of wanted BRN leader Masae Useng, indicated an interest in expanding propaganda activities into the *tadika* level. And since January 2004, the role of these schools has come under even sharper focus. The four religious school teachers arrested in December 2004 is perhaps the best proof that there is a link between militancy and religion. Furthermore, local intelligence sources believe that about 20 Muslim religious teachers are behind the almost daily shootings of security officials in Yala, Pattani, and Narathiwat. Military intelligence also suggests that in about 50 schools in the three provinces, students have undergone some level of military training.

Thai authorities report that as many as 300 *ustazs* from private Islamic schools may be active in the insurgency, serving as jihadist ideologues, recruiters, and operational leaders. Masae Useng, one of the key players, was a teacher at the Sampan Wittaya private Islamic school in Narathiwat's Cho Airong district. Another teacher, *Ustaz* Abdullah Akoh, who was arrested in July 2004 and admitted to being part of the network involved in the 28 April 2004 attacks, worked in Tham Wittaya Foundation School in Yala town. Ismael Yusuf, better known as *Ustaz* 'Soh', was described by several detained insurgents as having played a key role in mobilising youths for the attacks of 28 April 2004. He is also alleged to be involved in recruiting youths to undertake insurgent training outside Thailand. *Ustaz* Soh was employed at the Tarpia Tulwatan Mullaniti Islamic Boarding School in Yala for one semester during the period during 2001–2. According to sources in the school, *Ustaz* Soh was made to resign because of his 'rude behaviour.' Four of the persons who died in the 28 April uprising were students of this school. It is believed that Soh might have lured some of the students from this school to join his network, known as Talekat Hikmahtullah Abadan (Direction from God Towards Invincibility).[173] Similarly, Abdul Wahab Data, arrested by Thai security for the 28 April 2004 attacks, was also a former *ustaz* of the school. Wahab was also in the committee of the Al Amin Foundation and co-author of the book *Berjihad di Pattani*. Wahab, who also preached at the local mosque, admitted that he was persuaded by *Ustaz* Soh to join the movement. Owner and principal of Islam Burana Tonoh School, Maisuri Haji Abdullah and his son, Mujahid Haji Abdullah, have been in custody since June 2003 on charges of involvement with the regional terrorist network JI and allegedly plotting bomb attacks in Bangkok.[174] On 24 September 2004, police seized a large stash of ammunition in a raid on a house owned by Amad Tueyoh, an Islamic teacher at Thamma Withaya Foundation School in Yala's Muang district.

This reinforces the perception that though the schools in the southern provinces may not be directly involved in preaching jihad, some of the teachers might be doing so. Indoctrination is taking place only amongst individual teachers and in informal learning circles. Some charismatic persons have influenced a small and yet sufficient following to keep a low level insurgency going. The religious teachers in *pondoks* command a very high degree of influence in the local community. Unfortunately, many of the teachers have misused their influence with what Surin Pitsuwan terms 'sporadic outbursts of political opposition to the central government in their quest for a higher degree of self-rule.'[175] Even as the school administrations claim that they check the background of every teacher and *ustaz* before allowing them to work, there have been instances where these radical teachers have successfully embedded themselves into the Islamic educational system for the recruitment and indoctrination of insurgents. As Abdul Hamid Othman, the religious adviser to the Malaysian Prime Minister and a Malaysian government intermediary dealing with Thai Muslims, says, '[A]n insular Islamic education system is partly to blame for violence … in southern Thailand.'[176]

When police raided the hideout of Masae Useng, an important figure in BRN and GMIP as well as a religious school teacher, they found documents indicating that insurgent groups were reaching out to the younger generation. Another leading member of GMIP, Jaeku Mae Kuteh, believed to be living in Malaysia's Terengganu state, was also singled out as one of the masterminds of 4 January 2004 attacks. Investigators believe that, unlike older separatist groups such as Barisan Revolusi Nasional and the Pattani United Liberation Organisation, the new groups consist of smaller cells that carry out attacks as well as spread anti-government propaganda at the community level. Of the 10 persons arrested by Malaysian authorities during raids on shelters known to have been used by the KMM, which is known to be sympathetic to the cause of the Muslims in southern Thailand, four held dual Thai-Malaysian nationality. The others were Burmese and Pakistani nationals. In February

2004, police searched the residences in Narathiwat owned by three suspects—Ibrahim Hongyu, Mahama Puteh, and Giffari Vajeh. They found Malay-language documents detailing a plan to take over the three Muslim provinces. The same month, police arrested six Thai nationals in connection with Narathiwat army camp raid on 4 January 2004. Basae Bato, one of those arrested was allegedly connected with the BRN separatist group and was believed to be the right hand man of Masae Useng. Another person, Makata Harong, who was arrested in connection with 4 January 2004 incidents, was also a member of BRN.

Similarly, Nasori Saesaeng (also known as 'Awae Keleh' after the village in Narathiwat) is believed to be a veteran of the Afghan civil war and is said to have links to global jihadists. He founded the GMIP upon returning to Thailand in 1995.[177] Another key member of GMIP is Subay Useng, who was responsible for the bombing of a railway track in Yala's Raman district in August 2002. Subay Useng is a bomb expert who was probably trained overseas and is a close friend of Mahamae Maeroh, a GMIP leader. Mahamae Maero killed the Muang Pattani police chief and four other local officers and was later shot dead on 28 July 2004.

Some also attribute many of the attacks on government officials in Yala, Pattani, and Narathiwat to paybacks by local villagers for family members and friends they believe have been abducted and murdered by security officials. In March 2004, a worker, Lek Pinlamai, was shot dead by unknown assailants in Bannang Sata. Thai police found a letter near the body saying that they would continue killing innocent Buddhists in retaliation for the alleged abducting and killing of suspected Muslim terrorists. 'If you continue to abduct and kill innocent people,' it said, 'we will retaliate by killing innocent people.'[178] Another letter with a similar message was found in Yala's Betong district.

Apart from religious schools, evidence of the religion's complicity with militancy in southern Thailand can be seen in the 28 April 2004 attacks. Police discovered pamphlets in Arabic calling for the creation of a separate Muslim homeland. They said that this was evidence that the insurgents are fighting for a separate land on religious lines.[179] General Kitti Rattanchaya, a high-ranking security adviser to the government claimed that an underground shadowy movement that has been building its ranks for almost a decade was behind the recent spate of violence in the country. Some believe he may have been referring to PUSAKA. General Kitti claimed that, 'they (the separatists) are now reaching the sixth of seven steps towards establishing an independent Muslim state.

The sixth stage is the armed fight and the undeclared war and the final stage was a revolution and the formation of an Islamic state.'[180]

Interrogation of some of the suspects arrested after 28 April 2004 raids also revealed that a number of religious leaders, including Islamic provincial committee members with links to local politicians, played a key role in the uprising in the southern provinces of Pattani, Songkhla, and Yala. One of those arrested, Yusouf Yimadiyoh, said that he had been invited by a friend to join the group to fight for the liberation of 'Greater Pattani.' He also said that certain teachers in private Islamic schools had incited the young men to join the separatist movement. Yusouf told his interrogators that he had attended three training sessions at a secret location in Tambon Proon in Muang district in Yala. Training was given by coaches who had their faces covered. There were eight insurgents in his group and all of them came from Tambon Yupo. He said there was no gun training at all. Trainers would speak to the students in the Yawi language, urging them to fight for the freedom of "Greater Pattani" and that they should die fighting for their cause.[181] Yusuf claimed he was a 'jihad warrior' who was ready to die for Allah. 'At first, we drank holy water and swore we would keep our mission and activities secret. We were told not to tell parents or brothers as we had to work for God. If we told them, we were regarded as betraying God.' His leader gave them machetes and red clothes and said the outfits would make them invisible to the security forces. 'He told us to follow him and we would be safe. Nobody would see or injure us. We would sacrifice our lives for God. If survived (sic), we would get weapons.'[182]

After the incident, a 34-page booklet titled, 'The Fight for the Liberation of Pattani' (*Berjihad di Pattani*) was found on the bodies of some of the 108 insurgents killed. The handbook, written in Yawi, a Malay dialect written in Arabic script, urged Muslims to fight for greater autonomy of Pattani state and outlined steps which the author said would lead to the Pattani state gaining independence. 'Let us go and spark this fire and look for them everywhere, night and day, and kill those infidels to show non-believers that Muslims are strong while living in this world.'[183] The author compared the struggle of ethnic Malay-Muslims in southern Thailand to that of Muslims around the world against the non-Muslim rulers—disbelievers and *munafiks* (hypocrites) who are destroying Islam. These disbelievers, according to the author, 'make alliances throughout the world in order to annihilate Muslims.'[184] The book makes references to the Koran to justify an uprising to liberate the

predominantly Muslim provinces from non-Muslim rulers. The manual
maintained that once 'liberated', the state of Pattani must be ruled by
religious leaders. The book specifically singles out the adoption of *Shafi'ee*,
one of Islam's four schools of thought and jurisprudence, widely embraced
by Muslim communities in Indonesia, the Philippines, Brunei, and in
some areas of Africa. Addressing the local Muslims, specifically 'the
children of Pattani warriors and generally to every soul whose blood is
fused with faith and *taqwa* (god-consciousness),' the author urges Muslims
to 'wake up' and 'prepare an army to resurrect the greatness of Islam.'

> We should be ashamed of ourselves for sitting idly and doing nothing
> while the colonialists trampled our brothers and sisters. Our wealth
> that belonged to us is seized. The wealth of our country is confiscated.
> Our rights and freedoms have been curbed and our religion and
> culture have been sullied. Where is our commitment to preserve
> peace and security for our people? Remember, O Wira Shuhada
> brothers! Our late parents, brothers and sisters sacrificed their lives
> for their land as warriors; they left behind a generation with warrior
> blood flowing in their veins. Today, let us make a call so that the
> warrior blood will flow again and the generation will emerge again
> with us, even though we have to face pain and sorrow. With the
> blessings of the martyrs, the blood will flow. In every battlefield,
> they echo in the heart of every soul with 'There is no God but Allah
> and Mohammed is his Prophet. Allah is the Greatest' in them.
>
> Once again, I call upon all of you, O my fellow brothers, fighters of
> the land, join the army of Shuhada, enter the battlefields And I …
> and I will continue calling and motivating. Where is the blood of
> the past warriors? Where is the spirit of the warriors? Look at our
> elders, children and wives! Just how much suffering have they been
> through? Who else is responsible to protect them?[185]

The book appears to have been quite well-written in terms of jihadi
indoctrination, with very strong persuasive power. Prime Minister
Thaksin Shinawatra compared the book to the one written by Jim Jones,
an American cult leader who led about 800 people to a mass suicide in
Guyana in 1978.[186] However, not every Muslim in Thailand is taken in
by the book's preaching. Islamic clerics and civic leaders who discussed
the issue under the guidance of *Chularajamontri* Sawas Sumalayasak, the
spiritual head of the Thai Muslims, agreed that the book is nothing more
than propaganda and is in fact misleading. They believe it has put Islamic
teachings out of context. Consequently, it has not only tarnished the

image of Islam, but also affected national security.[187] The spiritual leader said that the 'book was neither a version of the Koran nor a textbook on Islam', rather a tool to deceive other Muslims into joining the separatist cause. Saman Korpitak, the Central Islamic Committee's public relations chief said that the book is 'a manual for outcast warriors to mobilise popular support in order to destroy Islam.' They urged Muslims to destroy all copies of the book.[188] Niti Hassan, president of the Council of Muslim Organisations of Thailand said that it is quite worrisome that young people are 'being attracted to the wrong teachings and interpretation of Islam.' He urged that 'the *ulama* (religious teachers) … release the correct facts about Islam to the youth.' Similarly, Ismail Ali, director of the college of Islamic Studies at the Prince of Songkhla University, in Pattani, said, 'The book has many verses of the Koran, but they have been taken out of context and included to fit into the argument the author is trying to make about violence. A young person unaware of the Koran's correct teachings could be tempted to violence after reading this book.' According to Ismail Ali, the book portends to destroy the communal harmony in Thailand between the Muslims and the Buddhists, and therefore, the message of the book must be challenged.[189]

It is now believed that the handbook was written by Issamul Yameena, (alias Isamail Jaafar or Pohsu), who resides in Malaysia's Kelantan state.[190] Isamail Jaafar was arrested by the Malysian authorities in August 2004. However, the Malaysians refused to hand him over to Thai authorities since he held dual citizenship.[191] Abdul Wahab Data (alias *Babor* Wahab), principal of Malayu Bangkok Ponoh School in the Muang district, reportedly confessed that he was a co-writer of the book. Abdul Wahab also confessed that he was among Muslim insurgents trained in Malaysia before they returned to stage the April 28 violence. The Malaysian authorities have also handed the written confession of Isamail Jaafar to Thai authorities.[192]

GLOBAL INSURGENT LINKS

The rapidly deteriorating situation in southern Thailand is indicative of the beginning of a new age of conflict in the south. At the beginning of the violence in January 2004, the Thai Premier insisted that 'international terrorists' were not behind the spiralling violence. According to him, some religious teachers from the south commuting between Thailand, Malaysia, and sometimes Indonesia were the masterminds. However, this perception has now changed. Many, including Thai government officials, are citing domestic insurgents' links with international terrorist organisations as the cause of the resurrection of violence in southern Thailand. Security agencies believe that the insurgents are getting outside help, 'possibly from the Kumpulan Mujahideen Malaysia' (KMM). Similarly, the London-based Asia Pacific Foundation in a report said that 'international insurgent groups may be behind the attacks and are contributing to increasing tensions' in the region.[193] It is no secret that covert ties existed between local separatists and regional Islamic insurgents, especially the KMM.[194] It was also suspected that JI and KMM have mobilised up to 300 million baht to incite unrest in the southern Thailand.

However, there is as yet no evidence of outside terrorist groups being directly involved in the conflict in southern Thailand. The following section explores the linkages that Thai groups have or have had in the past. This is based on the methods of analysis discussed earlier. Given the nature of the attacks at present, it is reasonable to conclude that so far there has not been any significant exchange of logistics and support between the groups in Thailand and those outside. At present, the capabilities of the Thai insurgents are rudimentary. They lack the sophistication necessary for large-scale escalation of violence, especially if they want to bring the attacks to Bangkok, as claimed by PULO. However, it is important to understand the linkages between the groups since these can be made use of by the insurgents in southern Thailand as the conflict escalates.

Leading members of PULO were known to have connections with the Free Aceh Movement in Indonesia, in terms of training. Interestingly, the getaway plan used by the insurgents in the January attacks on the army camp was similar to those used by Aceh rebels. Nails were scattered on the roads to delay forces pursuing the attackers. The Indonesian group, Front Pembela Islam (FPI) is known to be keenly interested with the developments in southern Thailand. For example, after the death of a significant number of Muslims on 28 April 2004, FPI gave a call for volunteers from Indonesia to join their co-religionists in jihad in southern Thailand. Similarly, seven of the 32 Muslims killed at Krue Se Mosque on April 28 following insurgent raids on government security outposts were not Thai citizens and were believed to have been Indonesians. Thai immigration officials reported that seven Indonesians had arrived in the country on April 18 and 19, through a border crossing between Thailand and Malaysia, and were not registered as having left the country.[195] There is however no confirmation yet about the true identity of the seven foreigners. Locals maintain that the unclaimed dead bodies were of those who were orphans or those whose family were not aware of their deaths. Given that it is a Muslim tradition to bury the dead within 24 hours, many unidentified dead bodies were left to the government agencies for burial.

Regional intelligence officials and terrorism experts believe that regional or international Islamic insurgents and local separatists could have been working together to stir up unrest in southern Thailand. As Thai Defence Minister Chettha Thanajaro puts it, "[W]e should not rule out the possibility of foreign terrorist groups taking advantage of the unrest to expand their network here."[196] In June 2003, Thai authorities arrested four Muslims, three from Thailand and one from Singapore, allegedly from the JI. They were apparently plotting to stage terrorist strikes in Bangkok, coinciding with the APEC summit in October 2003. Authorities recovered a tourist map of Bangkok with likely targets circled on it—reportedly including the embassies of the US, Britain, Israel, Australia, and Singapore from those persons. This followed the arrest in Bangkok on 16 May 2003 of Arifin bin Ali, a Singaporean alleged to be a senior member of the terror group.[197] Arifin, also known as John Wong Ah Hung, is an ethnic Chinese who converted to Islam. He received military training in a Moro Islamic Liberation Front (MILF) camp in the Philippines in 1999. Ali was arrested on a tip provided by Singapore intelligence, following the arrest of Mas Selamat Kastari who was the head of the JI cell in Singapore.[198] Thai Muslims, identified as Maisuri Haji Abdullah, his son Mayahi Haji Doloh, and medical doctor Waemahadi Wae-dao were arrested in the province of Narathiwat. Haji Abdullah and his son reportedly admitted to belonging to the JI and confessed that they were planning bomb attacks on embassies and tourist spots in Thailand such as Phuket and Pattaya.[199] Haji Abdullah was owner and teacher of the Islam Burana Tohnor School, funded by the Saudi charity Umm al-Qura (UAQ). The charity is believed to have been used by Al Qaeda to fund its own activities and that of its Southeast Asian associates such as the JI.[200] Thailand's Interior Minister said that the JI plan was for simultaneous explosions—an Al Qaeda trademark—with high-powered explosives to be concealed in vehicles at the targeted places.[201] Intelligence debriefing of Omar Al-Faruq, who was the Al Qaeda resident representative in Southeast Asia prior to his arrest, also revealed active involvement of Thai Muslims in the activities of JI. For example, representatives from Thailand were present in a meeting of the RM held sometime during May and July 2000 in Malaysia. Present in the meeting were many senior JI members such as Agus Dwikarna and representatives from Malaysia, the Phillipines and Singapore. In the meeting, the plans to attack Philippine interests in Indonesia, including the attack on the Philippine ambassador's residence in August 2000 was discussed. In another meeting of the RM held at Trobak Country Resort in Perak in November, 2000, Abdul Fatah, a key JI leader and arms procurement agent from Thailand was present. The meeting was arranged by Zulkifli Marzuki, a JI secretary for Malaysia and Singapore. In the meeting, the plans to bomb US interests in Singapore and the Christmas Eve bombings in Indonesia were discussed.[202] Faruq also told that senior Al Qaeda officials—Abu Zubaydah and Ibn al-Shaykh al-Libi—had asked him to 'plan large-scale attacks against US interests in Indonesia, Malaysia, (the) Philippines, Singapore, Thailand, Taiwan, Vietnam and Cambodia.'[203]

Another JI link to southern Thailand was Hambali, a key JI member, and Al Qaeda's point man in Southeast Asia. The suspected mastermind of the 2002 Bali bombings had taken shelter in Narathiwat before going to Cambodia. Hambali later returned to Thailand and went into hiding in Ayutthaya province until his arrest in August 2003. Apart from Hambali, other JI elements were found in Cambodia, some of them Thai. In June 2003, Cambodian authorities clamped down a religious school run by Umm al-Qura (UAQ), headed by an Egyptian, Esam Mohammad Khidr Ali. They also ordered the expulsion of 28 teachers, including some from Thailand. Two Thais were arrested on suspicion of having links with the JI.[204] One is allegedly a student of Dr. Ismael Lutfi.

Some intelligence agencies speculated quite early on that the violence in southern Thailand is perpetrated by JI. They believed that JI's Thai counterpart Jemaah Salafiyah (JS) was responsible for the violence. JS is very small group that was represented at the RM meetings. Ismael Lufti of the Yala Islamic College and Abdul Fatah of Pondok Hutan Tua are the leading figures of JS. The group has as yet not carried out any attacks but they have allegedly contributed to the funding of the Bali bombings. In March 2002, Malaysian JI member Wan Min Wan Mat passed over to one of the Bali bombers Mukhlas the sum of $15,000 in the province of Yala. Our research into JI and JS reveal that they are not behind the current wave of violence in Southern Thailand.

Ideologically, JI, JS, and Al Qaeda belong to the same family and their doctrines are incompatible with the groups perpetrating violence in Thailand today.

According to Thai Interior Minister Bhokin Bhalakula, a 'significant number' of Thai Muslims had taken part in the anti-Soviet jihad in Afghanistan. 'These veterans, who were regarded by the international community as mujahideen, or holy warriors, had adopted extremist ideologies while fighting against the Soviet Union. These ideologies have since been brought back to Thailand.'[205] The combination of the extremist ideology with local grievances has made it possible for the insurgents to expand their scope of targets to include civilians, non-security personnel and religious establishments, unlike the separatism of the previous decades.[206] It should be noted that Thailand forms part of *Daulah Islamiyah Nusantara*, the pan Islamic super-state that JI seeks to establish in Southeast Asia. The perceived oppression of the Muslims in southern Thailand offers avenues for trans-national terrorist groups such as Al Qaeda and the JI to co-opt ethno-nationalist Muslim resistance movement into the global jihad campaign. And as the southern Thai Muslims become more aware of the developments in the Muslim world—such as the US invasion of Iraq and Indonesia's offensive in the province of Aceh—these could become a source of inspiration for local insurgents who see their Muslim community as victims and under threat from foreign aggressors. There is now evidence that the insurgency is getting radicalized. Soon after the 28 April 2004 incident at the Krue Se Mosque, VCDs entitled *Global Jihad Movements* began to sell 'like hotcakes.' The businessman who opened his new shop near the Krue Se mosque after the incident revealed that these VCDs are a series on jihad movements in Afghanistan, Chechnya, and also about Osama bin Laden.[207]

Thai radical Islamic militancy has been mainly sustained by the radical groups that have cross-border linkages and patronage with Malaysia. Thailand has long alleged that PAS in Malaysia had nurtured and supported the PULO and New PULO groups with resources and safe haven and had facilitated the trans-shipment of arms from Cambodia.[208] The links were very strong during Operation Falling Leaves launched by PULO and New PULO. However, Thailand's pressure on Malaysia and cooperation through the trilateral Malaysia-Indonesia-Thailand Growth Triangle (MITGT) led to some action by the Malaysians to curb the linkages.

As mentioned, PULO used to have links with the Iranian Hizbollah. This was revealed during investigations in the aftermath of the attempted bombing of the Israeli Embassy in Bangkok in 1994.[209] The seizure of the saboteur and his trail led to the straining of Thai-Iranian relations. Nevertheless, as bilateral relations have now improved, the persistence of the Iranian connection cannot be overlooked, given the activities of the Iranian Cultural Centre in Bangkok and its financial support to many educational projects in the south.

Links to Radical Educational Institutions

There has also been extensive links between insurgent groups in South Asia and southern Thailand. *Madrasahs* have also been added to this equation as some are closely tied to the insurgent groups. According an intelligence analyst, Thai insurgents are using motorcycle drive-by shootings in recent targeted killings of individuals such as government officials and their relatives. This modus operandi closely resembles that used by the Sunni extremist Lashkar-e-Jhangvi (LEJ) and the Harkat-ul-Jihad-al Islami (HUJI) in Pakistan.[210] This tactic is taught in the *madrasahs* controlled by LEJ and HUJI in Pakistan, as well as those controlled by HUJI (Bangladesh). It is also well known that many Thai Muslims had been trained in *madrasahs* in Pakistan and Bangladesh. Before 11 September 2004, Pakistani *madrasahs* were host to more than 10,000 students from various countries, including those from Southeast Asia. These numbers have however substantially declined following the introduction of new regulations by the Pakistani government in 2002. According to Pakistani Interior Ministry reports, only about 1,500 foreign students studied in *madrasahs* in Pakistan in 2003. The number further dropped to only about 700 in 2004.[211]

Students from the Southeast Asian countries mostly enrol in Karachi seminaries, two of the most prominent being Darul Uloom Islamia Binori Town and Jamia Khalid Bin Waleed. According to reports released by the Sindh police, in 2004, there were about 200 students in Karachi seminaries and most of them were from Indonesia and Malaysia. Police sources claimed that these students have certificates from their respective governments allowing them to receive their education in Pakistan. However, inside sources claim that many foreign students in these seminaries do not have proper documentation. It is worth mentioning that the Binori *Madrasah* in Karachi is considered one of the most influential centres of hardline Deobandi Sunni Muslim ideology in the world. Many top ranking leaders of the former Taliban regime in Afghanistan were alumni of this school. Its head, Mufti Nizamuddin Sumzai, was the spiritual mentor of Mullah Omar, the leader of the Taliban, and was his unofficial adviser.[212]

Jamia Khalid Bin Waleed was established by the HUJI (Burma), an affiliate of HUJI International, the umbrella organisation for all HUJI groups. HUJI (Burma) operates in the Korangi area of Karachi. This area is a famous locality for Burmese and Bangladeshi immigrants. A few Thai Muslim families also live in this area. The majority of these people are poor and cannot afford education in formal educational institutions. Therefore, they send their children to *madrasahs*, which provide free education. There are 34 *madrasahs* in this area. Most of them are small and only provide primary level education with Koran memorisation. In the past, the Burma and Bangladesh chapters of the HUJI had used these localities and *madrasahs* for their activities. However, after continuous raids by law enforcement agencies, some of the HUJI leadership and teachers who were involved in jihadi organisations were arrested, while others fled.[213]

Apart from HUJI and LEJ, a large number of Muslims from Thailand also studied in some of the *madrasahs* run by groups such as Lashkar-e-Toiba (LET), Harkat-ul-Mujahideen (HUM), and Jaish-e-Mohammad (JEM).[214] All these groups have strong ideological and logistical affinity to Al Qaeda. According to an estimate published by the Human Rights Commission of Pakistan (HRCP), in 2002, there were 190 students from Southeast Asia in the *madrasahs* in the Sindh province of Pakistan. Of the 190, 86 were from Malaysia, 82 from Thailand and 22 from Indonesia. Similarly, 61 Malaysians, 49 Thai Muslims, and 41 Indonesians were in *madrasahs* in the Punjab province, while 21 Indonesians, 20 Malaysians and 18 Thais were in the *madrasahs* of Pakistan's North-West Frontier Province (NWFP).[215] The NWFP, the Federally Administered Areas (FAA), and the ruling coalition—the ultra-rightwing political conglomerate called Mutahidda Majlis-e-Amal (MMA)—are known for its amenability to radical teachings. Many of the *madrasahs* in these areas preach jihad and train insurgents, including those from Southeast Asia.

During the current phase of insurgency in southern Thailand, Lashkar-e-Toiba, one of the most violent insurgent groups fighting for the liberation of Kashmir from India, began to take an increasing interest in the area. It published a number of articles about the Muslim movements in Jamaatud Daawa[216] (JD) publications. A JD (Jamaatud Daawa is the parent organisation of LET) member mentioned that after the killings of Muslims in southern Thailand, the JD leadership had discussed the issue and offered their help to the Thai Muslims in their struggle against Bangkok. Although there is no clear evidence yet of any direct links between LET and the Thai groups, there was certainly an attempt on the part of JD to explore the possibility of providing assistance. The JD leadership reportedly sought information on whom to contact in southern Thailand should they want to assist in their struggle.[217]

It was also believed that teams from these Pakistani groups toured Southeast Asia posing as preachers of the Tablighi Jamaat (TJ), an international Islamic preaching setup. They recruited students and brought them back to Pakistan for training in the various *madrasahs*. Some of these students were also sent to Afghanistan and Kashmir to get jihad inoculation. It is to be noted, however, that the Tablighi Jamaat is not known to preach radical education. Its teachings are oriented toward the character reformation of Muslims. It has no links with insurgent organisations, although some insurgent group had misused the educational mission.

In October 2003, some Southeast Asian Muslims from two seminaries—Jama Darasitul Islamia Madrasah, a seminary run by the Jamaatud Daawa, and Abu Bakr Islamic University in Karachi—were arrested by the Pakistani security agencies. They were part of a JI cell in Pakistan codenamed 'al-Ghuraba' (meaning 'foreigners'). It was revealed that this cell was set up by Hambali in 1999, to train young Southeast Asian Muslims to become the next generation of leaders of the JI.[218] Hambali's brother Gun Gun Rusman Gunawan was the coordinator of the cell. He had been a student at Abu Bakr Islamic University since 1999. Of the 500 students in the university at any one time, around 200 are foreign nationals, mainly from Thailand, Indonesia, Malaysia, and Africa.[219]

In Bangladesh, the HUJI faction is known to have brought a small number of Thai Muslims, with the help of their Myanmar co-religionists to train in HUJI-controlled *madrasahs*. After the education and training they were then escorted back to Thailand. HUJI (Bangladesh) is a close affiliate of the Al Qaeda network. Its leader, Abdul Salam Muhammad (Fazul Rahman) was one of the signatories of the 1998 fatwa—the

International Islamic Front for Jihad against the Jews and the Crusaders—that was issued by Osama bin Laden and other Al Qaeda associates.

The HUJI (Bangladesh) has a long-established training infrastructure in Bangladesh. It is likely that this would be used to impart training and provide other facilities to jihadi elements from Southeast Asia, including Thailand. There are reports suggesting that funds are being channelled to Thailand from the Al Haramain office in Bangladesh for Arabic language classes and the dissemination of copies of the Koran in Arabic. The copies of the Koran come with exhortations to the local Muslims to study the Koran in the Arabic language only, and give up the use of the Thai language for this purpose.[220] There has so far been no indication of any supply of arms, ammunition and explosives to the Thai Muslims.

Madrasah education is not necessarily linked to insurgent training and indulgence in violence. However, as Maulana Fazalur Rehman, the chief of Jamiat Ulema-e-Islam (JUI) in Pakistan puts it, 'the seminaries are the nurseries of the Islamic revolution.'[221] Given the closeness of the groups running the religious schools with the ideology of Al Qaeda and the Taliban, some form of extremist indoctrination cannot be ruled out. Furthermore, these students, most of them young, are especially susceptible to being recruited for jihad. Vali Nasr, an authority on Islamic fundamentalism, interviewed 70 Malaysian and Thai students in Pakistani *madrasahs*. He found that these students were being educated side by side with those that fought in the Afghan jihad. According to Nasr, when these students return to their respective countries, they become, at best 'hot-headed preachers in mosques' coaxing listeners to wage war against the infidels; and at their worst, 'they actually recruit or participate in terror acts.'[222]

In southern Thailand, direct involvement of the Al Qaeda terrorist network has not been evidenced yet. The US National Commission which enquired into the 11 September 2001 terrorist strikes in the US (9/11 Commission) has provided few details of the Al Qaeda connections to Thailand in its final report. The report mentioned that Khalid Sheikh Mohammad who masterminded the 11 September operation, reportedly considered possibilities for terrorist attacks elsewhere. Al Qaeda operative Issa al Britani toured Southeast Asia and met Hambali. Although Hambali's JI operatives did a surveillance of possible targets, including possible targets in Thailand, Singapore, Indonesia, and the Maldives, the proposals were never carried out.[223] Britani was arrested by the British in August 2004. Nevertheless, Bangkok featured prominently in Al Qaeda's global jihad agenda. For example, Al Qaeda operative Tawfiq bin Attash (also known as Khallad), involved in the USS Cole attack, went to Bangkok in December 1999 to reconnoitre security arrangements in the airport as well as on board the aircraft. He carried a box cutter in his toiletries kit onto the flight to Hong Kong. The security officials at the airport searched his carry-on bag and even opened the toiletries kit, but just glanced at the contents and let him pass. Khallad returned to Bangkok again and met Nawaf al Hazmi and Khalid al Mihdhar, two of the September 11 hijackers, and discussed the maritime attack plan. Apparently they preferred to do this in Bangkok as they thought it would enhance their cover as tourists to have passport stamps from a popular tourist destination such as Thailand.[224]

NOTES

1   ICPVTR, IDSS, trans., *Berjihad di Pattani* (The Fight for the Liberation of Pattani), 2004.
2   'Suicide-bomb warning issued', *Nation*, 3 May 2004.
3   Richard C. Paddock, 'Thai Rebels at Mosque Knew Their Fate, Witnesses Say', *Los Angeles Times*, 30 April 2004: A3.
4   'Carnage in south of Thailand may unify separatists', *Straits Times*, 3 May 2004.
5   'Superstition, fear and loathing: the secret life of a Thai Muslim insurgent', channelnewsasia.com, 1 September 2004, available at http://www.channelnewsasia.com/stories/afp_asiapacific/view/104320/1/.html.
6   'Suicide-bomb warning issued', *Nation*.
7   'Carnage in south of Thailand may unify separatists', *Straits Times*.
8   'Suicide-bomb warning issued', *Nation*.
9   'Don't interfere, warns Thai PM', *Straits Times*, 3 May 2004.
10 'A symbolic date?' *Nation*, 30 April 2004.
11 Joseph C. Y. Liow, 'Violence and the Long Road to Reconciliation in Southern Thailand' (paper presented at the Conference on Religion and Conflict in Asia: Disrupting Violence, Arizona State University, 14–15 October 2004), 11.
12 '78 die in riot aftermath', *Straits Times*, 27 October 2004.
13 'Protest triggers deadly riot', *Straits Times*, 26 October 2004.
14 '81 more dead; riot toll hits 87', *Bangkok Post*, 27 October 2004.
15 '78 die in riot aftermath', *Straits Times*, 27 October 2004.
16 'Weapons show protest was planned', *Straits Times*, 27 October 2004.
17 '78 die in riot aftermath', *Straits Times*, 27 October 2004.
18 'Pulo "to set city ablaze"', *Bangkok Post*, 28 October 2004.

19   'Thai insurgent group threatens Bangkok with attacks', *Reuters*, 27 October 2004.

20   'Thai rebels warn of fresh attacks', *Straits Times*, 30 October 2004.

21   'Phone bomb kills owner of Yala noodle shop, 47 hurt', *Bangkok Post*, 17 January 2005; 'Bomb kills one, injures dozens in noodle shop', *Nation*, 17 January 2005.

22   'Army, police on high alert for cabinet meeting in South', *Nation*, 16 March 2004.

23   Areepen Uttrasin, *The Local Administration of the Special Area of the Five Provinces in the South of Thailand* (in Thai, unpublished, the Partial Fulfilment Report for the High Certificate, King Prajadhipok's Institute, 2002), 5.

24   'Some attacks "due to political rivalry"', *Nation*, 23 February 2004.

25   'TRT MPs and senator implicated', *Bangkok Post*, 22 March 2004.

26   Dana R. Dillon, 'Insurgency in Thailand: The U.S. Should Support the Government', *The Heritage Foundation, Executive Memorandum* #936 (10 June 2004), available at http://www.heritage.org/Research/AsiaandthePacific/em936.cfm.

27   'Thai PM blames militant for raids', BBC, 28 April 2003, available at http://newswww.bbc.net.uk/2/low/asia-pacific/2982101.stm.

28   'New security chief says he doesn't know who enemy is', *Nation*, 8 October 2004.

29   'Plan to capture province', *Nation*, 14 January 2004.

30   This section gives an overview of the insurgent groups that are still active in southern Thailand. For an in-depth look at these groups, see Appendix 9.

31   Lukman Iskandar, 'Deceiving Commander of Region 4 army to sign peace agreement with BRN: Time to speak the truth', BRN Information Department, 15 February 2000, available at http://members.fortunecity.com/patani_republic/fourarmy.html.

32   'Thai police put on alert against separatist attack', Xinhua News Agency, 5 August 2002.

33   Iskandar, 'Deceiving Commander'.

34   'Brief History: Patani Peoples' Revolutionary Commando Regiment', Institute of Patani Research & Strategic Studies, available at http://www.geocities.com/brn_president/resinstitu.html.

35   'Finding the truth behind the peace accord between BRN and Region Four Army', Institute of Patani Research & Strategic Studies, available at http://www.geocities.com/brn_president/resinstitu.html.

36   'Split in BRN – Patani Malay National Revolutionary Front', Institute of Patani Research & Strategic Studies, available at http://www.geocities.com/brn_president/resinstitu.html.

37   'Finding the truth', Institute of Patani Research & Strategic Studies.

38   'Sketch of "top rebel" released', *Nation*, 9 January 2004.

39.   'New Political Strategy & Reform', Institute of Patani Research & Strategic Studies, available at http://www.geocities.com/brn_president/resinstitu.html.

40 'National Armed Forces of Patani Republic', Department of Information of BRN, 13 March 1983, available at http://www.geocities.com/brn_president/patani.html.

41 Iskandar, 'Deceiving Commander'.

42 Ibid.

43 '22-Point Demand', PKRRP (Pasukan Komando Revolusi Rakyat Patani, or Patani People's Revolutionary Commandos Brigade), 18 November 1991, available at http://www.geocities.com/brn_president/22d.doc.

44 Lukman Iskandar, 'BRN's letter to General Chavalit Yongchayudh', 19 January 1996, available at http://www.geocities.com/brn_president/chava.doc.

45 'New Political Strategy', Institute of Patani Research & Strategic Studies.

46 Ibid.

47 'National Armed Forces of Pattani Republic', BRN Department of Information, available at http://www.geocities.com/brn_president/abrep.doc.

48 Iskandar, 'Deceiving Commander'.

49 'Pasukan Komando Revolusi Rakyat Patani (PKRRP)', Institute of Patani Research & Strategic Studies, available at http://members.fortunecity.com/pattanicity/amanat.html.

50 'Teacher arrested, explosives seized', *Bangkok Post*, 4 November 2002.

51 'Den Tohmeena builds his dynasty in Patani', Institute of Patani Research & Strategic Studies, 12 December 1989, available at http://www.geocities.com/brn_president/resinstitu.html.

52 'All State Officials At Risk', *Bangkok Post*, 11 July 2002.

53 T. Davis, 'Thailand's troubled south', *Jane's Terrorism & Security Monitor*, 1 October 2003.

54 'New Political Strategy & Reform', Institute of Patani Research & Strategic Studies.

55 'Counter Proposal by Barisan Revolusi Nasional Melayu Patani (BRN) to Privy Council of Thailand Regarding Peace Plan of BRN', The Office of the Secretary General, Patani Malay Revolutionary Front, 17 January 1996, available at http://www.geocities.com/brn_president/22d.doc.

56 'Muslim group volunteers from south Thailand reportedly going to Afghanistan', *Matichon*, 30 September 2001.

57 Wassana Nanuam, 'Army blames Muslim insurgents', *Bangkok Post*, 9 April 2001.

58 Rob Fanney, 'Pattani United Liberation Organisation', *Jane's Terrorism and Insurgency Centre*, 31 Oct 2002.

59 Ibid.

60 'Thaïlande: retour de la violence dans le Sud du pays' (in French), *Terrorisme.net*, 19 August 2002, available at http://www.terrorisme.net/analyse/2002/002_thai.htm.

61 'The Year of National Reorganisation (1988–1989)', Pattani United Liberation Organisation, available at www.pulo.org/reorg.html.

62 Ibid.
63 Peter Chalk, 'Separatism and Southeast Asia: The Islamic Factor in Southern Thailand, Mindanao, and Aceh', *Studies in Conflict and Terrorism* vol. 24 (July 2001): 241–269.
64 'Exiled PULO leader', *Nation*, 14 May 2003.
65 'Thailand Islamic Insurgency', GlobalSecurity.org.
66 Hj. Lukman Bin Lima, 'PULO calls for "self-determination in Patani"', *Pattani United Liberation Organisation*, 29 January 2003, available at http://web.archive.org/web/20030202022511/pulo.org/pulo/calls.htm.
67 Chalk, 'Separatism and Southeast Asia'.
68 Ibid.
69 Fanney, 'Pattani United Liberation Organisation'.
70 Ibid. See also Peter Searle, 'Ethno-Religious Conflicts: Rise or Decline? Recent Developments in Southeast Asia', *Contemporary Southeast Asia* vol. 24, no. 1 (April 2004): 78.
71 Chalk, 'Separatism and Southeast Asia'.
72 Fanney, 'Pattani United Liberation Organisation'.
73 Hamid Papang, 'Thai army launches operation against Muslims', *Muslim Media*, February 1998: 16–28, available at http://www.muslimedia.com/archives/sea98/thai.htm.
74 Ibid.
75 Ibid.
76 Chalk, 'Separatism and Southeast Asia'.
77 Fanney, 'Pattani United Liberation Organisation'; 'Child Soldiers Report 2001: Thailand', available at www.child-soldiers.org/report 2001/countries/thailand.html.
78 Fanney, 'Pattani United Liberation Organisation'.
79 'Primer: Muslim Separatism in Southern Thailand', Virtual Information Center, 23 July 2002, available at http://www.vic-info.org/0a256ae00012d183/626e6035eadbb4cd85256499006b15a6/e42514a843d9a3260a256c05006c2d84?OpenDocument.
80 Fanney, 'Pattani United Liberation Organisation'.
81 Ibid.
82 Ibid.
83 Chalk, 'Separatism and Southeast Asia'
84 Ibid.
85 Onnucha Hutasingh and Nauvarat Suksamran, 'Cross Border Terrorists Extorting Money from Businesses', *Bangkok Post*, 13 July 1997.
86 'Alleged Muslim rebels behead kidnap victims', *Phuket Gazette*, 6 June 2001.
87 Hutasingh and Suksamran, 'Cross Border Terrorists'.
88 Chalk, 'Separatism and Southeast Asia'.
89 Peter Chalk, 'Political Terrorism in Southeast Asia', *Terrorism and Political Violence*, vol. 10, no. 2 (1998): 118–134.

90 Pares Lohason and Don Pathan, 'Southern Violence: Four battalions hunting 60 separatist rebels', *Nation*, 8 January 2004; Jane Perlez, 'Cracks in Thailand's Peace', *New York Times*, 8 March 2004.

91 'Insurgents face treason charges', *Nation*, 15 January 2004.

92 Ibid.

93 Ibid.

94 Rob Fanney, 'Gerakan Mujahideen Islam Pattani (GMIP–Pattani Islamic Mujahideen Movement)', *Jane's Terrorism and Insurgency Centre*, 31 October 2002.

95 'Insurgents face treason charges', *Nation*.

96 Ibid.; 'Police claim to have located insurgents', *Nation*, 12 January 2004.

97 'Trouble in the South: Schools linked to attacks: PM', *Nation*, 12 January 2004.

98 'Bt1m reward for top suspect', *Nation*, 7 January 2004.

99 'Trouble in the South', *Nation*; 'Agency discord endangers region', *Nation*, 30 January 2004.

100 Jason Gagliardi, 'Behind the News—Fear and Fervour', *South China Morning Post*, 5 February 2004.

101 Fanney, 'Gerakan Mujahideen Islam Pattani'.

102 Anthony Davis, 'Thailand faces up to southern extremist threat', *Jane's Intelligence Review*, 1 October 2003.

103 Fanney, 'Gerakan Mujahideen Islam Pattani'.

104 Ibid.

105 Wassayos Ngamkham Yuwadee Tunyasiri, 'Malaysia-based units "running the show"', *Bangkok Post*, 3 April 2004.

106 Fanney, 'Gerakan Mujahideen Islam Pattani', *Jane's Terrorism and Insurgency Centre*.

107 Ibid.; Pares Lohason and Don Pathan, 'Two more suspects held on swoop in Pattani village', *Nation*, 9 January 2004.

108 Fanney, 'Gerakan Mujahideen Islam Pattani'.

109 'Attackers had "outside help"', *Nation*, 9 January 2004.

110 'Thai Islamic Insurgents', GlobalSecurity.org.

111 Fanney, 'Gerakan Mujahideen Islam Pattani'.

112 Ibid.

113 'ISOC Blames Separatists For Bombs', *Bangkok Post*, 3 July 2002.

114 Fanney, 'Gerakan Mujahideen Islam Pattani'; Pares Lohason, 'Malaysia hands over suspected terrorists', *Nation*, 11 January 2004; 'Bt1m reward for top suspect', *Nation*.

115 Tunyasiri, 'Malaysia-based units "running the show"'.

116 'Bt1m reward for top suspect', *Nation*.

117 Ibid.

118 Fanney, 'Gerakan Mujahideen Islam Pattani'.

119   BIPP is the new name of Barisan Nasional Pembebasan Patani (BNPP, or National Liberation Front of Pattani). Formed in 1959, the group is no longer considered to be active.

120   BNP is said to be made up of members who left the BNPP. Established in 1985, its aim was to consolidate the various separatist groups into one single entity. The group is no longer considered active.

121   'Payong' means 'umbrella' in Malay.

122   'Columnist Views Activities of Muslim Terrorist Groups in Southern Thailand', *Matichon*, 24 June 2001.

123   'Primer', Virtual Information Center.

124   'Police Put on Alert for Separatist Attack', *Bangkok Post*, 5 August 2002.

125   Ibid.

126   Don Pathan, 'Separatist wants to return: Bersatu leader Wan Kadir says he will work for peace if allowed to come back', *Nation*, 9 December 2004.

127   'Thailand: Leaders of Group Blamed for Southern Weekend Bombing Named', *Nation*, 11 April 2001.

128   Shawn W. Crispin, 'Thailand's War Zone', *Far Eastern Economic Review*, 11 March 2004.

129   Muhamad Ayub Pathan and Abdulloh Boonyakaj, 'Bersatu separatists blamed for bombs', *Bangkok Post*, 25 March 2004.

130   'Army Names Bersatu as Culprits', *Bangkok Post*, 11 April 2001.

131   Tunyasiri, 'Malaysia-based units "running the show"'.

132   Intelligence brief, ICPVTR, IDSS Registry.

133   Kavi Chongkittavorn, *Nation*, email interview, 5 March 2004.

134   'TRT MPs and senator implicated', *Bangkok Post*.

135   'Najmuddin granted Bt3m bail', *Nation*, 4 June 2004.

136   'MP faces treason charge', *Bangkok Post*, 23 March 2004.

137   Chidchanok Rahimmula, 'The Situation in Southern Thailand', Institute of Southeast Asian Studies Seminar, 12 April 2004.

138   Surasak Tumcharoen and Sermsuk Kasitipradit, 'MP denies being subversive', *Bangkok Post*, 2 April 2001; 'Thailand fears more attacks as Muslim separatists blamed for violence', channelnewsasia.com, 30 April 2004, available at http://www.channelnewsasia.com/stories/afp_asiapacific/view/82608/1/.html.

139   'Southern carnage: Kingdom shaken', *Nation*, 29 April 2004.

140   Nirmal Ghosh, 'Shadowy group behind violence', *Straits Times*, 1 May 2004.

141   'TRT MPs "fund body linked to insurgents"', *Nation*, 2 April 2004.

142   'Thailand fears more attacks as Muslim separatists blamed for violence', channelnewsasia.com.

143   Rahimmula, 'The Situation in Southern Thailand'.

144   Intelligence brief, ICPVTR, IDSS Registry.

145   Ghosh, 'Shadowy group behind violence'.

146 Intelligence brief, ICPVTR, IDSS Registry.

147 'Unrest in the South: Muslims pledge loyalty to King', *Nation*.

148 'I joined to liberate Pattani', *Nation*, 5 May 2004.

149 For a detailed analysis on Thailand's education and economy, see Pasuk Phongpaichit and Chris Baker, *Thailand: Economy and Politics* (Kuala Lumpur: Oxford University Press, 1995).

150 Anthony Davis, 'School System Forms the Frontline in Thailand's Southern Unrest', *Jane's Intelligence Review*, 1 November 2004.

151 Kazi Mahmood, 'Poverty Grips Muslims in Southern Thailand', *Islam Online*, 12 February 2004, available at http://www.islamonline.net/English/News/2004-02/12/article04.shtml.

152 Davis, 'School System Forms the Frontline'.

153 Ibid.

154 Input from ICPVTR, IDSS Outreach Researchers.

155 Davis, 'School System Forms the Frontline'.

156 See Hasan Madmarn, *The Pondok and Madrasah in Patani* (Bangi:Penerbit Universiti Kebangsaan Malaysia, 1999).

157 Davis, 'School System Forms the Frontline'.

158 Ibid.

159 Surat Horachaikul, 'The Far South of Thailand in the Era of the American Empire, 9/11 Version, and Thaksin's "Cash and Gung-ho" Premiership' (paper presented at MSRC-KAF Intercultural Discourse Series, Dealing with Terrorism Today: Lessons from the Malaysian Experience, Kuala Lumpur, 23 July 2004).

160 Pasuk Phongpaichit and Chris Baker, *Thailand: Economy and Politics* (Kuala Lumpur: Oxford University Press, 1995), 273.

161 Input from ICPVTR, IDSS Outreach Researchers.

162 Davis, 'School System Forms the Frontline'.

163 'Phone bomb kills owner of Yala noodle shop, 47 hurt', *Bangkok Post*, 17 January 2005.

164 Intelligence brief, ICPVTR, IDSS Registry.

165 Macan-Markar, 'Class dismissed in Thailand's South', *Asia Times Online*, 24 February 2004, available at http://www.atimes.com/atimes/Southeast_Asia/FB24Ae01.html.

166 Ibid.

167 'Sirichai Admits He's in the Dark', *Nation*, 8 October 2004.

168 John R. Bradley, 'Waking Up to the Terror Threat in Southern Thailand', *Straits Times*, 27 May 2004.

169 'Crown Prince to open Islamic college headquarters in Pattani', *Nation*, 6 March 2004.

170 Ibid.

171 'Terror cell headquarters moved to Malaysia, says suspect', *Agence France Presse*, 4 July 2003.

172   'Crown Prince to open Islamic college headquarters in Pattani', *Nation*.

173   'Imam admits to contact with separatists', *Nation*, 1 September 2004.

174   Davis, 'School System Forms the Frontline'.

175   Surin Pitsuwan, *Islam and Malay Nationalism*, (Bangkok: Thai Khadi Research Institute, Thammasat University, 1985), 179.

176   'Interview: South Thai violence due to school system – Malaysia', Yahoo! India News, 16 December 2004, http://in.news.yahoo.com/041216/137/2ihxu.html.

177   'Insurgents face treason charges', *Nation*, 15 January 2004.

178   'Sungai Kolok Blast: Bombers in Malaysia', *Nation*, 31 March 2004.

179   'Police to search dead insurgents' homes', *Bangkok Post*, 1 May 2004.

180   'Shadowy group behind violence', *Straits Times*, 1 May 2004.

181   'I joined to liberate Pattani', *Nation*.

182   'Detainee says hooded men trained rebels', *Bangkok Post*, 14 May 2004.

183   'Book found on dead insurgents a call to arms', *Nation*, 5 June 2004.

184   ICPVTR, IDSS, trans., 12.

185   ICPVTR, IDSS trans., 3.

186   'Govt seeks help from local clerics', *Nation*, 4 June 2004.

187   'Muslims told to destroy govt booklet', *Nation*, 11 June 2004.

188   'Call to destroy "jihad manuals"', *Asia Media*, 11 June 2004, available at http://www.asiamedia.ucla.edu/article.asp?parentid=11932.

189   Marwaan Macan-Markar, 'Muslim Leaders Take on Youth to Stem Southern Violence', *Globalinfo.org*, 14 June 2004.

190   'Imam admits to contact with separatists', *Nation*.

191   'Principal admits co-writing book', *Bangkok Post*, 1 September 2004.

192   Ibid.

193   Claude Salhani, Al Qaeda's 'second front', *Washington Times*, 2 May 2004, available at http://www.washingtontimes.com/commentary/20040501-114211-6697r.htm.

194   'Thailand Islamic Insurgency', GlobalSecurity.org.

195   'Thai officials urge reconciliation', *Taipei Times*, 5 May 2004, http://www.taipeitimes.com/News/world/archives/2004/05/05/2003154204.

196   'Sungai Kolok Blast: Bombers in Malaysia', *Nation*.

197   'Thailand Islamic Insurgency', GlobalSecurity.org.

198   Dan Murphy, 'Southeast Asia's 'mini-Al Qaeda' nests in Thailand', *Christian Science Monitor*, 13 June 2003, available at http://www.csmonitor.com/2003/0613/p07s01-woap.html.

199   'Four Thai Muslims Go on Trial over JI, Bomb Plot Charges', *Clari News*, 18 November 2003, available at http://quickstart.clari.net/qs_se/webnews/wed/ch/Qthailand-attacks-ji.RSwQ_DNI.html.

200   'The Hard Cell', *Time Magazine*, 16 June 2003, http://www.time.com/time/asia/magazine/article/0,13673,501030623-458843,00.html.

201 Murphy, 'Southeast Asia's 'mini-Al Qaeda' nests in Thailand'.

202 Intelligence debriefing notes, ICPVTR/IDSS.

203 'Confessions of an al-Qaeda Terrorist', *Time*, 15 September 2002, available at http://www.time.com/time/covers/1101020923/story.html.

204 'Cambodia meets Islam head on', *Asia Times*, 3 June 2003, available at http://www.atimes.com/atimes/Southeast_Asia/EF03Ae02.html.

205 'Govt seeks help from local clerics', *Nation*, 4 June 2004.

206 Ibid.

207 'Publicising 'jihad' with video discs', *Nation*, 27 May 2004.

208 Surin Pitsuwan, 'Issues Affecting Border Security Between Malaysia and Thailand', *Thammasat University Series* no. 4 (1982).

209 'Shi`ite-PULO Link Seen in New Hat Yai Blast Theory', *Bangkok Post*, 13 January 1995; 'Iranian Man Acquitted and Released', *Bangkok Post*, 19 February 1998.

210 B.Raman, 'Muslim Anger: The Thai Dilemma', *ORF Analysis* no. 309, (New Delhi: Observer Research Foundation, 2004).

211 Data from Amir Rana, research analyst, ICPVTR, IDSS.

212 Ibid.

213 Ibid.

214. B. Raman, 'Thailand & International Islamic Front', *South Asia Analysis Group*, Paper no. 890, 9 January 2004, available at http://www.saag.org/papers9/paper890.html.

215 Ibid.

216 Jamaatud Daawa is the parent organisation of LET.

217 Data from Amir Rana, research analyst, ICPVTR, IDSS.

218 '2 young Singaporean JI members arrested', *INQ7.net News*, 19 December 2003.

219 Owais Tohid, 'Awakening a Sleeping Giant', *Newsline*, October 2003, available at http://www.newsline.com.pk/NewsOct2003/newssepoct.htm.

220 B. Raman, 'Muslim Anger'.

221 'Religious students leaving Pakistan', *Daily Times*, 15 September 2003, available at http://www.dailytimes.com.pk/default.asp?page=story_15-9-2003_pg7_11.

222 'Analysis Madrassas, Interview with Vali Nasr', *PBS Frontline*, available at http://www.pbs.org/wgbh/pages/frontline/shows/saudi/analyses/madrassas.html.

223 *The 9/11 Commission Report: Final Report of the National Commission on Terrorist Attacks upon the United States* (Authorized ed.), (New York and London: W. W. Norton and Company, 2004), 150.

224 Ibid., 159.

CHAPTER 3

Strategies, Targets, and Tactics

STRATEGIES

A few new strategies have emerged in southern Thailand which cannot simply be put down as mere coincidences. For example, in inciting violence and unrest, especially after the 4 January 2004 raids, the perpetrators used unusual and unconventional methods. While these have baffled security personnel and analysts alike, the resort to such methods reflect the depth of indoctrination that the masterminds of the unrest have instilled in the disaffected population. This is also indicative of the future trajectory of the conflict and its escalation potential.

One of the strategies that have come to the fore recently is what security analysts call the use of agitprop methods similar to those used by the communists in the past. In such a scenario, the leaders, in this case Muslim clerics and community leaders, build up confrontational situations with the security forces in order to provoke them to overreact. Such agitprop methods were typically demonstrated on 28 April 2004, outside the Krue Se Mosque, and in the incident of 25 October 2004. Thai security forces are known to take heavy-handed measures to control the violence, which the present administration usually endorses as legitimate and necessary. Prime Minister Thaksin is a tough go-getter. His background in criminology and police work has made him supportive of the actions taken by the police. The overreaction by the security forces has however been counter-productive, resulting in excesses. This has fuelled Muslim anger further with a growing perception among the Muslims that the administration in general and the security forces in particular are anti-Muslim. It is apparent that the separatist leaders are exploiting the age-old Muslim anger and resentment against the security forces and the government. This sentiment dates back to the days when authorities employed exceptionally heavy-handed tactics against separatists, including the beheading of separatist leaders.[1]

The human rights violations, especially the type that occurred during the last week of October 2004, have further alienated the man in the street from the security forces as well as against the government. There have been instances in which community volunteers working with the security forces to restore normalcy have themselves handed over their weapons to insurgents and later attempted to cover them up as thefts. This was in fact what led to the riots in Tak Bai on 24 October 2004. When police enquiries lead to arrests or detention, they have been systematically resisted, leading to violent outcomes. This has also been the case when security forces attempted to search religious schools or arrest religious teachers. Haji Nideh Waba, president of the group Private Islamic Schools in Five Southern Border Provinces, railed against the government saying 'such acts show that the government is using dirty tactics on Islamic teachers.'[2]

Similarly, the insurgents may well be using one of the tactics that Thai security has been known to adopt to stir up more feelings of distrust. This involves abduction and the subsequent disappearance of suspects picked up by the police. In some cases, after the police have released the suspects, many of them were immediately abducted by masked persons, never to be seen again. One of the so-called disappearances that has provoked much resentment and outcry is the one involving Somchai Neelapaijit, a Muslim lawyer. While all the 'disappearances' may not be the work of the security agencies, with its past reputation, the blame almost invariably lands on the security forces, prompting further backlash. One such revenge attack was in March 2004 when a letter found near the body of a slain worker stated that the insurgents would continue killing innocent people in retaliation for the alleged abducting and killing of suspects by police.[3] The institution of inquiries by the country's human rights commission has not been able to address this problem successfully so far.

In many cases, clerics and community leaders have interpreted incidents of violence as stage-managed by the local security agencies in order to have Muslims discredited as terrorists. For example, after the armoury heist on 4 January 2004, Abdullah Ahamad, a religious teacher in Pattani, accused the police of selling the firearms issued to them to smugglers and blaming the Muslims for allegedly looting them. 'The arms were stolen not by Muslim Mujahideen or by separatists, but with the help of the soldiers in the camps. The schools were burnt by pro-government elements.'[4] Another retired teacher, Yapa Barahaeng, alleged,

'Muslim groups haven't done this. It seems the government itself or the police or military have done it.'[5]

For the most part, there have not been spontaneous outbursts of public anger, but carefully instigated and orchestrated violence. The orchestrated attempts to denigrate the professionalism of the security agencies and to project the local police force as anti-Muslim have unfortunately led to an overreaction by the authorities to even the slightest provocation from Muslim mobs. All these have also been aggravated by Muslim clerics projecting the use of force by the security agencies as serious incidents of state terrorism in order to attract international attention. The danger here is also that the incidents might not only draw the attention of the international community to the use of excessive force, but may most likely attract global terrorists to view southern Thailand as a new theatre for jihad.

TARGETS

In the new wave of violence in southern Thailand, government officials and security force personnel have been routinely targeted. The targets have so far included security forces personnel (from the armed forces as well as the police force, border patrol officers, customs officers, and guards in the religious schools and banks); officials from irrigation, agricultural, and education departments (including teachers); railway employees, employees of the Telephone Organisation of Thailand (TOT); provincial administration officials, village heads; healthcare workers, and a former Member of Parliament. The highest ranking official targeted was a judge in Pattani on 17 September 2004, indicating that the 'degree of violence will magnify and that people in any profession can be attacked.'[6] Insurgents have also threatened to kill well known forensics expert Dr. Khunying Pornthip Rojanasunan, who helped in the identification of dead insurgents and offered a bounty of 1million baht to anyone who takes her life. Insurgents are expected to attack more soft targets—high-ranking officials, clerics, and community leaders—in order to undermine the Thaksin administration and establish themselves as local leaders.

As the conflict escalated, civilians have not been spared. Civilian targets include religious teachers, plantation workers, workers in nightclubs and bars, construction workers (including contractors); in other words, all common civilians. Foreigners have also been targeted, including two Chinese hawkers and tourists from Malaysia.

Property targets include government offices (buildings belonging to the Provincial Waterworks Authority, a deserted public health office in Pattani and TOT offices), police stations, outposts, army installations, railway infrastructure (including rail tracks and station buildings), residences of government and security officials, piers and boats, roads, bridges and pipelines, commercial centres (including night clubs and beer bars in Sungai Kolok), prawn farm storage sheds, banks and telecommunication networks, fruit orchards, rubber plantations, residential buildings, club buildings, Buddhist temples, and religious as well as government schools.

Most of those targeted were unprotected places as there was no security presence at any of the buildings and in some cases no occupants. Attacks against railway tracks, the backbone of transportation in the region, and roads and water pipelines are meant to undermine civic administration in the restive provinces.

Intelligence sources have warned that Hat Yai airport, government agencies, and state symbols on display—plus 'soft targets' like entertainment venues—could become targets for future terrorist attacks. The perpetrators were reportedly planning attacks at tourist spots in the Hat Yai district of Songkhla, the Betong district of Yala, and the Sungai Kolok district of Narathiwat. Phuket, one of the kingdom's top tourist destinations, is also a potential target. As already mentioned, in October 2004, the Pattani United Liberation Organisation repeated its warning to stay away from the southern provinces and cautioned tourists against visiting the tourist centres of Phuket, Krabi and Bangkok. 'If you are in the above-mentioned provinces, we advise you to avoid police stations, music concerts, cafes, bars, nightclubs, railway stations and airports.'[7] Other potential targets include shopping malls, hotels and banks. Military intelligence has also warned that the commercial heart of Hat Yai, the capital city of Songkhla province, could be targeted, and that young men were known to have purchased large amounts of chemicals that could be used in attacks there.

TACTICS AND WEAPONS[8]

So far the most common form of attack have been drive-by shootings in which insurgents riding motorcycles have shot at and more often than not killed their victims. The use of both sharp—such as knives and machetes—and blunt weapons are also not uncommon. A tactic that has generated a lot of concern among the southern Thai community is beheading. Assailants have generally decapitated victims from other religions.

Arson attacks against public buildings, schools and residential complexes have also been common, using mosquito coils or Molotov cocktails as incendiaries. M-60 grenades and rocket-propelled grenades launchers have also been used. The miscreants have also resorted to sabotage, in which saboteurs had ring-barked trees in fruit orchards to make them wither and die, or had poured acid on the fruit trees. This was meant to ruin the local economy.

There have also been instances of bombings, most of them small, although there are some large explosions as well, including the car bomb explosion on 17 February 2005. The insurgents are increasingly turning to radio-controlled devices to attack officials who were lured to the scene by decoy explosions or attacks. In some cases, the insurgents would tip off the police about the planted bomb, and when bomb disposal units try to deactivate the device, they would trigger the explosion. In many cases, bombings have been multiple and simultaneous. On 21 November 2004, five bombs went off simultaneously in Pattani. This pattern of coordinated simultaneous attacks suggests that the insurgents are getting increasingly sophisticated and organised, moving upwards in the matrix of the threat dynamics.

An analysis of the types of bombs and detonators used in the attacks suggests massive improvisation and a shift towards greater sophistication and lethality. Cellular phones or remote controlled triggering devices are increasingly replacing timing devices as detonators. The assailants have also used motorcycle bombs and car bombs in August 2004 and February 2005. On 12 June 2004, insurgents exploded a device made from ammonium nitrate that was housed in a plastic box. In another attack in which four policemen were injured, the insurgents used a new type of explosive gel. The gel used is virtually undetectable; even police dogs are not able to sniff it out. Interestingly, the Thai military does not have this kind of explosive, which implies that the substance had been imported, possibly from Indonesia. An operator waiting nearby detonated the device remotely. The bomb was connected to a radio frequency (RF) receiver and the operator had an RF transmitter to send a signal to activate the receiver to detonate the bomb. The bomb planter was said to be an expert in electronics as a walkie-talkie or wireless telephone was adapted as a detonator for this device.

The most powerful explosive device that was defused before detonation was a 10-kilogram bomb found outside the Military Bank branch office on 21 August 2004 in the Tak Bai district of Narathiwat. It was made from ammonium nitrate, nails, and two types of plastic explosive—C-4, and Power Gel, which is commonly found at mining and construction sites. Had it exploded, it could have resulted in the loss of many lives and caused serious damage to property. On 29 August 2004, another bomb, assembled with 10 kilograms of ammonium nitrate and dynamite was defused in Narathiwat.

According to General Chavalit Yongchaiyudh, who oversees national security, the insurgents seem to have shifted their tactics from shootings to bombings, which is more devastating in terms of casualties. They aim to damage the public trust in the government's ability to provide safety to the general public. This trend is all the more worrying as insurgents are known to be in possession of explosive material such as ammonium nitrate and dynamite that were stolen from a quarry in Yala on 30 March 2004.

Initially, the bombings have largely been targeted at security forces. However, due to the hardening of these targets, insurgents have switched to softer targets such as the 27 March 2004 bombing of a stretch of nightclubs at Sungai Kolok which injured 30 people, as well as the 17 February 2005 bombing which killed five and injured about 40 civilians. There has also been a shift towards more dramatic attacks. On 28 August 2004, a bomb exploded at a Caltex petrol station in Narathiwat. It destroyed a pickup truck and caused minor damage to the station and nearby houses. The fallout from that attack was limited but if the explosion had reached the oil pump, the result would have been disastrous. A Siam Gas tanker-refuelling factory, also in Narathiwat, was attacked on the same day, but the bomb was defused in time. These are meant to keep the regional and international attention focused on southern Thailand as the insurgency escalates.

New patterns in attacks are also evolving over time. Motorcycles are favoured vehicles for planting bombs, as seen in the attack at the market in Narathiwat and in the simultaneous attacks outside two hotels and a karaoke bar in Yala. There have also been a number of roadside bombings, targeting mobile security forces. On 1 September 2004, a group of police providing security for teachers in Narathiwat narrowly escaped twin blasts from concealed roadside explosives. This looks to be an effective strategy as security forces are most vulnerable while travelling along narrow roads flanked by thick vegetation, which provides excellent cover for the insurgents. This new tactic has also led some analysts to speculate that the insurgents are consciously turning to methods employed by those in Iraq. This copycat effect was also demonstrated when on 29 May 2004, insurgents beheaded a 63-year-old rubber tapper, and threatened to carry out more such killings if security forces continued to arrest 'innocent Muslims.'[9] Further on 1 June 2004, the shrine of a popular Chinese goddess Lim Ko Niew near the Krue Se Mosque was ransacked by suspected Muslim insurgents. It is important to note that the Lim Ko Niew cemetery and Krue Se Mosque are symbols of communal tension between the Chinese Buddhists and Malay Muslims in southern Thailand.[10] This could be a deliberate attempt to incite communal tension. On 21 November 2004, PULO announced on its website that it would offer financial rewards for the assassination of the governors of the southern provinces or any prominent government official. It said that a sum of 90,000 baht or USD$2,250 would be paid to anyone who kills the governor in any of the three southern provinces. The separatist group also said that the same price would be paid to any one who assassinates any prominent government official, their deputies or high-ranking army and police officers. The photos of the three governors were published on the website. This is reminiscent of the ongoing jihad in Iraq, where militants offered cash prizes to anyone who kills American soldiers and officials. It is also suggestive of what the Thai Interior Minister Bhokin Bhalakula admitted, 'that Muslim extremism had taken root in the region.'[11]

Intelligence sources have warned about the possibilities of car bombings, in addition to military-style raids and hit-and-run attacks. The likelihood of bombings has increased, especially after the Tak Bai riots in October 2004. In fact, the most lethal attack that has taken place in southern Thailand at time of printing was the car bomb on 17 February 2005. Thai authorities have also revealed that they received intelligence from their Israeli and American counterparts about the possibility of suicide-bomb attacks, with suicide bombers wearing explosives vests, or with explosives loaded into their vehicles.

GOVERNMENT RESPONSE

Responding to the January 2004 armoury raids, Bangkok imposed martial law in troubled areas of the provinces of Yala, Pattani, and Narathiwat.

Thailand requested Malaysia to seal its border and both the countries strengthened joint Thai-Malaysian border patrols and communication networks. Bangkok also proposed to build a fence to prevent free movement across the Thai-Malaysian border. The Prime Minister ordered a radical review of security and intelligence standards. The Fourth Army, which is responsible for security of the southern provinces and administration of the martial law, launched rapid-deployment night patrols jointly with local police to hunt down the insurgents responsible for the attacks. The government also announced that the task forces under the '*Tai Santisook*' (Peaceful South) scheme would include soldiers, police, and local administration officials. Bangkok proposed to set up an anti-terrorism unit combining excellence in intelligence collection with the ability for swift manoeuvre to combat acts of violence. The security agencies installed technology to intercept telephone conversations and made use of satellite surveillance and unmanned gliders to track down the stolen weapons. In June 2004, the martial law was extended to cover more areas in Narathiwat, Pattani, and Yala, giving the military powers to search and arrest 'suspects'.

Subsequently, the government announced a number of measures to address the local grievances and dilute the process of indoctrination. The National Economic and Social Development Board (NESDB) was instructed to prepare short-term 'special projects' for the provinces of Yala, Pattani, and Narathiwat to 'free the region from all its deep-rooted problems.' These targeted projects were aimed at creating new jobs, building more public utilities, and improving exports.[12] Government officials willing to work in the troubled provinces for at least three years were offered incentives. Announcing the plans, Prime Minister Thaksin Shinawatra said that 'we are going to build sustainable strong communities ... with no more separatism after three years.'[13] He announced that the government would create more opportunity for the locals to develop their potential to the fullest and improve their economic conditions with more jobs and better education. He hoped that this would make it difficult for the insurgents to manipulate local discontent 'as a groundswell to galvanise support' for separatism.[14]

The army also planned to set up a 'political school' based at the Sirindhorn Camp in Pattani. The re-education camp would bring separatist sympathisers and former insurgents to correct their negative attitudes towards the administration and instil a sense of Thai nationalism. Special psychological operation teams were set up to prevent local

Muslims being misled by false rumours and to convince them that Thai security forces respect Islamic values. The Thai government also urged educational institutions to keep a close watch on students at risk of being exposed to separatist indoctrination by the insurgents.[15]

The Thai government also announced its intention to bring the private *pondok* educational system under some form of regulation. This is to ensure that these institutions of learning—popular among the local Muslims—are not misused as centres of indoctrination and insurgent recruitment. Deputy Education Minister Aree Wongaraya who was tasked to implement the reform project said that *pondoks* need to be changed to make them valuable assets for the society. 'The new curriculum will have to be of use for the local communities.'[16] Since there is a perception that the violence is being fuelled by the teaching of 'deviated' Islamic ideas, the government requisitioned respected religious leaders such as Sawas Sumalayasak, the *Chularajamontri* of Thailand to give guidance on the 'correct' understanding of Islam.[17]

Apart from working with the *Chularajamontri*, Bangkok has also seen the need to consult with religious leaders in the southern provinces. This is because they acknowledge that some Muslims in the south do not feel that the *Chularajamontri*, who is based in Bangkok, can accurately reflect the needs and sentiments of the Malay Muslims in the south. Prime Minister Thaksin Shinawatra has spent some time on his visits to the south engaging the leaders of the Islamic community. Some groups such as the Yayasan Muslimin have welcomed the move. 'We have to build the south and if Thaksin is helping with monetary advances, we are keen to bring development projects to the Muslims,' said Wan Abdullah, an influential member of the Yayasan Muslimin.[18] However, because of the Thaksin administration's heavy-handed responses to the violence, many other Muslim leaders in the south have refused to work with the government. The chairman of the private Islamic schools in the southern provinces, Nideh Waba, has even gone so far as to suggest a petition to the King for a royal government to replace the Thaksin government.[19]

Assessment of the Thaksin administration's responses

In all fairness, barring instances of overreaction by Bangkok, the policies and measures adopted by the government to combat insurgency in southern Thailand appears to be sound. However, there is a huge gap between intentions and accomplishments. What explains this failure?

Thailand is no stranger to insurgency. In the sixties, the Thai government encountered the communist insurgency, which it managed to contain by the early eighties. The key to that success was due to a calibrated approach in which civil confidence building measures preceded police and military intervention. The use of force was a measure of last resort. At the beginning of the communist insurgency in the sixties, the Thai military, schooled in World War II combat doctrines, 'had tremendous difficulty understanding counter-insurgency, rebellion, and the fundamental causes which fed revolt.'[20] The initial response—Communist Suppression Operations Command (CSOC)— was overwhelmingly force-oriented. Their approach focused on the use of firepower, cordon and search operations, and large-scale military deployment. These tactics were largely unsuccessful. Over a period of time, the military became more proficient in understanding the dynamics of the threat in the particular geographical environment and in its social and cultural context. There was an understanding that firepower and conventional counter-insurgency tactics were counter-productive, driving more and more people into the ranks of the insurgents. The government then began to focus more on political than military means. The key to that strategy—enshrined in the then Prime Minister Prem Tinsulanonda's Order (naiyobai) Number 66/2523, better known as the 'Policy to Win Over the Communists' and Prime Minister's Order Number 65/2525, also known as the 'Plan for the Political Offensive'—was to isolate the common people from the insurgent indoctrination and win them over by addressing the issues of corruption and poverty.[21] These lessons were drawn from famous the Civil-Police-Military (CPM) tactics used successfully against communists in Malaya by British counter-insurgency expert Sir Robert Thompson and others.[22] This strategy first sought civilian solutions to address the grievances that lay at the root of discontent. The police were used to deal with the breaches of law. 'Troops were used only when it was necessary to confront a sudden rise in disorder or the insurgents' open militarisation.'[23] However, at present, Thai government policy privileges the use of force and intimidation, placing the police and the military too much at the centre of events. This has undermined its ability to implement its security and development policies with any measure of success.

There are many important lessons that the Thai administration and its security establishment can learn from their experience with the communist insurgency. To begin with, there was a conscious attempt to study and understand the causes of discontent which the insurgents exploited. At a more basic level, the roots of discontent in Thailand, as in the past and as with insurgencies in other parts of the world, lie in perceived political, economic, and social injustices and the lack of avenues of expression through alternative (democratic) means. Power and wealth differentials make the impoverished masses vulnerable to the collective predation and exploitation by a handful of the privileged and the entitled. The Prem Tinsulanonda administration understood this dynamic and took steps to correct the prevailing imbalances. For example, it initiated rural development programmes aimed at eliminating the socio-economic injustices prevailing in the countryside. It launched mass movement programmes to develop democratic governance at the grassroots level. Popular participation through genuine engagement distanced the masses from the crippling ideology of the communists and helped bring the insurgency to an end. Similar methods were also employed by Harn Leenanon, the 4th Army Commander in the southern provinces, to deal with Muslim separatists in 1981 and 1983 with a very large measure of success.[24]

The present administration led by Prime Minister Thaksin Shinawatra is known for its corporate-style governance. Many critics argue that this has eroded many of the political reforms of the past and dissuaded alternative agendas, 'particularly agendas which prioritise rights, democracy, or equity above growth.'[25] Treating democracy as 'a tool not, (a) goal,' the administration threatens civil society and reduces citizens to mere consumers.[26] The Prime Minister's "Governors as CEOs (Chief Operating Officers) Program,' which empowered provincial governors in terms of their ability to operate without much of the bureaucratic oversight from Bangkok, has largely failed especially in the south. This was because of its failure to take into account the unique social, cultural, and religious context of the south.[27] The result was that the southern Thailand has become a complex cocktail of corruption, bureaucratic mediocrity, and mismanagement, as grievances and alienation continue to feed the insurgency.

Response in Thaksin's Second Term

On 6 February 2005, the Thai Rak Thai (TRT) Party swept the country's general elections, winning more than 70 per cent of the seats contested.

The picture in the south, however, was drastically different. Out of 11 seats at stake in the three southern provinces of Pattani, Yala and Narathiwat, the Democrats won 10 and the Chat Thai managed to gain one seat. This is significant when compared to 2001 election results. In 2001 elections, TRT won the majority (six) of the seats while the Democrats took five. The 2001 results boosted TRT's confidence so much that they predicted they would sweep 10 seats in the 2005 elections. This of course was not to be. Most importantly, in 2005, established TRT Members of Parliament (MPs) such as Deputy Prime Minister Wan Muhamad Nor Matha, were unseated by political novices. Many analysts attributed TRT's dismal showing in the south to the locals' disapproval of Thaksin's heavy-handed policies in dealing with the violence. However, Thaksin claimed that it was due to misconceptions the people in the south had about the government and its policies.

Post-elections, Thaksin has sent out mixed signals as to how he would deal with the south. Fresh from his victory, he declared there would be no change to his methods of handling the violence-plagued region. 'We will adjust nothing. Now, the people there do not believe us, but they will one day because what we have done is right.'[28] Despite this, he said he would take into account suggestions from opposition MPs and send teams to gather opinions from locals so as to adjust policies if necessary. Days later, Thaksin did an about-turn, calling security forces to be more cooperative with one another and to come down hard on religious teachers suspected of involvement in militant activity. He also called for the full implementation of martial law to authorise intensive military operations, and authorised the deployment of the 12,000 strong 15th Infantry Division to be permanently stationed in the south. According to Thaksin, the division would be a psychological warfare unit that would transform itself into a combat force whenever necessary. Its headquarters was likely to be in Pattani, but each of the three restive provinces would have a battalion stationed there. In response, Muslim leaders questioned the government's decision, saying that the new government should respect the wishes of the Muslim people who had asked for a withdrawal of troops, the lifting of martial law, and the fair treatment of Muslim suspects. Nimu Makajae, deputy chairman of the Yala Islamic Committee said, 'If the new division is really stationed in the south, then we want it to listen to the voices of the local Muslim people ..., rather than listening only to (the) government. If the division only listens to the government, we believe that the problem of violence is unlikely to be solved in the next four years.'

On 16 February 2005, Thaksin announced the introduction of a zoning scheme to identify trouble spots in the south. Villages in the three southern provinces would be divided into red, yellow, and green zones, depending on the level of violence, the number of core insurgent leaders suspected of involvement in the violence, and the extent to which villagers cooperate with officials to provide information.[29] According to authorities, the classification could be changed at any time if the situation in the villages improves. 358 villages—most of them in Narathiwat—have been designated red zones, or the most violence-laden areas which are least cooperative and the most difficult for authorities to access, and where most people are sympathetic to insurgents. These zones will not receive any help from provincial development funds worth 30 billion baht or the 20-billion baht budget for the SML (Small, Medium, and Large) village scheme. Villages in the yellow zone where violence sometimes occurred would get some help and villages in the green zone where villagers had worked well with authorities and had no record of violence would get full access to funds. Justifying this scheme, Thaksin said, 'We won't give a single baht to those "red villages" because we don't want them to spend the money on explosives, road spikes or assassins. No one can use our money to separate (the deep south) from Thailand.'[30]

The measure, which some have called desperate, has come under fire by many of Thaksin's critics, and even some from the establishment. They say that excluding communities from state aid will backfire in the battle for hearts and minds of the people in the south. Chaiwat Satha-anand from Thammasat University argued, 'The policy drive of the government is based on the assumption that the south is underdeveloped, and that to develop it will lessen the problems of violence. Now, if I understand the prime minister, because the area is violent, or prone to violence, we will leave it underdeveloped. It is very strange logic.'[31] Indeed, many analysts point out that the new policy is the exact opposite of the successful method adopted against the communists in the 1970s and the 80s. During that time, Bangkok poured in money to develop the red zones, so as to win over the locals from the insurgents. Instead of winning over the locals, the new move to deny funds may even push the villagers over to the side of the militants. Insurgents may now find it easier to recruit new members from red and even yellow villages. People in these villages may also feel that the government has abandoned them and has conceded defeat, handing over these areas to the insurgents.

Many also argue that the move is unconstitutional. People like National Human Rights Commissioner Pradit Charoen-thaithawee say the new policy is an act of discrimination against local residents. According to Section 30 of the Thai Constitution, discrimination against a person on the grounds of origin, race, language, sex, age, physical condition, health, personal status, economic or social standing, religious belief, education, or political view is not permitted. Dr. Pradit said he would seek a Human Rights Commission ruling if the government's policy is found to be against the spirit of the Constitution.[32]

In the bigger picture, the denial of funding is likely to deepen the alienation already writ large among the Muslims in the south. Already feeling neglected, southern Muslims living in the red and yellow zones will feel even more like second-class citizens. This move, along with the weight of increasing violence and disharmony, could widen the crack into a fault line. This is especially so in the backdrop of the February 2005 elections where the rest of the Kingdom voted overwhelmingly to put Thaksin back in power a second time around. In fact, many analysts suspect that Thaksin's new policy stems from the confidence he has gained from the 19 million voters behind him, and also his anger at the southern voters' rejection of his TRT party. However, there are signs that the support behind Thaksin may not be that strong after all. A poll of Bangkok residents by Assumption University done soon after the new policy was announced found that 63 per cent of the respondents opposed the zoning scheme.[33] Most also feared that cutting the budget to the south would only lead to the stagnation of the local economy and hurt innocent residents. 62 per cent did not believe that the government's handling of the unrest through force would bring peace to the region. As it was, the tension in the region was being augmented by an enhanced security presence in the region, and exacerbated by high-handed security tactics, such as what happened on 25 October 2004, and an overwhelming sense of neglect. The proposed measures would make it more difficult for the government to counter the sense of marginalisation and grievance felt by Thai Muslims and exploited by the insurgents.[34]

ESCALATION POTENTIAL

Despite what some analysts might say about the southern Thai conflict being propelled onto the global jihad bandwagon, our research found that the insurgency is currently a domestic one. The present lack of sophistication in the attacks conducted by southern insurgents suggests the lack of training, resources, and professionalism. If indeed the southern Thai insurgents had received help from trans-national terrorist groups such as Al Qaeda or the JI, this would have been reflected in the lethality of their attacks. The death toll from bombings in the south is usually small, with one or two killed in each attack. Furthermore, in terms of ideology, the southern Thai insurgents also differ from those with a global jihad orientation. An analysis of the *Berjihad di Pattani* reveals that it is not in the same vein as Al Qaeda literature and is not pan-Islamic. It instead has a nationalist character. Thus, the insurgency as yet has not developed an external dimension.

However, the indoctrination of the Muslims in the south appears to be at a very high level at present, and this can be exploited. A good example can be found in the incident on 28 April 2004. While the youths were told that they would be impervious to bullets if they chanted and truly had faith in their cause, some also showed an understanding that they may end up sacrificing their lives in the fight. Some of them told their kin before the incident that they wished to be buried as martyrs should they die. Mana Matiyoh, one of the suspects arrested in connection with the 28 April 2004 raids, said during his interrogation that 'all of us were sacrificing ourselves for God.'[35]

This willingness to die was apparent in they way they fought, with some commentators saying that they appeared almost suicidal in their motivation. It was said that they appeared as if they wanted to die in order to send a message about their beliefs to their fellow religionists. Here, death was seen not as a cause for mourning. Instead, it was to be respected and celebrated. As the study of radical movements suggests, political and religious revisions of history, and interpretations of present situations based on such revisions, exacerbate the conflict with fanatic intensity.[36] It is interesting to note here that the author of *Berjihad di Pattani* glorified death in combat in order to use it as a potent motivational tool.

> Let us realise, O Wira Shuhada, how glorious we will be if we fall as warriors of our land. O Brothers, understand! When the martyrs

were killed, they are not dead, but they are alive next to God. Allah placed them to rest temporarily. Allah will place them in the most honourable place. They will continuously receive sustenance from Allah. They will watch and listen to every piece of news, if their children will follow in their footsteps.

O my Brothers! Are you afraid that you are going to die? Never think like that! Know that death will come to each of you when it is destined, even if you try to hide.

The martyr blood flows in every one of us fellow Muslims who believe in Allah and the Prophet, which we inherited from our ancestors who had sacrificed their lives in the path of Jihad. This blood is eager to be spilled onto the land, to paint it red and illuminate the sky at dawn and dusk, from east to west. So it is known that the Pattani land produce Jihad warriors.

According to some of the suspects arrested after the incident, the insurgents took part in the uprising voluntarily because they intended to declare an Islamic state and were willing to die for Allah. The insurgents, some of whom wore shirts bearing the slogans 'There are no other gods but Allah' and 'Follow the Path of our God' in Arabic, attended prayer sessions led by an Islamic cleric before the attacks. This level of indoctrination suggests Islam's potential to increasingly become the organising principle of the resistance. Southern Thailand has indeed become a fertile recruitment ground for groups willing to exploit it for producing suicide volunteers, which could then close the gap in the insurgents' capability to bring jihad to the doorsteps of Bangkok and spread it to other parts of the kingdom in a very real way. This trend is also in line with the modus operandi of the global jihadists and the two may find this an opportunity for further collaboration.

Monitoring of Islamist websites and chat rooms and forums on the internet, especially Arabic sites in the Middle East, reveals that the latest deaths of the Muslims at the hands of the Thai security in Tak Bai has not featured prominently in the agenda of the international jihadists. This is surprising though not unusual given the preoccupation of the Mujahideen in Iraq. It was only as late as January 2005 that an Islamist discussion forum under the banner of Al-Sunnah wal-Jamma'h (a jihadi website) carried a discussion on the situation of the Muslims in southern Thailand. The discussion appeared under a section titled, 'The news of jihad and al-Mujahideen from the battlefields.' A subtitle described the discussion as 'The Muslims in Thailand—Horrible Images.' The web page featured a lot of images from southern Thailand, intended to highlight the plight of the Muslims in Thailand. There was a map of Thailand under which the following sentence appeared: 'Justice for Muslims in Thailand'. The images were followed by the comments of members. Most of what they said however was a kind of *du'a* (supplication), asking Allah to help the Muslims in that country. For instance, one member said, 'We pray to Allah to raise the position of al-Mujahideen and give them support and victory.' Another one expressed his sadness to what has happened to the Muslims. A third member made a long *du'a* in which he prayed to Allah to defeat and destroy the Christians, the Jews, and the hypocrites. Another member said that whatever they (the Thai security forces) do to Islam, 'they forget that Allah has made a promise that only his sincere worshippers will inherit the earth in the end.' In another comment, a member said that 'the sufferings of the Muslims didn't attract the attention of the world although the whole world has reacted swiftly, particularly the Christians nations, to support and defend the Christians in Indonesia'.[37]

Another website, www.altebyan.com, carried a story about the conditions in southern Thailand. Titled 'The Hell of the Muslims in Thailand', the author, Shaban Abdul Rahman, described the Muslims' reaction as 'a natural and legitimate feeling' against oppression, restriction, and a life full of bitterness and injustice. Though it did not glorify violence, it said that the 'Muslims' reaction to what is happening to them differs from one person to another and from one group to another but there is no doubt that some have reached the conclusion that a military resistance movement is the best response to oppression.' The discussant deplored the killings of Muslims, especially what it called the 'black Monday massacre' of October 2004. Importantly, the discussant expressed his sadness about the fact that the plight of the Muslims in southern Thailand is being ignored by their co-religionists.

> The strange thing is that the Muslim world is silent, as if it has become deaf and dumb. Even the statements of denunciation have disappeared. It is strange that the bloody campaign against the Muslims in Thailand has coincided with a strong media campaign in which the Muslims are accused of terrorism and training of the terrorists in other countries.[38]

Still another website, www.islammemo.cc, carried an article on the conditions of Muslims in Southeast Asia. It equated the oppression of Muslims in Southeast Asia with that in other parts of the world both in terms of its method and form—to eradicate their identity, spread vice, consolidate ignorance and poverty, and create division among the different groups. It lamented that 'in spite of these evil steps which are directed against the Muslims in Thailand, the Muslims in other parts of the world are not aware of what is happening to their brothers in religion and leaving them alone to face the enemies of Islam from inside and outside the country.' (The article also gave a detailed narrative of the struggle of the Muslims in Pattani with an historical account of the Muslim grievances and the methods used by Thai authorities to 'fight the Muslims.')[39]

There is thus an increasing indication that fellow religionists in other parts of the world are beginning to take an increasing interest in what is happening in southern Thailand. This portends that the insurgency in southern Thailand will not remain domestic for long. In the past, trans-national terrorist organisations, especially Al Qaeda, have hijacked home-grown Muslim insurgencies and transformed local conflicts into global jihad campaigns in the name of oppressed co-religionists. One of the most significant accomplishments of Osama bin Laden was the effective 'melding of the strands of religious fervour, Muslim piety and local grievances into a powerful ideological force'[40], and turning it into an 'effective weapon with the technological munificence of modernity'.[41] As Peter Bergen puts it, 'this grafting of entirely modern sensibilities and techniques to the most radical interpretation of holy war, is the hallmark of bin Laden's network.'[42] In Southeast Asia, for example, the Indonesian Darul Islam movement, which since the 1940s was an indigenous Islamic revivalist struggle, was transformed into a movement for Daulah Islamiyah Nusantara, envisaging the establishment of an Islamic Caliphate inclusive of all the Southeast Asian nations including Thailand. If the southern Thai conflict is allowed to linger and government crackdowns begin to touch sympathetic cords outside, we may see external elements getting involved, resulting in the escalation of the conflict. This may eventually spill over to other parts of the kingdom and beyond.

Given Thailand's strategic proximity to the United States, its troops commitment for Afghanistan and Iraq, and its non-NATO ally status, there would not be much difficulty for jihadi elements to find identity of purpose with the cause of Muslims in southern Thailand. Anti-Americanism has already begun to manifest in the south, especially in the realms of economy and commerce. In the province of Yala, for example, people have boycotted American commercial products in accordance to directives of the National Association of Muslim Youth (NAMY). NAMY has erected billboards terming the province as 'US product-free zones.'[43] There has also been a strong reaction against the US-Thailand Free Trade Agreement. The handover of Hambali captured in Thailand in August 2003 to the US has also inflamed the Islamic sensitivity. Southern Muslims are also very sensitive about the Counter Terrorism Intelligence Centre (CTIC), a Thai-US joint initiative, which was instrumental in the capture of Hambali. Local residents allege that CTIC is manipulating the violence in the region to push the Thai government closer to the US.[44]

Another potentially disturbing dimension to the present conflict is the nexus between organised crime networks and southern insurgents. The nexus between the terrorists and organised crime which is premised to supplement each other's capabilities—both financial and logistical—has now become a matter of serious concern internationally. Thailand is notoriously famous for trans-national criminal networks engaged in illegal arms and narcotics trade. In June 2004, Thai authorities seized a large amount of radioactive material, Cesium-137, in Bangkok. Stolen from Russian stockpiles and smuggled into Thailand through Laos, this was reportedly meant for making a dirty bomb.[45] Thailand has long been an arms transit point and procurement base for the Liberation Tigers of Tamil Eelam (LTTE) in Sri Lanka. The country's criminal establishment was even involved in the construction of a partially completed submarine at a shipyard in Phuket. In the latter half of 2004, Bangkok police seized 11 guns from a Silom Road apartment believed to be delivered to the LTTE in Sri Lanka. Francis Subrama, a Sri Lankan, rented the apartment, but the rent was being paid by Nicho, believed to be a part of gun-smuggling network.[46]

In fact, until the recent surge in violence, the separatists were themselves better known for their criminality than their politics.[47] If the capabilities of the criminals and the terrorists do meet in Thailand, Bangkok may well have to brace itself for spirals of violence and bloodshed. The violence will involve both domestic as well as international targets—symbols of authority, business and economic infrastructure, as well as civilian life—in line with jihadi terrorism elsewhere in the world. When that happens, it will become exceptionally difficult for the government to contain and control it.

There are already signs that the violence in the south is reaching new heights. In the week immediately following the February 2005 elections, there were bombings on an almost daily basis. The most significant attack took place on 10 February 2005 when a bomb exploded near a group of senior military officials who were watching a parade at Narathiwat stadium. It was seen as an attempt to assassinate the governor of Narathiwat province. Governor Pracha Terat narrowly escaped injury but others were not so lucky. Six were hurt and one person was killed in the bombing. This may be linked to the bounties that PULO had placed on the heads of the southern provincial governors in November 2004. Incidentally, the announcement of the bounties was posted on the jihadi website www.goalalaldyn.com on 14 January 2005.[48]

The most lethal bombing in the history of the southern Thai insurgency took place on 17 February 2005. The explosion ripped through the busy nightclub strip of Sungai Kolok, killing at least five people and wounding more than 40. Malaysian citizens were reported to be among the victims. The new tactic, as well as the size of the bomb—estimated at 50 kilogrammes—again raised questions about militant links to outside groups. This is the type of weapon used in attacks in Indonesia (Bali, Marriot and Australian Embassy) and in Iraq. Thaksin has however denied that foreign militants were behind the attack. At time of writing, Thai authorities have detained two suspects, both Thai nationals. One is said to be Buraheng Waemama, a former member of the now defunct Communist Party of Malaya. He is allegedly a bomb-making specialist who later joined Bersatu.[49] However, General Sonthi Boonyakarin, a top army commander in the region, believed that the BRN was responsible for the attack.[50]

The incident came a day after Prime Minister Thaksin unveiled his controversial plan to deny funding to villages suspected of aiding separatists, and while he was touring the three southern provinces. Thus, many observers have pointed out that the incident could have been a response to the proposed budget cuts. The militants have sent an unmistakable message that they are not happy with Thaksin's policies in the south. They have upped the stakes, increasing the level of sophistication in their attacks. The adoption of the car-bomb tactic is a sign that the southern Thai militants are surveying successful methods used by militants in other parts of the world and incorporating them into their own battle with Bangkok. It may only be a matter of time that they will begin using the tactic of suicide bombings. With the 17 February bombing, the insurgents have not only shown that they will spare no one in their quest to achieve their political aims, but also that they are becoming increasingly capable of terrorising the locals, foreigners who visit the region, and security officials. Their motivation will only increase if Bangkok continues to use force and other drastic measures in the attempt to keep a lid on the violence.

NOTES

1   'Plan to capture province', *Nation*, 14 January 2004.

2   'Teachers call on military to tread softly', *Nation*, 14 September 2004.

3   'Arsonists strike 14 more targets', *Nation*, 31 March 2004.

4   'Thai troops arrest scores of Muslims', *Islam Online*, 9 January 2004, http://www.islamonline.net/English/News/2004-01/09/article03.shtml.

5   Ibid.

6   'Judge killed by gunmen in Pattani', *Bangkok Post*, 18 September 2004.

7   'Thai rebels warn of fresh attacks', *Straits Times*, 30 October 2004.

8   For a comprehensive review of the tactics employed in the southern Thai insurgency, see Anthony Davis, 'Southern Thai insurgency gains fresh momentum', *Jane's Intelligence Review*, 1 August 2004.

9   Ibid.

10   A tourism billboard at the cemetery describes the myth of Lim Ko Niew. It says that she came from China's Hokkien speaking region to Pattani to see her brother, Lim To Khiam, who was married to a Pattani woman and had become a Muslim. When she failed to persuade her brother to return to China, Lim Ko Niew prayed that her brother would not finish construction of the Krue Se Mosque. The mosque was left unfinished for a period of time. Local Muslims, however, dismiss this version. According to them, the mosque was destroyed during wars between Pattani and Siam more than two centuries ago, rather than by Lim Ko Niew's black magic. In 1990, Muslims held a huge demonstration at Krue Se demanding that the government stop promoting the legend. See 'Popular shrine looted', *Nation*, 2 June 2004.

11   'Situation in South needs honest appraisal', ThinkCentreAsia.org, available at http://www.thinkcentreasia.org/opinions/honestappr.html.

12   'Govt to pour funds into South', *Nation*, 12 February 2004.

13   'Development plan mapped out for South', *Nation*, 16 February 2004.

14   'PM offers cash for peace', *Nation*, 15 February 2004.

15   'Police seek arrest warrants for southern Muslim separatists', *Bangkok Post*, 15 January 2004.

16   'Sirichai admits he's in the dark', *Nation*, 8 October 2004.

17   'Army warns of more soft target attacks', *Nation*, 21 September 2004.

18   Kazi Mahmood, 'Thai Muslim groups preach non-violence', *Islam Online*, 16 April 2004.

19   Yuwadee Tunyasiri, 'Prime minister says post report awful', *Bangkok Post*, 31 October 2004.

20   Saiyud Kerdphol, Thai armed forces supreme commander (retired), cited in Anthony Paul, 'Can Thailand end insurgency?' *Straits Times*, 3 November 2004.

21   'Primer: Muslim separatism in southern Thailand', Virtual Information Center, 23 July 2002, available at http://www.vic-info.org/0a256ae00012d183/626e6035eadbb4cd85256499006b15a6/e42514a843d9a3260a256c05006c2d84?OpenDocument.

22   Anthony Paul, 'Can Thailand end insurgency?'

23   Ibid.

24   'Primer: Muslim separatism in southern Thailand', Virtual Information Center.

25   Pasuk Phongpaichit, 'A country is a company, a PM is a CEO' (paper presented at the international forum 'Statesman or Manager? Image and Reality of Leadership in Southeast Asia' at Chulalongkorn University, 2 April 2004), 4–5.

26   Surat Horachaikul, 'The far south of Thailand in the era of the American empire, 9/11 Version, and Thaksin's "Cash and Gung-ho" Premiership' (paper presented at MSRC-KAF Intercultural Discourse Series, Dealing with Terrorism Today: Lessons from the Malaysian Experience, Kuala Lumpur, 23 July 2004).

27   'Primer: Muslim separatism in southern Thailand', Virtual Information Center.

28   'PM: No change in handling of south; Blames TRT loss on local 'misconceptions'', *Bangkok Post*, 10 February 2005.

29   Anucha Charoenpo, 'Sirichai: Zoning idea military's brainchild', *Bangkok Post*, 19 February 2005.

30   Amy Kazmin, 'Thai PM's aid threat comes under fire', *Financial Times*, 18 February 2005.

31   Ibid.

32   'PM warned of backlash over southern aid threat', The Nation, 20 February 2005.

33   Preeyanat Phanayanggoor, 'Letter urges PM to drop zoning policy', Bangkok Post, 21 February 2005.

34   Joseph C. Y. Liow, 'Are Al-Qaeda and Jemaah Islamiyah in southern Thailand?' *Asian Analysis*, September 2004, available at http://www.aseanfocus.com/asiananalysis/article.cfm?articleID=777.

35   Nirmal Ghosh, 'Shadowy group behind violence', *Straits Times*, 1 May 2004.

36   Rona M. Fields, Salman Elbedour, and Fadel Abu Hein, 'The Palestinian suicide bomber', in *The Psychology of Terrorism, Volume Two: Clinical Aspects and Responses*, edited by Chris E. Stout (Westport, C.T.: Praeger, 2002), 208.

37   'Justice for the Muslims, Thailand in the jihadi websites', 11 January 2005. Translated at the International Centre for Political Violence and Terrorism Research, Institute of Defence and Strategic Studies. See Appendix 4.

38   The Hell of the Muslims in Thailand, Thailand in the Jihadi Websites, 16 January 2005, Translated at International Centre for Political Violence and Terrorism Research, Institute of Defence and Strategic Studies, See Appendix 6.

39   The Forgotten Muslims, Thailand in the Jihadi Websites, 18 January 2005, Translated at International Centre for Political Violence and Terrorism Research, Institute of Defence and Strategic Studies. See Appendix 7.

40   Karim Raslan, 'Now a Historic Chance to Welcome Muslims into the System', *International Herald Tribune*, 27 November 2001, available at http://www.asiasource.org/asip/raslan.cfm.

41   Ibid.

42   Peter Bergen, *Holy War Inc.: Inside the Secret World of Osama bin Laden* (New York: Free Press, 2001), 28.

43   Horachaikul, 'The far south of Thailand in the era of the American empire.'

44   'CIA-backed unit "may be involved in violence"', *Nation*, 19 April 2004.

45   Salhani, 'Al Qaeda's "second front"', *Washington Times*.

46   'Arms were heading for Sri Lankan rebels', *Bangkok Post*, 6 March 2004.

47   John R. Bradley, 'Thailand's Muslim insurgency has "Wahhabi" ties', *Daily Star*, 6 May 2004, available at http://dailystar.com.lb/article.asp?edition_id=10&categ_id=5&article_id=3286.

48   Islamic Organisation in Thailand offers financial rewards for the assassination of Buddhists officials, Thailand in the Jihadi Websites, 19 January 2005, Translated at International Centre for Political Violence and Terrorism Research, Institute of Defence and Strategic Studies. See Appendix 2.

49   Waedao Harai, 'Bomb Expert Nabbed for Hotel Blast', *Bangkok Post*, 20 February 2005.

50   Sasithorn Simaporn and Panarat Thepgumpanat, 'Car Bomb Planted by Militants' Relatives: Thai PM', *Globe and Mail*, 19 February 2005.

4

Responding to the Threat

This part of the analysis is based on independent research carried out by the International Centre for Political Violence and Terrorism Research at the Institute of Defence and Strategic Studies in the conflict zone, intelligence reporting, and analysis of insurgent documents recovered by the Thai authorities. There is no dearth of literature about what do with the problem in southern Thailand. Many analysts and strategic commentators have spoken at length about what the government must do to restore normalcy and confidence in the troubled provinces. Most of the recommendations have merit and need to be pursued seriously by the agencies concerned, in order to contain the insurgency in southern Thailand. We make our own contribution to the same from the perspective of observers of conflicts in many other parts of the world and how they correlate to what is now happening in Thailand.

The new face of the insurgency is significantly different from the insurgency of the 1970s and 1980s. As the complexion of the insurgency in southern Thailand is changing rapidly, the Thai government should consider developing new capabilities to meet future challenges. The key, however, lies in Bangkok's ability to disrupt the insurgent networks and their leadership in the short term and delegitimise their grievances over a period of time. By arresting the escalation of the insurgency at the threshold, it would be possible to prevent the transformation of the conflict from a domestic one into a regional or even global jihad.

First, the nationalist-separatist struggle in southern Thailand is rapidly transforming into a politico-religious conflict. Insurgent ideologues are increasingly politicising and mobilising the target audience, using religion rather than nationalism. Religiosity, a more powerful ideology, is steadfastly replacing ethno-nationalism. An analysis of the *Berjihad di Pattani* suggests that the *Shafi'ee* ideology of the insurgents is increasingly coming under the influence of the *Salafi* jihadi ideology.

Islamism, the radical political interpretation of Islam, is generating recruits and support.

Second, the character of the insurgent campaign is changing from guerrilla warfare into urban terrorism. In the past, the insurgents targeted military, police, and government officials. Today, the targets are mostly civilians and civilian infrastructure. In the past, the insurgents engaged in ambushes and raids. Today, the insurgents mostly conduct assassinations and bombings. In the past, the fighting formations were organised as guerrilla units. Today, the structure is secret, compartmentalised, and cellular. In the past, the insurgents operated mostly in the jungles and mountains. Today, the insurgents mostly operate in the villages, towns, and cities. Compared to the groups of the previous generation, the strategies, tactics, techniques, and training of the current generation of groups are externally influenced. There is thus a likelihood that beheadings, mass fatality, spectacular and even suicide attacks—the hallmark of the global jihad campaigns—would soon become trends in the surging spirals of violence in Thailand.

Third, external insurgent-insurgent and insurgent-support linkages are growing. Although the insurgents are largely driven by domestic grievances, they are drawing inspiration, finance, and training from external sources. These include Malaysian, Indonesian, and Philippine Islamists belonging to various groups and political dispositions including PAS, MILF, JI, and Al Qaeda. Thai insurgents are not only getting trained in southern Thailand, Malaysia, and Indonesia, a few Indonesian militia (*Laskar*) groups have also expressed their interest to directly participate in jihad in southern Thailand. During the Cold war era, many separatist groups were extensively state-sponsored. Even as the state sponsorship has significantly declined, the terrorists and insurgents today are supported by groups which share similar ideology, religion, and empathy. They continue to receive funds from myriad sources including from religious and philanthropic institutions and charities as well as through self-financing criminal activities such as low level crime, drugs trade, kidnapping, exhortation, and the like. In the case of southern Thailand, although the support to the insurgents is largely from domestic sympathisers, the ideological empathy and operational linkages with external actors seem to be on the increase.

Most Islamist conflicts in Southeast Asia—Mindanao in the Philippines and Ambon (Maluku), Poso (Sulawesi) in Indonesia—have attracted foreign *mujahideen*. It is only a question of time that the insurgency in southern Thailand will attract Malaysians, Indonesians, Filipinos, Singaporeans, and other nationalities. The steadfast growth of external linkages will have a profound impact on both Thai national and regional security. It is therefore essential to prevent the emergence of southern Thailand as a new theatre of conflict with trans-national implications and the integration of southern Thailand into the agenda of global jihad.

KEY TO THREAT MANAGEMENT

The single biggest weakness of the Thai national security apparatus has been its inability to develop intelligence dominance in the south. After the 4 January 2004 attacks, Prime Minister Thaksin Shinawatra himself admitted that 'intelligence was flawed and under-utilised.' He was particularly concerned about the poor coordination among different government agencies especially on the issue of intelligence management among the police and the military.[1] The problem has also been exacerbated by an undercurrent of tension and competition among various security agencies for influence and resources. As a result, the security agencies appear to have little understanding of the organisational composition, command structure, or the nature and extent of international connections of the insurgent groups operating in the south.[2]

The Thai security apparatus and the policy establishment have improved its understanding and knowledge of the problem at hand after the arrests made in the last quarter of 2004. However, the rapid pace in the evolution of the terrorist threat requires a more aggressive intelligence collection effort. It entails building new platforms for collection of intelligence, not only in Thailand but also in Malaysia, especially in areas where the Thai insurgents have found support and refuge. Failure to invest in counter-terrorism intelligence at this stage runs the risk of significantly challenging the Thai national security apparatus in the coming years. Instead of attempting to overwhelm the southern provinces with a huge military presence, the government must seek to develop an intelligence network covering not only the conflict zone but also in its immediate neighbourhood, including the bordering areas in Malaysia.

As Sheldon Simon puts it, 'hunting down terrorists only deals with the symptoms but not the underlying disease.'[3] The key to successful conflict management rests on a robust political will to balance the short-term tactical response mechanism and the long-term strategic initiatives.

This involves not only a sustained intelligence-led operational effectiveness, but also a credible framework to engage religious and community leaders from the disaffected population in the south. Thailand also needs to work closely with Malaysian authorities in border management, intelligence sharing, and other operational tasks.

As the terrorist violence in the south is significant and growing, the management of the threat is a priority and requires the most immediate attention. The essential ingredient to effectively combat the terrorist threat is to develop high quality intelligence. Until late 2004, the quality of intelligence with the security forces about the insurgent movement was rather poor. Both the knowledge and understanding of the Thai military of the situation was gravely weak. As a result, the Thai military has been ineffective operationally. For instance, only one single firearm out of nearly 400 stolen by the insurgents in January 2004 was recovered; the same firearms were used by the insurgents in some of the subsequent attacks. Furthermore, Krue Se and Tak Bai outcomes clearly favoured the terrorists.

To prevent terrorism and to deter attacks, it is crucial to maintain the flow of intelligence and operational effectiveness on the ground. To ensure that the insurgents are accurately targeted and that there is no overreaction, the overall campaign must be intelligence-led and intelligence-driven. More than the knowledge *about* the adversary, an understanding *of* the adversary is necessary. The government should allocate and invest more resources in developing a robust intelligence capability through training and operations. This would mean a combination of smart technology as well as a pool of professional undercover agents with some degree of competence in the local Malay dialect. They must be able to imbed themselves into the community and relate to Malay-Muslim culture.[4]

Until a robust information network is put in place, the authorities should co-opt or work closely with mainstream Muslim community leaders, and where necessary and possible, with faction leaders and members of groups such as Bersatu, BRN, New PULO, PULO and others. The government should place a permanent and credible amnesty process for those who wish to abandon violence. This is especially important given the fact that there is now a huge misperception about government's intention in this regard. Many local Muslims allege that Thai security forces have executed some among those who have accepted amnesty.[5] It is to be noted that amnesty was one of the policies that successfully calmed the communist insurgency in the past. The government must also offer attractive rewards for information, and build a professionally trained informant/undercover scheme. To detainees who cooperate, the government should offer security for their families, reduced sentences, and other benefits. More than the desire to prosecute detainees, the government must seek to enlist them in counter-terrorism intelligence and strike operations. To create and encourage a culture of success within the counter-terrorism community, the government should appoint and promote officials who perform exceptionally well in investigations—both intelligence gathering and strike operations—and offer financial rewards and provide other benefits.

Containing the Threat

The presence of a significant Muslim community in the rest of the kingdom, including Bangkok, and free and easy travel within the country has the potential to disperse the threat beyond its current epicentre in the south. The security apparatus in rest of the country is already under pressure due to the large concentration of armed forces personnel in the south. Furthermore, the government's decision to try insurgent leaders in Bangkok is likely to encourage terrorist attacks in the capital. Dispersal of the threat would mean damage to tourism and investment. Already, southern Thailand has suffered gravely from the disruption of tourism and the lack of investment. The resultant unemployment has created a ready pool of potential recruits for militancy. The insurgent leaders appear to be preying 'on young people who do not have jobs, do not have education, cannot get into universities and get into drugs.'[6] It is only a question of time that the insurgency would spread to the north in the form of terrorist attacks.

Although there is a multiplicity of violent groups, the vanguard in the current phase of the insurgency is BRN Coordinate. BRN Coordinate affiliate, PUSAKA, through its 23 sub-groups comprising 529 centres, with a total number of 59,097 students and 3,160 teachers, has provided a significant proportion of recruits and support to the current instability. It is therefore very important that the capability and the support structure of the insurgents are effectively neutralised. The key personnel of BRN Coordinate must be neutralised and their infrastructure dismantled on both sides of the border, especially on the Malaysian side. At present, most of the attacks are being directed and coordinated by operational leaders living in areas of Malaysia bordering Thailand. With experience, their operational reach and lethality will grow. Mobile and static checkpoints at places linking the south to the rest of the country will not help appreciably to contain the threat. Bangkok must enlist the confidence and support of Kuala Lumpur to disrupt the operational cells operating on Malaysian soil. Failure to cripple insurgent capabilities on both sides of the border in the short term will mean an escalation of the insurgency, with terrorist attacks outside the southern provinces, including in the capital city of Bangkok. Its spillover to other parts of the region also cannot be ruled out.

Public Support

To consolidate security measures, the government must match military methods with non-military initiatives. In 2004, as the security situation in southern Thailand rapidly deteriorated, the Thai government lost significant public support. The overreaction by security agencies, abuse of authority and corruption, intimidation tactics, and lack of sensitivity to local religious and cultural values aggravated the situation further. The climate of fear and suspicion has distanced even the moderate Muslims from the government policies and actions. The political leadership has unnecessarily been critical of and suspicious about local community and religious leaders. This has critically squeezed the space for the moderate elements to speak out against the radical propaganda of the insurgents. Even the local residents, who do not necessarily support the violence, keep quiet because they do not trust the authorities. Indeed, southern Thailand has now become a 'frustrated community whose mistrust of state agencies has reached one of its lowest points in recent history.'[7] As Thaksin himself admitted, 'they (the local residents) do not trust the authorities because they (officials) do not engage them.'[8] In this respect however, the southern Thai insurgency is not very different from Islamist terrorism elsewhere in the world.

Sustaining the success of counter-terrorist (CT) and counter-insurgency (COIN) operations is dependent on the incremental increase of public confidence and the recovery of lost public goodwill. As insurgents seek to replenish human losses and material wastage, it is paramount to retain and nurture public support and win over the mainstream community leaders and influential religious teachers from the *pondoks*. To win public confidence, it is essential to empower the

Muslims by co-opting Muslim leaders to join the decision-making structures in the south. The government must invest in forming trust-building relationships through advocacy campaign and continuous dialogue. Muslims should be allowed to express the insurgency problem as they perceive it. The government must also encourage community vigilance. As Somboon Bualuang, an academic from the Prince of Songkhla University at Pattani put it, 'the government needs to understand the (complex relationship) of culture, ethnicity and religion. They should not view Muslims with distrust. It also should engage local communities in any development projects.'[9]

The Thaksin administration should also adopt a policy of large-scale recruitment of Muslims into the police, army, and the intelligence community. The Muslim leaders and members who work with the government—that are vulnerable for insurgent targeting—should be monitored, protected, and rewarded. Another aspect of confidence-building measures is the appointment of the right type of leaders (military and civilian) to key government positions in the southern provinces. This must come with developing appropriate training for these officials to sensitise them to local customs and traditions so as to ensure that law enforcement and security measures as well as social and economic policies do not trample over local sensitivities. The officials themselves must be provided with the right kind of incentives such as fast-track promotions so that they do not consider themselves as refugees from the north and do not consequently channel their personal frustrations to demonising the population in the south. Appropriate financial incentives would go a long way in preventing the propensity to indulge in corruption.

The political leadership should announce, periodically appraise, and, more importantly, begin implementing, credible and robust political and economic development policies for the southern provinces. It is a misconception that public support can be obtained by granting political autonomy for the provinces. While in many instances greater autonomy has worked in ameliorating political grievances such as the issue of representation in the administration and decision-making processes, autonomy is not necessarily concomitant to long-term peace and stability. As it stands today, the southern provinces now have a sufficient number of Muslims who are highly politicised and radicalised. This represents the critical mass that sits on a very thin line between autonomy and separatism. Granting regional political autonomy at this late stage will not improve the situation. The Islamist leaders will use the autonomy granted as a launching pad to fight for independence. However, investing in economic development of the south and appointing Muslims to key positions will dissuade public support for insurgency and dissolve the aspiration for independence in time. This should be matched by development of robust institutions both in the government and private sectors and the empowerment of the civil society at the grass roots level, which would work to reinforce national identity and national unity.

Traditionally, religious institutions in the south have been the centres used by local Malay-Muslims to reinforce their identity, which was perceived to be threatened by the policies of assimilation by successive Thai governments. Islamist education in *pondoks* has been extensively used to revive and sustain pan-Malay nationalism. At the same time, these are the centres which can train 'a future leadership that offers hope for the region'.[10] Attempts to regulate the religious schools have systematically been opposed as government incursion into Islamist teaching. The measures are seen as policies adopted to dilute Malay-Muslim identity. Additionally confronted with the challenge of making themselves relevant in the context of social, political, and economic changes, some institutions of learning have taken to the path of greatest resistance, preaching the message of separatism and jihadi violence against the 'oppressive' Thai government. Already, the discontent in the religious institutions has manifested in targeted killing of some vocational training teachers who are being seen as 'government spies.' Regulation of the curriculum in these institutions would also mean confrontation between traditionalism and modernity, and between spirituality and materialism.[11] The real challenge for the government therefore will be refraining from approaching the problem with a 'one-size-fits-all' policy that will only serve to further alienate the Malay-Muslim community and heighten the legitimacy of radicalism and separatism among the religious teachers in the south.[12]

The *pondok* education in southern Thailand continues to emulate the intellectual learning processes among the institutions in medieval Islam. The appeal of the traditional Islamic education continues to be very strong in southern Thailand. It is therefore imperative to encourage the schools to modernise general Islamic education in a manner that not only fosters knowledge of religion, but also practical skills that will empower and equip graduates from the Muslim education system for mainstream life.[13] Creation of avenues and opportunities for higher education would prevent Muslim students from going abroad, especially to Middle Eastern, Pakistani, and Indonesian universities to get radicalised.[14]

Public response to regulation of the *pondoks* has been one of concern. There has been a perception that registration of the schools would leave them open to greater government intervention. This stems from their experience from the way the security agencies are dealing with the institutions especially after January 2004. As an Islamic scholar put it, the indiscriminate targeting of religious schools on the assumption that they all foster militancy among students and that these youths have the potential to become terrorists, is proving to be counter-productive. This only confirms Muslim suspicion that the government is bent on 'weakening [their] social fabric.'[15] Our own interaction with the majority of the teachers and the management of the *pondoks* in southern Thailand reveal that they do not mind putting their institutions under some form of government regulation. The perception has largely been that the government should recognise and support the role of the *pondoks* as centres of alternative learning, and more specifically determine which government agency should be responsible for the regulation of the *pondoks*.

Collaboration with Malaysia

Military and security measures alone will not reduce the threat of insurgency. Similarly, political and economic measures alone will not reduce the threat. Both military and non-military measures must be married and collectively applied. Restoring security in the short term (one to two years) depends on targeting the armed insurgents that engage in terrorism (against civilians) and guerrilla attacks (against armed personnel). Restoring stability in the mid term (five years) depends on the effective targeting of ideologues that preach hatred. These ideologues living in southern Thailand and northern Malaysia have a very high capacity for producing fresh recruits and galvanising support to sustain a campaign of violence. To sustain bold initiatives and robust security measures to weed out the terrorists, it is necessary for Thailand to develop a special relationship with Malaysia.

Northern Malaysia remains an active intellectual and material support base for the insurgent groups active in southern Thailand. Malaysian Islamists living in Kelantan provide ideology and haven (refuge, finance, physical training, and ideological indoctrination) to key Islamists from southern Thailand. Without sustained political and security assistance from Malaysia, Thailand will fail to contain the threat successfully. Malaysian Prime Minister Abdullah Badawi has agreed to assist Thailand and his offer should be taken seriously. Malaysia is aware that the threat will spill over and will galvanise its own Islamists.

In framing a common response, differences of opinion on the targeting strategy periodically emerge. For instance, Malaysia has released Issamul Yameena (alias Isamail Jaafar or Pohsu), the author of *Berjihad di Pattani*, the most important ideological manual of the insurgents active in southern Thailand. Bangkok continues to be suspicious about the role of their co-religionists across the border in the simmering discontent in the southern provinces. The close contact between inhabitants on both sides of the border has long been sustained on kinship, culture, commerce, and trade. This contact has long been manipulated and misused by the insurgents for their support and other logistical requirements such as training and safe haven. Thailand and Malaysia have an anti-terrorism pact since March 1970 to fight both the communist insurgency and separatist movements. However, the political will on both sides to work together is marred by occasional hiccups especially during the current phase of insurgency. For example, Thailand's Prime Minister's 16 December 2004 statement that many separatist guerrillas have been trained in northern Malaysia evoked a strong reaction from Kuala Lumpur. Even though Thaksin did mention that Kuala Lumpur was unaware of the clandestine activities, Malaysian state news agency Bernama quoted Malaysian Prime Minister Abdullah as expressing 'shock' when told of the allegations that Malaysian territory was being used as a base to train Thai insurgents. Abdullah was particularly concerned about the manner in which the issue was raised by his Thai counterpart publicly, instead of going through the usual diplomatic channels.[16] Thai politicians were similarly incensed about the report that money from a trust-fund—the Kelantan branch of the Malaysian Islamic Welfare Organisation (Perkim)—had gone to help Muslim insurgents in Thailand.[17] Despite the differences, it is essential for Thailand to nurture a special relationship and cooperate and collaborate with their Malaysian counterparts.

Contemporary networked insurgencies and terrorist campaigns are fought by the target governments in collaboration with partners. To meet the present challenge, current Thai security arrangements with Malaysia should shift from cooperation to collaboration. Thailand should propose a special security agreement and the creation of a joint operational infrastructure in which officers from both Thai-Malaysian intelligence and enforcement agencies could interact. It is also essential that both the countries jointly establish and develop a common database, exchange personnel, arrange joint training programmes and combined operations, and share expertise and experience.

KEY TO ENDING THE THREAT

Due to years of neglect, a substantial percentage of the Muslims in the south are disappointed with the central government in Bangkok. They especially resent the officials posted to the south from Bangkok. They express their anger by pointing at Prime Minister Thaksin Shinawatra and his style of governance. Nonetheless, at present, public support and sympathy for the insurgency is not overwhelming. To prevent the insurgents from gaining support, it is critical for government not to overreact to insurgent and insurgent-inspired actions such as what happened at Krue Se and Tak Bai. The conventional mindset of the Thai military establishment of projecting force has not helped to improve the security situation but is instead feeding the insurgent. Large-scale deployments to show force or use of force are counter-productive. Furthermore, key Thai leaders must develop a thorough understanding of the south. Dropping white origami birds will not help but will fuel the anger of the aggrieved Muslims.

Traditionally, Bangkok posted officers to the south on punishment. Often, these corrupt and incompetent officers failed to impart or govern with justice. Continuing with such policies and practices would be counter-productive. Only the best and the brightest officials should be posted to the south. For postings to these provinces, the government must select the very best, whether they are from the military, police, or civilian administration. They should be selected based on merit, ability, and performance, and paid higher wages, placed on a fast track for promotion and appointment, and regularly monitored. Whenever possible, Muslims—preferably from the south, or those knowledgeable about Islam—should be appointed. If not religiously sensitised, those appointed should follow a course on Islam and Muslims. Irrespective of rank, service, family, or personal and political ties, the government should discipline and if necessary punish military, police, and administrative officers that fail to perform or execute their responsibilities. Government failure to charge and try the military officials who ordered the storming of the Krue Se Mosque on 28 April 2004, and those responsible for tragic death of detainees during October 2004 demonstrations at Tak Bai has damaged the image and credibility of the Thaksin administration. The administration must demonstrate a sense of justice and fairness to win back the trust of the Muslims.

The majority of Thai Muslims are not radicalised. There is a willingness to assist the government in managing the threat of violence. However, public trust and support can never be won through mere rhetoric. It requires empowerment and continuous dialogue. The government must also encourage community vigilance. Ultimately, policies grounded in transparency, honesty, and sensitivity are the pillars of a successful strategy to counter local grievances. Collaboration and partnership with the disaffected would be the key to manage and control the insurgency in southern Thailand.

Rethinking Government Strategy

The current military dominated strategy adopted by Bangkok to improve the situation in southern Thailand is flawed. The situation in the south today is fundamentally different from the insurgency of the past. The primary concern in southern Thailand is that the insurgency is an unconventional threat and not a military one. A group of power-hungry Islamist leaders are using and misusing religion to politicise and mobilise the masses through the religious schools and mosques. A conventional military response to a political and ideological threat is likely to worsen the problem. As the threat has militarised and is widespread, the presence of the military is necessary. Nonetheless, large-scale military presence will not solve the problem, and is likely to worsen the climate of fear and suspicion. Furthermore, the police-military rivalry and lack of collaboration has impeded counter-terrorist and counter-insurgency operations. In phases, the primacy for maintaining law and order should be handed over to the police—a force oriented and trained to deal with the public—and the governance of the south should be transferred to the political authority. The military should only assist the police and the political authority.

While the police working with the intelligence community and the military can restore law and order, the conflict can be ameliorated only by the political authority. The bottom line is for the Muslim elite to feel that it is advantageous and profitable to be a part of the Thai state rather than to secede from it. The mismanagement of the south by successive Thai governments has created the opportunity for secessionist and Islamist ideologies to take root in the minds of the Muslim elite and Islamic community institutions. While intelligence-led operations can target the terrorist network that has penetrated the religious and educational institutions, the political authority working with the Muslim political and religious leaders should offer a counter-ideology. The government should work towards strengthening the educational and religious establishments in the south to prevent future extremist and terrorist infiltration. The government should direct, hold responsible, and provide resources and incentives to Muslim councils to manage the religious and education centres through self-regulation and other means. By systematically co-opting moderate Muslim leaders—both educators and religious leaders—the government should build a norm and an ethic in the community against the preaching of hatred. Each school, mosque and especially teacher—both government or privately funded—must be registered and if necessary monitored by an independent Muslim council working in partnership with government. The government should prosecute religious and educational leaders that preach hatred, incite violence, and participate or provide military-style training, with or without firearms. The trial and prosecution must be fair and under established legal procedures. To discourage and dissuade extremism, the government should strengthen existing and build new institutions with resources and authority, set deliverable goals, and monitor progress. As there is no standard textbook for restoring normalcy in the south, the government should develop sound and timely policies and practices that will encourage moderation and instil toleration—which is the hallmark of traditional Thai norms and values.

INTERNATIONAL AND REGIONAL IMPLICATIONS OF A DOMESTIC INSURGENCY

The conflict in southern Thailand is a domestic insurgency but with regional and international implications. Like other nations in the developing world, Thailand too is apprehensive about foreign governments and foreign nationals commenting on Thailand's security situation. It is a very ASEAN characteristic to be sensitive to criticism, especially by its neighbours. Even if such criticism is made politely, some Thai officials regard such comments as foreign interference. Nonetheless, the citizens of Thailand must realise that the escalation of the conflict in southern Thailand will affect the security of the region. Therefore, it is in the individual and collective interest of Thailand's neighbours to ensure that Thailand recovers from the current crisis. Unlike the Cold War era, no one country can protect itself without the cooperation of their neighbouring countries. Enlightened Thai leaders must recognise this predicament.

When any internal conflict matures, it develops security implications for its neighbours. It is inevitable that foreign governments will be concerned about and take keen interest on the developments in southern Thailand. Although ASEAN was structured and developed during the Cold War, the post-Cold War realities dictate a more cooperative and collaborative approach. Although Thailand is blessed with resources, Thailand can benefit from the experience and expertise in some countries in the region in its efforts to manage the threat.

The insurgency in Thailand is rapidly becoming a catalytic conflict. Like Palestine, Kashmir, Chechnya, Mindanao in the Philippines, Algeria, Afghanistan, and Iraq, the conflict in Thailand is likely to be placed on the global jihad map. Any conflict involving Muslims has a special significance today and Thailand is no exception to this trend. Due to the concept of Muslim brotherhood, wherever Muslims are affected, suffering, and dying, fellow Muslims perceive the obligation of giving alms, participating in training, and volunteering to fight. Therefore, most contemporary conflicts in which Muslims are participants will sooner or later attract foreign volunteers as combatants, and aid and assistance from charities and other questionable organisations. A number of Muslim leaders from southern Thailand visited MILF camps and held discussions in 2003 and 2004. Southeast Asian nationals—Indonesians, Malaysians, Thais, Singaporeans, and Filipinos—fought in Afghanistan in the 1980s and 1990s. Similarly, Arabs (Saudis, Jordanians, Egyptians, Iraqis), Asians (both South and West Asians), and Westerners (Australians, Spaniards) participated in the conflicts in Ambon and Poso in Indonesia. More than two dozen nationalities including Muslims from Southern Thailand trained in the MILF-run guerrilla and terrorist training camps in Mindanao in southern Philippines. Similarly, a few thousand Muslims from southern

Thailand trained in Malaysia (mostly ideological training) and in Indonesia. Although the number of Muslims from southern Thailand that participated in Afghanistan and the Philippines was numerically small, they gained significant expertise. Today, the Afghan and Filipino veterans as well as the Malaysian and Indonesian trainees form the core of the groups perpetrating violence in southern Thailand.

Unless the insurgency in southern Thailand is contained and resolved early, its nature, characteristics, and implications will not be very different from other regional conflicts, where volunteers from different nationalities help their local Muslim brethren in their struggles. In southern Thailand, signs of foreign involvement are emerging. In January 2005, an Arabic web site carried graphic images from southern Thailand. Muslims from southern Thailand trained with several foreign Islamist groups in the region. There is a likelihood that old camaraderie among the trained veterans would be called in to augment the capabilities of the insurgents in southern Thailand.

Considering the fact that the insurgency in Thailand is an internal conflict but with international implications, the Thai authorities should work closely with their foreign security, intelligence, and law enforcement counterparts. Branding the conflict in southern Thailand as an internal affair and neglecting the rapidly developing international dimension will be advantageous to the insurgents. The immediate challenge facing the Thai authorities is to disrupt existing links between the insurgents and foreign organisations—both insurgent groups and charities—and prevent the formation of new linkages. In the past few years, Thailand was the home of Hambali, the most important Al Qaeda and JI leader in Southeast Asia, and was visited by Issa Al Brittani, the Al Qaeda leader in the UK who was developing a template to attack financial targets in New Jersey, New York, and Washington DC. Working with their foreign counterparts, the Thai authorities should monitor and disrupt the travel of leaders and members of Al Qaeda, Jemaah Islamiyah, and other violent groups. As much as managing the domestic threat, developing and sustaining a special relationship with Malaysia as well as liaison with the other regional countries is central to constraining the conflict from assuming global dimensions. As one senior Muslim cleric from southern Thailand put it, 'if the government gets this wrong, ..they could have a Baghdad here.'[18]

CONCLUSION

State building, especially one involving ethnic minorities is a complex process. When minority needs face inadequate accomplishment or when minority interests are ignored, it leads to 'identity conflicts,' prompting defensive reactions from the minority community. In the context that established state systems fail to accommodate minority reactions, then insurgency becomes the alternative mode of expression. Complete consolidation or assimilation, such as the policies being adopted by successive Thai governments, are not necessarily the solutions to violent ethnic identity conflicts. The minority identity cannot be completely erased or assimilated into the majority.[19] The use of force is also not a sustainable option. Some forms of political space and means of expression must be provided to the disaffected population to satisfy their distinct needs and preserve their unique culture. As Larry Diamond puts it, 'ethnic cleavages do not die. They cannot be extinguished through repression or assimilation; however, they can be managed so that they do not threaten civil peace, and people of different groups are able to coexist tranquilly while maintaining their ethnic identities.'[20]

NOTES

1   'Barrack raided, 20 schools torched in South', *Nation*, 5 January 2004.
2   Tony Davis, 'Are Thailand's Southern Insurgents Moving to Soft Targets?', *Jane's Terrorism and Intelligence Centre*, 5 April 2004.
3   Sheldon Simon, 'Managing Security Challenges in Southeast Asia', *National Bureau of Asian Research* vol. 13, no. 4 (2002), 37.
4   Joseph C. Y. Liow, 'Violence and the Long Road to Reconciliation in Southern Thailand' (paper presented at the Conference on Religion and Conflict in Asia: Disrupting Violence, Arizona State University, 14–15 October 2004).
5   'In the South, an Iron Fist in a Velvet Glove', *Far Eastern Economic Review*, 12 August 2004.
6   Nirmal Ghosh, 'Shadowy group behind violence', *Straits Times*, 1 May 2004.
7   'Chaturon's solution leaves Thaksin in a difficult situation,' *Nation*, 10 April 2004.
8   'Plan to capture province', *Nation*, 14 January 2004.
9   'PM Offers Cash for Peace', *Nation*, 15 February 2004.
10 Surin Pitsuwan, 'Abode of Peace', *Worldview Magazine* vol. 17, no. 2 (Jun–Aug 2004), 3.
11 Anthony Davis, 'Thailand faces up to southern extremist threat', *Jane's Intelligence Review*, 1 October 2003.

12   Joseph. C. Y. Liow, 'The *Pondok* Schools of Southern Thailand: Bastion of Islamic Education or Hotbed of Militancy?' *IDSS Commentaries*, 32/2004, 25 August 2004.

13   Hasan Madmarn, *The Pondok and Madrasah in Patani* (Bangi:Penerbit Universiti Kebangsaan Malaysia, 1999), 66.

14   S. P. Harish, 'Conflict in Southern Thailand: Removing Education from the Security Agenda', *IDSS Commentaries*, (33/2004), 25 August 2004.

15   Cited in Marwaan Macan-Markar, 'Class dismissed in Thailand's south', *Asia Times*, 24 February 2004.

16   'Malaysia informed about insurgent training', *Reuters Alert*, 19 December 2004, available at http://www.alertnet.org/thenews/newsdesk/BKK70155.htm.

17   Ibid.

18   Anthony Davis, 'School System Forms the Frontline in Thailand's Southern Unrest', *Jane's Intelligence Review*, 1 November 2004.

19   Linda J. True, 'Balancing Minorities: A Study of Southern Thailand.' SAIS Working Paper Series, Working Paper No. WP/02/04 (May 2004).

20   Larry Diamond, 'Three Paradoxes of Democracy,' in *The Global Resurgence of Democracy*, 2nd ed., edited by Larry Diamond and Marc F. Platter (Baltimore: Johns Hopkins University Press, 1996), 121.

Appendixes

Berjihad di Pattani (The Fight for the Liberation of Pattani)*

PREFACE

Start with Do'a (supplication).

May peace be upon all of you.

From a room for *ibadat* (worship) in Suluk cave, the voice of *Jihad Sabilillah* (Struggle in the Path of Allah) by fellow Muslim brothers of Pattani called this pen (writer) to advance all sacrifices (for the liberation of Pattani). This pen (writer) felt weak to fulfill such hope. Nevertheless, he (writer) will try to answer the call with all his might and courage by writing. May this writing benefit all fellow warriors.

This pen (writer) hopes that this book will represent the writer in every battlefield. For that reason, please remember that the writer is always at your side at all times. Fight, my brothers, till the last drop of your blood. Allah is the Greatest, Allah is the Greatest, Allah is the Greatest (*Allahu Akhbar*). All praises to Allah, Amin.

by
Writer
Ismuljaminah
Kuala Tiga Tanah Merah – Kelantan
1 Jamadil-Akhir 1423 Hij. (Fourth month in Hijrah Calender)
10 August 2002

In the name of Allah, the Most Gracious and the Most Merciful.

---

* Translated at International Centre for Political Violence and Terrorism Research, Institute of Defence and Strategic Studies.

Day One

From Allah we come and to Him we shall return.
Every soul will taste death…

The pen (writer) will also die, but the writing shall continue to survive. Carried over by religious preachers (*Da'wah*), they shall inherit words and take over the leadership. I name them as *Wira Shuhada* (martyrdom fighters), Imam *Shaheed*, the Radiance of Jihad. The *Wira Shuhada* will rise in Pattani with the radiance of *Jihad Fi-Sabilillah* (Struggle in the Path of Allah). *Wira Shuhada* will come to the children of the land (Pattani) who are in a state of ignorance and obsessed with material wealth and power.

With wisdom, *Wira Shuhada* shall greet (the people) with 'May peace be upon you' (*Assalamualaikum Warrohmatullohi Wabarokatuh*). May his *salaam* (greeting) receive replies from general public, men and women, the poor and the rich, old and young, the healthy and the ill. The aforementioned *salaam* is dedicated specifically to the children of Pattani warriors and generally to every soul whose blood is fused with faith and *taqwa* (god-consciousness). My brothers! Wake up from your slumber. My brothers! Wake up from your ignorance. Remember, my brothers who forgot. Know, my brothers who still do not know, that Prophet Mohammed (PBUH) was a general of the army of *Shuhada*. He brought with him verses of Allah. He recited them and called all the people to believe in Allah and His Prophet.

To the believers, Prophet Mohammed (PBUH) had called them to establish Allah's religion and to re-capture Mecca. The Prophet Mohammed (PBUH) was our greatest general and he will lead you at all times.

I am a *Wira Shuhada*. I am the father of all warriors of this motherland. I will always be with you, respecting our greatest general Prophet Mohammed (PBUH). Let us listen to his words and adhere to them together. Listen and examine verses (in the Holy Book of the Koran) that our greatest general read:

> O Prophet! Rouse the Believers to the fight. If there are twenty amongst you, patient and persevering, they will vanquish two hundred; if a hundred, they will vanquish a thousand of the Disbelievers: for these are a people without understanding.
> **Al-Anfal [8:65]**

119

Our greatest general called us to prepare an army to resurrect the greatness of Islam the disbelievers destroyed. The Prophet called us to unite in preparing army to re-capture the land of Mecca from disbelievers ... Will this call lead to destruction? No, brothers ... But God and His Prophet commanded such actions. Indeed, whoever distances himself from this command or disobeys it will face Allah's wrath, and be punished in Hell as stated in the following verse:

> And why should ye not fight in the cause of Allah and of those who, being weak, are ill-treated (and oppressed)? Men, women, and children, whose cry is: 'Our Lord! Rescue us from this town, whose people are oppressors; and raise for us from thee one who will protect; and raise for us from thee one who will help!'
> **An-Nisaa [4:75]**

Wira Shuhada ... We should be ashamed of ourselves for sitting idly and doing nothing while the colonialists trampled our brothers and sisters. The wealth that belongs to us have been seized. Our rights and freedom have been curbed, and our religion and culture have been sullied. Where is our commitment to peace and security for our people? Remember, O *Wira Shuhada* brothers! Our late parents, brothers, and sisters sacrificed their lives for their land as warriors; they left behind a generation with warrior blood flowing in their veins. Today, let us make a call, so that the warrior blood will flow again and the generation will emerge again, even though we have to face pain and sorrow. With the blessings of the martyrs, the blood will flow. On every battlefield, they echo in the heart of every soul with 'There is no God but Allah and Mohammed is his Prophet. Allah is the Greatest' in them.

How sweet our brotherhood and how strong our army! Remember that we all come from the only One (Allah). We are united by the only One (Allah). Together we unite under the protection of the only One (Allah). We shall raise our voices to ask support from the only One (Allah) with '*Lailahaillaha*' (There is no God but Allah) *Alif Lam Jall Allah*. (recited during battle):

> So do not lose heart, nor fall into despair: for ye must gain mastery if ye are true in Faith.
> **Al-Imran [3:139]**

The above is the explanation from Allah (SWT). It is revealed to us so that we would not feel weak to face our enemy. Let us learn from Allah (SWT) and follow the guidance of the Prophet in every battlefield that we enter. Always remember that whoever transgresses Allah's teachings and His Prophets and disobeys the leader will lose the strength of the army, physically and spiritually.

> As to those who turn (for friendship) to Allah, His Messenger, and the (Fellowship of) Believers, it is the Fellowship of Allah that must certainly triumph.
> **Al-Maidah [5:59]**[1]

O Brothers, fellow fighters, let us adhere to the principles of God and the Prophet in our action ... and let us carefully elect a suitable leader who fears Allah. Together, let us take vows to obey the leader until God grants victory upon us.

> O ye who believe! Obey Allah, and obey the Messenger, and those charged with authority among you.
> **An-Nisaa [4:59]**

Allah is the greatest. We will obey, O Allah. May Allah help us as we face the disbelievers.

DAY TWO

May peace be upon you all.

> Nor can a soul die except by Allah's leave, the term being fixed as by writing.
> **Al-i-Imran [3:145]**

> Nay, Allah is your protector, and He is the best of helpers.
> **Al-i-Imran [3:150]**

Allahu waliyi Insha Allah Lailah Illallah Alif lam JallAllah Allahu Akbar (Allah is my guardian. If Allah is willing. There is no God but Allah. Alif Lam is the Greatness of God. Allah is the Greatest. Allah is the Greatest. Allah is the Greatest).

In this most precious and valuable hour, this pen (writer) stands up with courage and calls upon *Wira Shuhada* to stand up and unite to capture

121

our beloved Pattani and to bring back the pride and strength to our religion that has been tarnished. Let us join hands to protect our children, wives, possessions, and wealth of the country. If we fall, Allah has promised heaven to us.

> From Abuhuroirah, a companion of the Prophet Mohammed (PBUH), said: 'There was a man who went to meet the Prophet Mohammed (PBUH) and asked him, 'O Prophet, what is your view if somebody steals my possessions?' The Prophet replied, 'Do not surrender at all cost. Protect it with all might.' The man asked further, 'What should be done if he wants to kill me?' The Prophet replied, 'You should kill yourself.' The man asked further, 'What if I am killed?' The Prophet answered, 'You died as a Shaheed.' The man asked another question: 'What if a person who stole possessions is killed?' The Prophet answered, 'He will go to hell.'
> **Hadith Saheeh Muslim,** *book 1, page 65, Hadith 113*

Praise be to Allah Almighty. The answers and explanations that the Prophet elucidated above are true. It is also proof that every possession that belongs to an individual legally belongs to that individual. These include housing estates, material possessions, financial wealth, children and wives, country, and cultural traditions; and the most important thing of all is religion. Thus, let us work together to protect all these, even if it costs us our lives.

Once again, I call upon all of you, my fellow brothers, fighters of the land: join the army of *Shuhada*, enter the battlefields. And I ... I will continue calling and motivating. Where is the blood of past warriors? Where is the spirit of the warriors? Look at our elders, children, and wives! How much suffering have they been through? Who else is responsible to protect them?

Let us realise, *Wira Shuhada*, how glorious we will be if we fall as warriors of our land. Brothers, understand! When martyrs are killed, they are not dead but alive next to God. Allah places them to rest temporarily. Allah will place them in the most honourable place. They will continuously receive sustenance from Allah. They will watch and listen to every piece of news to see if their children will follow in their footsteps. My brothers! Are you afraid that you are going to die? Never think like that! Know that death will come to each of you when it is destined, even if you try to hide:

Even if you had remained in your homes, those for whom death was decreed would certainly have gone forth to the place of their death.
Al-i-Imran [3:154]

Think not of those who are slain in Allah's Way as dead. Nay, they live, finding their sustenance in the Presence of their Lord.
Al-i-Imran [3:169]

Then fight in Allah's cause – thou art held responsible only for thyself – and rouse the Believers (so that they will have the courage to fight). It may be that Allah will restrain the fury of the Disbelievers (not achieving their goals); for Allah is the strongest in might and in punishment.
An-Nisaa [4:84]

Come, fight in the path of Allah until He grants us victory, which is, either we depart this life as martyrs or we defeat our enemy and the enemy of Allah. Know that the martyr blood flows in every one of us fellow Muslims who believe in Allah and the Prophet, which we inherited from our ancestors who had sacrificed their lives in the path of Jihad. This blood is eager to spill onto the land, paint it red, and illuminate the sky at dawn and dusk, from east to west, so it will be known that the Pattani land produces Jihad warriors. Both male and female warriors will shout out '*takbir*' in all directions, while facing and attacking the enemy, *Allahu Akhbar ... Allahu Akbar ... Allahu Akbar* (Allah is the greatest). Such chanting will arouse life in the weak and pampered. The sound vibrates with anger and vengeance, answering the call of Jihad. *Labaika Ya Allah Fi Sabilil! Assalamualaikum Ya Ashhabal Jihad.* Come and flow, O warriors' blood in the body. Flow out to warm the faith in the warriors. Look and listen! How brave are our parents and children who pray to Allah that you will be elected as leader ... or as saviour of our destiny. Therefore, be prepared, and do not feel weak or afraid. Allah will always be with us ... Don't be sad, Allah will be with us ...

Ye who believe! When ye go abroad in the cause of Allah, investigate carefully (in individuals' behaviours).
An-Nisaa [4:94]

Against them make ready your strength to the utmost of your power, including steeds of war, to strike terror into (the hearts of) the enemies, of Allah and your enemies, and others besides, whom ye may not know, but whom Allah doth know. Whatever ye shall spend

123

in the Cause of Allah, shall be repaid unto you, and ye shall not be
treated unjustly.
Al-Anfal [8:60]

Have I not mentioned before … that God will always be at our side?
Examine … and listen … God has advised us not to forget our weapons.
Bring and use anything that will strike fear and slay the disbelievers,
your enemy. We have been commanded by Allah to prepare to face our
enemies. My brothers! Always remember that … we Muslims, who believe
in Allah and the Prophet, never rely only on modern weapons. It is an
obligation for us to hope for Allah's help. For He is the only One who
has weapons that are most powerful and have the greatest capabilities.
Know that no matter how large the army is, Allah is capable of defeating
and chasing them away. Although we may have small army, we will receive
support and help from God. Certainly we will receive victory.

> Remember thou said to the Faithful: 'Is it not enough for you that
> Allah should help you with three thousand angels (specially) sent
> down?'
> **Al-i-Imran [3:124]**

> Yea, if ye remain firm, and act aright, even if the enemy should rush
> here on you in hot haste, your Lord would help you with five
> thousand angels making a terrific onslaught.
> **Al-i-Imran [3:125]**

On the battleground, the believers should not become arrogant with the
possession of modern weapons and large numbers of troops. Instead, the
believers should be happy to seek support and help from Allah Almighty.
With this in mind, we must remember Allah in every action, even in war.
Keep in mind and mention the name of Allah many times. By doing so,
hopefully we will achieve victory. Therefore, recite, mention, and
memorise frequently.

Laila Haillallah Alif Lam JallAllah (Allah is the Greatest Alif Lam,
the greatness of God).

DAY THREE

May peace be upon you all.

Fighting is prescribed upon you, and ye dislike it. But it is possible
that ye dislike a thing which is good for you, and that ye love a thing
which is bad for you. But Allah knoweth, and ye know not.
Al-Baqarah [2:216]

My brothers and sisters *Wira Shuhada*! Protecting our rights is an
obligation ... whether in the form of material possessions, children and
wives, parents or relatives, fellow Muslims and citizens. Above all we
must protect the purity of Islam from being tarnished by whoever wants
to annihilate the teaching of Islam. For that reason, God has stated in
the Holy Koran as follows:

Your enemies, and others besides, whom ye may not know, but whom
Allah doth know.
Al-Anfal [8:60]

Yea, to those who take for friends Disbelievers rather than Believers:
is it honour they seek among them? Nay all honour is with Allah.
An-Nisaa [4:139]

The Hypocrites will be in the lowest depths of the Fire; no helper
wilt thou find for them.
An-Nisaa [4:145]

My brothers *Wira Shuhada*! ... Though it is difficult for the believers
to identify who our enemies, the real hypocrites, are, eventually there
will be a way in which Allah will guide the believers. The believers
can identify them (the hypocrites) easily. Allah has elucidated with
clear words to the believers that ... those who take and support
disbelievers as their leaders with the intention of seeking their favour
or to destroy our honourable Islam are hypocrites. They are the most
dangerous enemies of Allah. They are our enemies too, because they
live among Muslims.

Sometimes you may see them carrying out obligations to Allah by
praying, fasting, giving alms, etc. In reality, their actions or practices are
a disguise, for their hearts are filled with hatred and fury against Islam.
And they fear and are against the teachings of Islam. For those who waste
their lives away and the wicked ones, they will certainly be frightened
when they face the truth from Allah. Therefore, these groups will never
be with the believers, except to sneer at them. Truly, they are people
with two faces.

125

My brothers *Wira Shuhada* ... Do feel sorry for them, and love them, for they are your most dangerous enemy today ... And the punishment that they will receive from Allah in the Hereafter is hell at the lowest level. Know that they are no longer your relatives and parents.

> O ye who believe! Take not for protectors your fathers and your brothers if they love infidelity above Faith: if any of you do so, they do wrong.
> **At-Touba [9:23]**

My brothers *Wira Shuhada*! ... Those who are against the teachings of Allah are not only named as '*Munifikoon*' (hypocrites), they are also cruel. It is a pity to know that those who have intelligence can live happily under control of oppressors. Be aware my brothers! ... Allah not only forbids us from electing the hypocrites as leaders, but Allah also forbids the believers from offering prayers for the dead hypocrites and from standing at their graves to offer prayer. It is disgraceful to be followers of the hypocrites.

> Nor do thou ever pray for any of them that dies, nor stand at his grave; for they rejected Allah and His Messenger, and died in a state of perverse rebellion.
> **At-Touba [9:84]**

My brothers *Wira Shuhada*! To avoid being part of such people, the hypocrites, it is thus our duty not to turn away from the teachings of Allah and His Prophet ... Have you all already forgotten the history? ... Has not history taught that during the Prophet's times, there was only a man who was against Allah and His Prophet (the teaching of Allah and the Prophet). The man was Abdullah Bin Ubai. Later on, through his voice and those who were under his influence, he was able to congregate large numbers of supporters and followers. This consequently created a group of people known as the hypocrites (*Munafik*). This group was never pleased with the believers. Due to this, let us come together to fight and eradicate them until we are safe from their disturbances.

> O Prophet! Strive hard against the Disbelievers and the Hypocrites, and be firm against them. Their abode is Hell, an evil refuge indeed.
> **At-Touba [9:73]**

In this present time, it is evident that the disbelievers and the hypocrites are our enemies and God has given us ample opportunity to fight them. Certainly, no one among the believers will oppose the writer and the readers of this book ... except the disbelievers and the hypocrites. For them, the publication of this book is like a sophisticated weapon that will stab every part of their bodies and will destroy every single one of their groups and organisations. O my brothers, the disbelievers and the hypocrites begin to fear the truth. Many of them will start to seek answers to 'Who am I? What will be my fate?' Allah has cultivated fear in their hearts. Their minds are not functioning anymore. This is because they know that Allah has revealed to them with clarity in the Holy Book of Koran.

> If any do fail to judge by (the light of) what Allah hath revealed, they are (no better than) those who rebel.
> **Al-Maidah [5:47]**

That is the status that Allah has given to the disbelievers and the hypocrites. There are people who claim that they believe in Allah, but they do not follow the teaching that has been revealed. These are the people who rebel against the teachings of Allah. These are the hypocrites. They pretend to believe but their hearts rebel against Allah and the Prophet.

> Remember thy Lord inspired the angels (with the message): 'I am with you: give firmness to the Believers: I will instill terror into the hearts of the Disbelievers: smite ye above their necks and smite all their finger tips off them.'
> **Al-Anfal [8:12]**

Read Do'a.

DAY FOUR

May peace be upon you all.

O My brothers *Wira Shuhada*! Today, we know who the enemies of Allah are and who our true enemies are. We also know the unfortunate place where they will be rewarded as hypocrites. We also know that they are afraid of the believers ...

> Soon shall we cast terror into the hearts of the Disbelievers, for that
> they joined companions with Allah.
> **Al-i-Imran [3:151]**

Remember that God has given these commands in his Holy Book:

> Let not the Believers take for friends or helpers Disbelievers rather
> than Believers.
> **Al-i-Imran [3:28]**

> O ye who believe! Take not into your intimacy those outside your
> ranks: they will not fail to corrupt you. They only desire your ruin:
> rank hatred has already appeared from their mouths: what their
> hearts conceal is far worse. We have made plain to you the Signs, if
> ye have wisdom.
> **Al-i-Imran [3:118]**

Therefore, from the above explanation that Allah has given ... In the
name of Allah, I call upon you, sons of Patamala, wake up and unite ...
and before we enter the battlegrounds, let us listen and renew our loyalty
to our leaders who will lead responsibly and with determination. And let
us not rebel because it will lead to disunity and defeat in our struggle.

> And obey Allah and His Messenger; and fall into no disputes, lest ye
> lose heart and your power depart; and be patient and persevering:
> for Allah is with those who patiently persevere.
> **Al-Anfal [8:46]**

> O ye who believe! Obey Allah, and obey the Messenger, and those
> charged with authority among you.
> **An-Nisaa [4:59]**

Keep in mind all the time, *Wira Shuhada* brothers and sons of Patamala
... The war of Uhud taught Muslims today the greatest lesson. The
soldiers during the battle disobeyed the orders of the commander, who
was the Prophet at that time. The archers, responsible for guarding
the hilltop of Mount Uhud, abandoned their position to collect the
booty left behind by the defeated disbelievers. The disbelievers' army
then took the opportunity to launch a counter-attack from the rear of
Mount Uhud that was left abandoned. The attackers were under the
command of Khalid Ibni Waleed. So let us be vigilant and follow the
orders of the commander.

Here is another point that we should remember: In the upcoming battle in the near future, beware! ... Nobody among us should kill children, women, or destroy houses and farms due to anger, because Allah will not be pleased with such actions. And if any of you are elected as a leader who commands the army, do not be too strict with those who are under your command. Forgive them if they make any mistakes. Your firmness may cause them to leave the army. Hasn't Allah made your heart gentle? ...

> It is part of the Mercy of Allah that thou dost deal gently with them. Wert thou severe or harsh-hearted, they would have broken away from about thee: so pass over (their faults), and ask for (Allah's) forgiveness for them.
> **Al-i-Imran [3:159]**

Wira Shuhada brothers and sons of Patamala! ... Maybe in the near future and within the next few moments, we will start attacking the enemy lines. Are all your weapons prepared? ... If you have not prepared them, then seek for them. Prepare yourself also. Remember, besides physical preparation, you should also prepare yourself by remembering Allah. It is the knowledge that will strengthen your spirit to face the enemy. Utter the name of Allah regularly. May the warrior blood continue to flow in our veins and strengthen our muscles to carry weapons into battlefields.

I will not forget to call upon you, daughters of Patamala, that you should stand up together, side by side with your fellow people ... They are your fathers, your husbands, and they are also your children. You should not just look passively when they are slaughtered by their and your enemy; you will go through fire to save your children. This is the power of your forefathers' ideals that seek vengeance and restoration. That is the sign of love and loyalty to your parents, husbands, and your children. Daughters of *Shuhada*! Your cry will arouse the spirit of men in the battlefields. The softness at each end of your fingers will be the power that heals the wound. The charming and gentleness of mothers toward their sons make them tolerate no longer to chase their enemies out. The praying words from weak ladies who are in sorrow will be the power that unites these warriors with the blessing of Allah... That is how daughters of Patamala should be. You have an important role to fulfill for your people, nation, and religion. Let us recapture our beloved homeland together.

After we build the spirit of these warriors and unite them in one rank and each of them is impatient to fight, while waiting for the time that Allah commands, in this time of opportunity, let us utter the name of Allah and offer praises to Him Almighty together. Allah is the Greatest (*Allahu Akhbar*).

> Fight in the cause of Allah those who fight you, but do not transgress limits; for Allah love not transgressors.
> **Al-Baqarah [2:190]**

> And slay them wherever ye catch them, and turn them out from where they have turned you out. False accusation is more evil than killing.
> **Al-Baqarah [2:191]**

Thus, be mindful not to allow them to bring *fitnah* (tribulation) on you by corrupting you with wealth, beautiful women, etc., which will weaken you and cause you to stop from fighting against them. All these will cause you to lose.

> And fight them on until there is no more tumult or oppression, and there prevail justice and faith in Allah; but if they cease, let there be no hostility except to those who practice oppression.
> **Al-Baqarah [2:193]**

> And spend of your substance in the cause of Allah, and make not your own hands contribute to (your) destruction; but do good; for Allah loveth those who do good.
> **Al-Baqarah [2:195]**

Sons and daughters of Patamala! ... Know that in every struggle, there are always sacrifices to be made, especially in the fight for Allah and the Prophet. This is a struggle to liberate us from continuous oppression by the disbelievers and their alliances. They will never be pleased with the presence of Muslims who uphold the teaching of Islam, because they will not feel free to do what they like. Our struggle is also for the liberation of our beloved country, one which is continuously under occupation by heretic imperialists and their alliances. That is why we need the support and sacrifice of the believers. Thus, quickly provide your support according to your capability. Listen to what has been commanded by Allah with regards to the obligation to provide support and sacrifices.

Those who believe, and suffer exile and strive with might and main, in Allah's cause, with their goods and their persons, have the highest rank in the sight of Allah: they are the people who will succeed.
At-Touba [9:20]

My fellow fighters! ... There are many forms of struggle that everybody can individually participate in. For instance, we play our part by separating ourselves from the disbelievers. Instead, we should associate with our own brothers. We should socialise with people of the same nationality and religion only. We should banish our yearning for material possessions. We should build the passion in helping others who need help. Expel yourself from your past ignorance, repent and *taqwa* (God-consciousness). These are initial forms of exile and sacrifices for Muslims. To make sacrifices at the next level is to sacrifice material wealth such as finance, valuable goods, and others. The highest form of sacrifice is to forego our lives including our soul and energy. This means that we should be prepared to sacrifice our lives for Allah, community, beloved nation, and religion.

Shuhada sisters and brothers! The followers of the Prophet Mohammed (PBUH) had sacrificed their lives as shields in order to protect the Prophet from enemies' weapons. They were willing to lose their lives to save the Prophet from harm. They fell as martyrs. With those sacrifices, the Prophet remained alive and was able to fulfill his responsibility in guiding mankind towards the path of Allah's blessing. At the same time, the rest of the world was in need of the Prophet's guidance to save them from ignorance and deviation in their life. These are examples of which we often hear and see from news about our Muslim brothers who sacrifice themselves as death units. They are not people who commit self-destruction but they are the ones who have truly responded to Allah's call in the battleground. Brothers, do you dare say that the followers of Prophet Mohammed (PBUH) were fanatics who committed suicide? We should not listen to information that comes from the disbelievers and the hypocrites because it is clear that they are the enemies of Allah and the Prophet.

Be patient, fighters, and persevere ... because patience is needed in every struggle.

O ye who believe! Persevere (in doing good actions) in patience and constancy; vie in such perseverance (in facing various

131

obstacles); strengthen each other (guarding army); and fear Allah;
that ye may prosper.
Al-i-Imran [3:200]

Read Do'a.

DAY FIVE

May peace be upon you all.

> For my Protector is Allah, Who revealed the Book (from time to
> time), and He will choose and befriend the righteous.
> **Al-A'raf [7:196]**

Therefore, let us unite and fight in battle to regain our rights and liberate
our people from the disbelievers' occupation. Let it be known, sons and
daughters of Patamala, that it is better to die as martyrs or die under the
wrath of Allah.

> Unless ye go forth, He will punish you with a grievous penalty, and
> put others in your place; but Him ye would not harm in the least.
> For Allah hath power over all things.
> **At-Touba [9:39]**

For those who refuse to go to battle, they have no real excuses except
fear of death or pain of wound. They sit idly in their houses or make
excuses that the brothers will believe. Allah has warned them with the
following statement:

> O ye who believe! What is the matter with you, that, when ye are
> asked to go forth in the Cause of Allah, ye cling heavily to the earth?
> Do ye prefer the life of this world to the Hereafter? But little is the
> comfort of this life, as compared with the Hereafter.
> At-Touba [9:38]

Praise to Allah, today we are grateful to Allah who gives us mercy and
guidance because all the believers have responded and none rejects the
teachings of Allah. They are now inpatient to enter into battle. They are
made up of men and women, the young and old. They are the *Wira Shuhada*,
sons and daughters of Patamala. Their tears trickle down resembling oil
lubricating the engine. Their chests are heavy for holding themselves

patiently. Their bodies shiver as they wait for battle. The sound of *takbir* resonates across the sky as the Angels (Malaikat) of God receive it.

Allah is the greatest (*Allahu Akbar*).

I am your leader and commander. *Shuhada* fighters, know that Allah and the Prophet will always be at our sides and have faith that large numbers of Angels of God, with Allah's permission, will descend to give us support. The spirit of our greatest leader (Prophet Mohammed (PBUH)) is praying for us before Allah so that we will achieve victory. Therefore, let us together praise the Prophet Mohammed (PBUH). *Allah Hum Salli ala saidina Muhammed Wa ala Ali Saidina Muhammed*! Allah is the greatest (*Allahu Akhbar*).

Read Do'a.

DAY SIX

Allah is the greatest.

May peace be upon all of you.

Today, let us come together to pray to Allah and seek repentance for many mistakes that we have done. Let us all raise our hands and pray.

> Our Lord, please forgive all our sin and that of our relatives. Our Lord … please forgive the sins of our parents, teachers, leaders, and our warriors for what they have done in the past. Dear Lord, you are the greatest and you know everything. Your servants will not commit sin with the exception of the weaknesses you created in them. Only you are perfect. Make us happy with the fulfillment of your promises in the Hereafter or honour us with victory. O God Almighty, Lord of the universe, please accept our prayers.

Today, in the name of God who commands us to go to war, I release all of you to enter the battlefield either alone or in groups.

> O ye who believe! Take your precautions, and either go forth in parties or go forth all together.
> **An-Nisaa [4:71]**

For this reason, God has sent the warriors of Islam to enter the battlefields.

> O ye who believe! When ye meet the Disbelievers in hostile array, never turn your backs to them.
> **Al-Anfal [8:15]**

133

If any do turn his back to them on such a day—unless it be in a stratagem of war, or to retreat to a troop (of his own)—he draws on himself the wrath of Allah, and his abode is Hell, an Evil refuge (indeed)!
Al-Anfal [8:16]

As mentioned, God has added another commandment as follows:

O ye who believe! When ye meet a force, be firm, and call Allah in remembrance much (and often); that ye may prosper.
Al-Anfal [8:45]

Come forward; do not be ignorant. Let us together praise Allah by saying there is no God but Allah. *Alif Lam*. The Greatness of God (*Lailahaillalah Alif Lam JalAallah*). If Allah is willing, a rain of bullets could not harm us unless Allah has pre-ordained it.

Go ye forth, (whether equipped) lightly or heavily, and strive and struggle, with your goods and your persons, in the Cause of Allah. That is best for you, if ye (but) knew.
At-Touba [9:41]

O sons and daughters of *Shuhada*! If you have good reason not to be with us in battle, support us because it shows that you are part of the struggle in the path of Allah. Are there not sufficient commandments in the Holy Book calling the believers to join the war? It is elucidated in verse 216, Surat Al-Baqarah:

Fighting is prescribed upon you, and ye dislike it. But it is possible that ye dislike a thing which is good for you, and that ye love a thing which is bad for you. But Allah knoweth, and ye know not.
Al-Baqarah [2:216]

O Believers! Migrate or fight in the path of Allah with your wealth and your life. It is known that, firstly, based on Surat Al-Baqarah, verse 216, it is clear that fighting to uphold the truth is a compulsory obligation, *fardhu ain*, that every one must fulfill. Whereas the duty to propagate and lead is *fardhu kifayah* for those who are able to perform it. It is adequate for one person in a *mukim* (district) to go out as leader.

O fighters and *Wira Shuhada*! Let us examine why Allah said you may hate war because you think it is bad and you may think of something else as good; instead, it is bad for you. Truly, Allah knows more than you do.

Why did Allah describe the characteristics of humans as such from the beginning? This is to prove that Allah is the Omniscient, Most-Knowing. It is known today that among Muslims, there are those who say that wars are acts of self-destruction. Sometimes, some may ask what is the purpose of war; it is a burden after all, whereas we can spend time leisurely with our families? Are we not allowed to profess and practice our religion? We are forced to worship idols. Do we wait till death comes near us to ask for repentance? Or do we stand up and fight only after the disbelievers oppress us? No, please do not be narrow-minded. How can we disappoint our people and insult the teaching of Allah? Do not sell your faith at a low price. Remember that one day we will return to Allah. O sons and daughters of *Shuhada*! Be patient! And do not be angry with those who possess the aforementioned attributes. They read the Koran, but pretend as if they do not understand. Far worse, they neglect His commands. They read *hadiths* but they remain silent as if they have not read them at all. Therefore, leave them to Allah.

O sons and daughters of *Shuhada*! This is not the time for us to idle. Observe and look in every corner of the world: the disbelievers are hunting down our Muslim brothers and sisters. The disbelievers make alliances throughout the world in order to annihilate Muslims. The time may not arrive yet for you to cry or listen to your children and wives cry for the cruel treatment they received, or for you to hear them cry as they are chased out from their land by the disbelievers, as your possessions are confiscated or your people enslaved.

Do we wait until such a situation occurs to act? Remember! Do not fall into the group which Allah's wrath will befall: those who violate the commands of Allah; those who prefer this world to the Hereafter. It is shameful if there are such people among our warriors in this present time because Allah has sternly warned us:

> Those who love the life of this world more than the Hereafter, who hinder (men) from the Path of Allah and seek therein something crooked: they are astray by a long distance.
> **Ibrahim [14:3]**

Brothers who adhere and have faith toward the commandments of God and the Prophet ... Allah will not treat you unjustly and humiliate his slaves. On the contrary, it is His people that forget and violate the teaching of Allah. Such peoples since the time of Prophet Mohammed (PBUH) are adamant with their false practices. Today, these are the ones who always look for an easy way, appear in the community to seek support and resist the *Ulama* (religious scholars) and their followers. Before *Dajjal* (impostor) distribute wealth to people, this group of people will be allowed first in order to see if humans on earth will like or dislike in collecting wealth.

One day, *Dajjal* will appear with heaven and hell on his shoulders. Those who disobey him will be tortured in his hell. However, to those who obey him and violate the commandments of Allah are safe from *Dajjal*'s torture. Probably, my brothers and sisters, you have already seen this happening today.

Young Warriors of *Shaheed* ... Though our leaders and supreme commander has commanded all of us to enter into battle, those who live should congregate around the leader and listen to his advice. Peace be upon you, Allah's mercy and blessings too.

Read Do'a.

DAY SEVEN

May Peace be upon you all.

Today, let us again listen and examine together the explanation that will be read to you. Believers, you will feel sad to know that there are people who are against the teachings of Allah and His Prophet. But do not feel so because those people will no impact on whether you are invited to the path of Allah or not.

> As to those who reject Faith, it is the same to them whether thou warn them or do not warn them; they will not believe.
> **Al-Baqarah [2:6]**

Sisters and Brothers, why are they so stubborn to that extent? This is because they have chosen a wrong path from the start and they enjoy the path that they have already taken. Therefore, Allah has permanently decreed that this group of people could never accept the truth.

> Allah hath set a seal on their hearts and on their hearing, and on their eyes is a veil; great is the penalty they (incur).
> **Al-Baqarah [2:7]**

Young Warriors of *Shaheed* ... Are there among our fathers, sisters and brothers who are inclined to take such path? ... Certainly there are. If not Allah will not mention them as we have read and listened in the previous verse. Believers .... Do not take your fathers, brothers, and sisters as leaders if they incline towards disbelieving and rejecting true faith.

In the above verses, Allah has stated clearly to the believers that on the surface they may appear as our parents and relatives but the truth is they are no longer among us.

> Those who believe, and adopt exile, and fight for the Faith, in the cause of Allah, as well as those who give (them) asylum and aid, these are (all) in very truth the Believers: for them is the forgiveness of sins and a provision most generous.
> *At-Touba [9:20]²*

Sons and daughters of Patamala! Be prepared for it is uncertain whether we will enter battleground tomorrow or later. Look for the best methods and tactics to defeat your enemy.

The Saying of Prophet Mohammed (PBUH)

(Hadith Muslim, Book 3, Page 274, Hadith 1722)
Meaning: "From Jabir.... Said that Prophet (PBUH) said that... war is a deception."

The Saying of Prophet Mohammed (PBUH)

(Hadith Muslim, page 270, Hadith 1716)
Meaning: "From Sulaiman Bin Buraidah, from his father... said... when Prophet Mohammed (PBUH) appointed a person as a commander of the army, he advised the commander and the soldiers to uphold *taqwa* (God-consciousness) and to perform good deeds. He said: 'Fight in the name and in the path of Allah. Fight those who disbelieve.'"

When the Prophet appointed a person as a battle commander, he would advise him and the Muslim soldiers to 'uphold *taqwa*'. This means that in war there are limits that you should not transgress. 'Fight in the name of Allah' is also an act of devotion. You should defend the religion of Allah and fight those disbelievers who do not believe in Allah.

Sisters and brothers of *Shaheed* warriors ... giving advice is the duty of a leader and it is the duty of soldiers to listen to and obey orders.

The Saying of Prophet Mohammed (PBUH)

(Hadith Muslim, Book 5, page 22, Hadith 1809)

Meaning: "From Abu Huroirah… The prophet said … 'A leader is like a shield. Behind it a soldier fights and seeks protection. If the leader leads the army to uphold *taqwa*, with justice, he will be rewarded, if not he will be punished."

Sisters and brothers, use and protect your leader as you would protect your shield and weapons. For you, without a leader is like fighting a battle without a shield.

Young brothers and sisters! By entering the battle, we are actually trading our lives for Allah's blessing, because war means death. This means that all of us are willing to sacrifice life to defend Allah's religion. Such death is called martyrdom.

The followers of the Prophet before were ever ready to trade their life. They acted as the shield to protect the Prophet from enemies' arrows. Many of them died as martyrs. They were not considered fanatics. Today, we have also heard about those who are willing to die. They are members of daring units that seek Allah's blessing and attempt to save their people, nation and religion.

> And Allah is full of kindness to (His) devotees.
> **Al-Baqarah [2:207]**

Peace be upon you, O people of Jihad, and fear not, as Allah is always with us.

May you be in safe custody, O my fellow fighters! Never should we have fear and be sad because Allah is with us at all times and wherever we are.

O my brothers! Another important point to remember is that you should never allow a disbeliever to enter the house of Allah, the mosque, where we perform our rituals because they are impure in the eyes of Allah unless they embrace Islam.

> O ye who believe! Truly the Pagans are unclean; so let them not, after this year of theirs, approach the Sacred Mosque. And if ye fear poverty, soon will Allah enrich you, if He wills, out of His bounty, for Allah is All-knowing, All-wise.
> **Al-Baraah [9:28]**

The Muslim world is in shame. Verses such as 'For you, your practices and for me, my practices' and 'For you, your religion and for me, my religion' mean that Muslims have their own rituals and cannot be mixed with others. Also, the disbelievers have their own religion and we have our own religion. When Allah frees us, we will cleanse ourselves from such practices. With the will of Allah, our religion will be cleansed.

Remember, sons and daughters of Patamala! Fight in the name of Allah, slaughter and kill the disbelievers until they are defeated. Do not run.

> O ye who believe! When ye meet the Disbelievers in hostile array, never turn your backs to them.
> **Al-Anfal [8:15]**

> Others you will find that wish to gain your confidence as well as that of their people: Every time they are sent back to temptation, they succumb thereto: if they withdraw not from you nor give you (guarantees) of peace besides restraining their hands, seize them and slay them wherever ye get them: In their case, we have provided you with a clear argument against them.
> **An-Nisaa [4:91]**

Remember, brothers! During battle, do not kill those among the enemy who give Salaam to you. Do not generalise that they all are disbelievers just because you want booty from them.

> O you who believe! When you go to war in Allah's way, make investigation, and do not say to anyone who offers you peace: You are not a believer. Do you seek goods of this world's life! But with Allah there are abundant gains; you too were such before, then Allah conferred a benefit on you; therefore make investigation; surely Allah is aware of what you do.
> **An-Nisaa [4:94]**

Shuhada brothers and sisters! Observing and adhering to the limits that Allah has determined is necessary for victory. Muslims are fighting in the name of Allah, and not as they please. Thus, follow and adhere to Allah's orders and do not do as you please. You must truly believe in Allah's support and have faith that the victory will be ours. March forward and look for the enemy, day and night, in every place and also in your neighbouring countries, and kill them. Let the disbelievers know that Muslims are strong in this world.

O ye who believe! Fight the Disbelievers who gird you about, and
let them find firmness in you: and know that Allah is with those who
fear Him.
At-Touba [9:123]

Thanks to Allah who gives us support in both times of joy and sadness,
and hope that Allah will bless us with happiness in this world and the
Hereafter.

And remember! Your Lord caused to be declared (publicly): 'If ye
are grateful, I will add more (favours) unto you; but if ye show
ingratitude, truly My punishment is terrible indeed.'
Ibrahim [14:7]

Read Do'a.
I praise and thank God with highest gratitude for providing us
abundant support and for bestowing knowledge to me and mankind,
bestowing the light of goodness to me in conditions that God permits
and favours. We and I are highly grateful to God for everything that
God has bestowed upon us, and let all of us raise our hands to give support
to our warriors who are fighting for the cause of Allah.

The Saying of the Prophet Mohammed (PBUH)

(Hadith Muslim, Book 2, Page 180, Hadiths 948)
Meaning: 'From Tsauban, the Prophet's followers said that the
Prophet said the best money and wealth are spent first on family members,
then on food for his horse which is used for the path of Allah (jihad),
then on those who struggle on the path of Allah.'
Read Do'a.
For the day of Freedom
May peace be upon all of you.

And say not of those who are slain in the way of Allah: 'They are
dead.' Nay, they are living, though ye perceive (it) not.
Al-Baqarah [2:154]

The meaning of the above verse is that Allah, the administrator of
the universe, has said to us, the believers, not to think of our brothers
who lost their lives in battle as dead. In reality, they are alive. They

have gone to meet Allah in the same bodies that were cloaked in blood. Their wounds and blood drops remain fresh before Allah as clear proof that they are fighters and martyrs in the path of Allah. On the day of Judgement Allah will resurrect them in such a condition. Their physical bodies will become new as they enter Paradise. Before the Day of Resurrection, Allah permits them to visit their relatives and their people every night to see if they have been saved from oppression. Therefore, in response to Allah and His Prophet's call and to make our martyred brothers happy, let us unite to save our people starting from today. Know that if we take a wrong step today, we and our children will suffer more and endure further hardship in the future. It is not impossible that Muslims will suffer more hardship under the rule of Muslim government than under the colonisation of non-Muslims.

Therefore, this pen (writer) calls sons and daughters of *Shuhada* and children of the land, especially our fellow Muslims. Embolden yourself to draft a constitution for the land that will guarantee the security of the religion, land, and people. If not, the life and wealth that we have sacrificed would mean nothing. Our brothers have sacrificed themselves as martyrs in the path of Allah to free our children from the suppressive government that accumulates wealth by oppressing the people. Thus, we have to be careful in selecting the leader of our country. He must be a person who possesses faith, is God-fearing, and is humble. As the governor of the land, he must appoint leaders who are true believers.

Look properly! The people are the true owners of the country and they have the right to appoint any one as King or Sultan, one whom they will respect and obey, just as they did. The people of Pattani did not have its own king in the past. But when a royalty related to King of Kelantan visited this land, all the people of Pattani agreed to establish him as the first King of the state of Pattani. Therefore, this pen (writer) hopes that one day we will be able to appoint and establish (a ruler). As the pillar of our government, it is better to have someone of royal descent because the image of a royalty reflects the image of the people. Having a king or a just leader is the people's greatest pride. The people will give their loyalty and love to the just ruler.

Children of the land, how can we have a king who will bring our people and children security and blessings from Allah? Here, the writer is pleased to suggest ways that you all may consider as follows:

1.   The people must set up a body or a high council that alone has the power to select and appoint a ruler. It also holds the power to remove all office bearers, including the King or Sultan, and governmental officials of all levels. The name of the body is 'The Council of Constitution and Traditional Custom of the State of Pattani'.

   For the stability and efficiency of the administration, the council must consist of *Ulama* from the *Shafi'i* school of jurisprudence only. Never should you include other schools of jurisprudence or other community. Otherwise, it is impossible to attain unity. The resolution of the council will remain as the constitution forever. For example, all kings orheirs of the throne of Sultan or Amirul Mukminin must be a close descendant. He must also have deep knowledge of religion. If the closest descendant has little knowledge of religion or he is not a true believer or not humble, then other legitimate heirs can be appointed as the King, Sultan, or Amirul Mukminin.

   Any king or governor who does not please the people because he is unjust may be removed by the Council, which has the power to remove and appoint another person. The advisers to the King or governor must also come from members of the Council.

   With that, the people and the country will live under a just and pious King or Sultan. The King or Sultan will also have to educate the heir of the throne with religious knowledge of the highest level. Consequently the people will feel proud of their ruler and love him.

2.   The Council of the Constitution and Traditional Custom of the Pattani State must establish another lower council. That council is responsible for establishing various bodies for the development of the country, for example, a finance and economics ministry, an internal security ministry, and so on.

   Those who will sit on this lower council must be selected by the people. It must consist of professionals who are educated in different fields. Thus, they are well suited to develop the country. We call this council 'The Council of the People'.

   If Allah is willing, if this happens, this pen (writer) thinks that Pattani will prosper, and will be recognised throughout the world. Courts all over the country must function. It must follow the *syariat* law. Citizens of different faith must obey and submit to the *syariat* law.

   Sisters and brothers of the motherland, do not be afraid or weak to implement the *syariat*. You must be brave to implement the *syariat* just as you were brave to wage jihad, and sacrifice wealth and life to retrieve the independence of our beloved motherland from the hands of the colonialists, for the sake of Allah's blessing. Believe, Children of Pattani, that if you do anything for the sake of Allah only, and obey His orders, He, the Most Merciful, the Most Compassionate, the Most Powerful and the Most Wise will help his obedient servants. Listen to the saying of Allah:

> So lose not heart, nor fall into despair: for ye must gain mastery if ye are true in Faith.
> **Al-i-Imran [3:139]**

> Nay, Allah is your protector, and He is the best of helpers.
> **Al-i-Imran [3:150]**

O Children of the land ... What good is it to proclaim ourselves as faithful Muslims, pray to Allah for the return of our land and the opportunity to rule the country if we are ungrateful and disobey Allah's commands? Who are we? ... Where are we going? What is our final destiny? Therefore, we should think and ponder the following verses:

> If any do fail to judge by (the light of) what Allah hath revealed, they are (no better than) those who rebel.
> **Al-Maidah [5:47]**

Believers! Is it right for us to fight and retrieve the land of Pattani from the disbelievers, only to give it to an unIslamic government? If the people and the rulers are not willing to rule according to the law of Allah, it would be better for us to remain under the rule of disbelievers to protect our own rulers from becoming apostates.

Remember always the warnings and the promises of Allah. If we truly want to worship Allah and obey His commands and follow His rules, surely Allah will help and surely also we will achieve victory. Is not Allah the Omniscient? Remember! If the intention of our struggle is not purely for the sake of Allah's blessing, all the sacrifices of wealth and life will be wasted. They will be worthless to Allah.

Children of the land and sons and daughters of *Shuhada*! Another point that we need to remember is that we must safeguard ourselves from *syirk* (associating Allah with others). It will destroy all our good deeds, so will negligence, arrogance, and hypocrisy. Allah has warned us not to be arrogant about our accomplishments, for example if we succeed in killing and retrieving our rights from the disbelievers:

> It is not ye who slew them; it was Allah: when thou threwest (a handful of dust), it was not thy act, but Allah's: in order that He might test the Believers by a gracious trial from Himself: for Allah is He Who heareth and knoweth (all things).
> **Al-Anfal [8:17]**

The above verse means that Allah wants to tell His servants through His Prophet not to be arrogant. The best gift that Allah has given us is the spirit to fight in the battle, strength, power, confidence, and perseverance in facing various tests and tribulations. Allah has provided our body with strength to enter the battle. If He does not will it, the body will not be able to function. That is the best gift from Allah to us. In addition, Allah bestows us with many other gifts. Is it appropriate for us to neglect His commands?

Finally, the writer would like to advise that if Allah permits and provides opportunity for us to govern the country, do not cause injustices to our people or others. Be just and if we are called as witnesses, be truthful:

> Allah doth command you to render back your trust to those to whom they are due (responsibility in jobs and positions); and when ye judge between man and man, that ye judge with justice: verily how excellent is the teaching which He giveth you! For Allah is He Who heareth and seeth all things.
> **An-Nisaa [4:58]**

> O ye who believe! Stand firmly for Allah, as witnesses to fair dealing, and let not the hatred of others to you make you swerve to wrong and depart from justice. Be just: that is next to Piety: and fear Allah. For Allah is well-acquainted with all that ye do.
> **Al-Maidah [5:9]**[3]

My brothers and sisters, may Allah honour you ... We must brace ourselves to establish a state under the guidance of Allah and the Prophet. Together we will enjoy life with Allah's blessing, the Most-Compassionate, who provides us with various forms of sustenance. Sisters and brothers! ... Before we are willing to sacrifice everything to seek Allah's blessing, why are we not willing to fulfill His commands? If we truly observe His commands, we will prove ourselves as people who have performed exile and Jihad in the path of Allah.

Finally, sons and daughters of *Shuhada* and the *Wira Shuhada*! ... This pen (writer) would like to end this writing with tears of gratefulness to Allah and seeks love from all of you. The land of Pattani is my land also. All the believers of Pattani are my brothers. All of its *Ulama* are my fathers and teachers. To them, this pen (writer) would like to appeal that they accept this pen (writer) as their son who always looks for their guidance and teachings. This pen (writer) hopes that they will guide my brothers so they will remain under the blessing of Allah and will always follow your footsteps.

Do'a.

EPILOGUE

Praise be to Allah...this pen (writer) is grateful to Allah for providing motivation and inspiration that opens the heart of this pen (writer) to write this book as a contribution to brothers who are answering the call for the independence of their land. At the same time, the writer would like to pray that Allah blesses the Prophet Mohammed (PBUH), his relatives, and his followers.

This pen (writer) hopes that this book that is called *Berjihad Di Pattani* (The Fight for the Liberation of Pattani) will be useful in opening windows of confidence and will arouse the spirit of patriotism in the children of the motherland. This pen (writer) also hopes for this book to be my contibution towards the struggle. May all my sisters and brothers be blessed with success. *Allahu Akbar Walillahilhamd* (Allah is the greatest).

Amin.

From the Writer

ENDNOTES

1   Translator's note: This is the wrong citation. It should be Al-Maidah [5:56]
2   Translator's note: This is the wrong reference. The prescription is actually quoted from Surat Al-Anfal [8:74] instead of At-Touba [9:20].
3   Translator's note: This is the wrong reference. The prescription is actually quoted from Al-Maidah [5:8] instead of Al-Maidah [5:9].

Islamic organisation in Thailand offers financial rewards for the assassination of Buddhist officials*

An Islamic group in Thailand has offered financial rewards for the assassination of the governors of the southern provinces or any prominent government official. The statement appears on a website last Friday.

The Organisation (PULO) said that a sum of 90,000 baht or (US$2,250) will be paid to any one who kills the governor in any of the three southern provinces that Muslim majority.

More than 550 persons were killed in the military operations by the Buddhist government. Most of them were Muslims.

The statement explained that the same prize would be paid to any one who assassinates any prominent government official, their deputies, or high-ranking army and police officers. The photos of the three governors were published on the website. It is worth noting that the Thai government has offered big rewards to those who provide information that may lead to the arrest of the 74 Muslims accused of involvement in violent acts in the south. The Muslims who represent the majority in southern Thailand want autonomy in order to safeguard their identity and their lost rights. However, the Buddhist government rejects that.

---

* Taken from www.goalalaldyn.com, 19 January 2005

Justice for the Muslims*

THE FORUM OF AHL AL-SUNNAH WAL-JAMMA'H (ONE OF THE JIHADI WEBSITES)

The news about Thailand comes under the section: 'The news of jihad and al-Mujahideen from the battlefields'. The subtitle reads: 'The Muslims in Thailand—Horrible images'. (No doubt the images intended to highlight the plight of the Muslims in Thailand.)

There is a map of Thailand under which the following sentence appears: Justice for Muslims in Thailand. The images were followed by the comments of the members.

Most of what they said were supplications (do'a), asking Allah to help the Muslims in that country.

For instance, one member prayed to Allah to raise the position of al-Mujhideen and give them support and victory.

Another one expressed his sadness over what has happened to the Muslims.

A third member prayed to Allah to defeat and destroy the Christians the Jews, and the hypocrites. (Interestingly there is an advertisement in the middle of the page, reminding the Muslims not to buy Pepsi or Coca-Cola, as the two companies provide the Zionists with 4.6 billion dollars annually.)

Another member said that whatever they do to Islam, they forget that Allah has made a promise that only his sincere worshippers will inherit the earth in the end.

In another comment, a member said that the sufferings of the Muslims did not attract the attention of the world, whereas the whole world reacted swiftly—particularly the Christians nations—to support and defend the Christians in Indonesia.

---

* Taken from www.islam-minbar.net/modules/newbb, 11 January 2005

The Hell of the Muslims in Thailand*

by Shaban Abdul Rahman

One cannot describe the scenes of blood, destruction, and ethnic cleansing against the Muslims in the world. I do not exaggerate if I say that the eyes are no longer able to follow the funerals of the dead Muslims in different parts of the world in Palestine, Iraq, Kashmir, Burma, Chechnya, Afghanistan, the Moro region in the Philippines, and Pattani in southern Thailand. Every day, we see on TV the injustice and oppression practiced against the Muslims, as if an agreement was signed between the big and small oppressors to deprive the Muslims—countries and nations, majority and minority—of any factors of development and progress so that they remain weak and backward.

Let us look at what is happening to the Muslims in Thailand. According to official statistics, the Muslims form 10 per cent of the population (the population of Thailand is 63 million). Like many minorities groups, they used to have their own state, which was destroyed by the colonisers. To weaken and disunite the Muslim population, the tyrannical authorities bring in non-Muslims (mainly Buddhists) so that, over time, the Muslims will become a minority in the small area they were forced to live. Moreover, the Muslims are subjected to strict military observation and deprived of human rights and a peaceful life.

No doubt that oppression, restriction, and a life full of bitterness generate a feeling of injustice and a wish to get rid of it. It is a natural and legitimate feeling. However, the Muslims' reactions to what is happening to them differ from one person to another, and from group to another,

---

* Taken from www.altebyan.com, 16 January 2005

but no doubt that some have reached the conclusion that a military resistance movement is the best response to oppression.

Instead of wisely dealing with the issue, conducting extensive dialogue with the Muslims and differentiating between those who peacefully protest against their bad condition and those carry weapons, the regime reveals an ugly face of racism and a bloody plan against the Muslims. The government instigated the majority and the security forces against the Muslims and that was very clear in the responses of the security forces and the head of the government (Prime Minister) during the protests in 2004 when more than 400 martyrs were killed and ten of thousands were arrested. The crime was that they have opposed and rejected the policy of bringing in more Buddhists to their areas. In Oct 2004 (the black Monday massacre), more than 85 martyrs were killed and the Muslims are expecting more massacres.

The strange thing is that the Muslim world is silent, as if it has become deaf and dumb. Even the statements of denunciation have disappeared. It is strange that the bloody campaign against the Muslims in Thailand coincides with a strong media campaign in which the Muslims are accused of terrorism and training terrorists in other countries. Isn't our right to doubt that there is an announced and agreement between the wicked tool of colonisation that aims to destroy the Muslims and the political and media tool?

The article appeared in the 'Outstanding Articles' section and received the approval and acceptance of the members of the forum.

The Forgotten Muslims*

Any observer to the condition of the Muslims in South East Asia (Thailand, Malaysia, Singapore, the Philippines) knows the war against Islam and the Muslims in this region takes the same method and form that was used in other parts of the world. The plan aims to eradicate (wipe out) their identity, spread vice, consolidate ignorance and poverty, and create differences among the different groups.

In spite of these evil steps directed against the Muslims in Thailand, Muslims in other parts of the world are not aware of what is happening to their brothers in religion and are leaving them alone to face the enemies of Islam from inside and outside the country. As an obligation towards our brothers there, we provide here some information about the history, the struggle of the Muslims and the present situation in Thailand.

WHERE IS PATTANI?

The size of Thailand is about 520,000 square kilometers with a population of about 45 million, the majority are Buddhists. About 18 per cent of the populations are Muslims. They are Malays who speak the Malay language. The area lies between Malaysia and Thailand. Islam arrived in the area in the fifth century AH, through trade and gradually spread until the whole region was Islamised and under the rule of the Muslims in the eighth century. Pattani became an independent Islamic kingdom. However, when the Portuguese occupied Thailand, they encouraged the Thai leaders to occupy Pattani and end the Islamic sultanate. In 917 AH the Thais occupied Pattani but could not continue due to the fierce Islamic resistance. However, the Thais didn't stop their conspiracies against the sultanate. The British encouraged and supported the Buddhists to attack Pattani and crush the Muslim revolts. In 1320, Thailand officially annexed Pattani.

---

* Taken from www.islammemo.cc/historydb/Print,18 January 2005

THE STRUGGLE OF THE MUSLIMS IN PATTANI

The brave peoples of Pattani did not only face an infidel enemy, but also the disregard of other Muslims. However, they have remained strong and proud of their religion.

THE REVOLT OF AMIR ABDUL QADIR

He was the last king of Pattani. When he revolted in 1321, he was arrested, and the Thais, who were helped by the British, mercilessly crushed the revolt. The Muslims played an important role in the military coup that took place against the monarchy in 1351. However, they were denied their rights by the new government. Their demands were as follows:

- Appoint only one governor for the four Muslim provinces.
- 80 per cent of the government officials (in Pattani) must be Muslims.
- Make Malay the language of instruction in the schools and the official language for the Pattanis.
- Apply *shariah* in the region.
- Form an Islamic Council to look after the affairs of the Muslims.

In 1367, the military ruler of Thailand issued the following decisions against the Muslims.

- All Muslim names must be changed into Thai names.
- All Muslims must adopt the Thai attire and the Thai language.
- The use of the Malay language (in Arabic script) was prohibited.
- Mosques were closed and the Islamic missionaries were stopped.
- The Muslims were denied entry into universities, schools, the army, and the police.

THE MOVEMENT OF AL-HAJ MOHAMMAD

He was a religious scholar. In 1367, he presented a petition to the Buddhist government that included all the previous demands. In the same year, he wrote another petition to the UN, and as result he was arrested together with his colleagues and sentenced to three years in jail. They were secretly and suspiciously assassinated in 1373.

THE METHODS USED TO FIGHT THE MUSLIMS

As Thailand is considered a colonising occupier of Pattani, which used to be a Muslim state for a long time, its methods in fighting the Muslims are not different from the ones used by western colonisation in Africa and Asia. The government applied the following policies.

1. Immigration

As the land in Pattani is very fertile, the government plans to bring in new settlers to live there permanently. Therefore it established many camps to receive these new settlers—who are Buddhists—and arrange their settlement. The objectives of this policy are:

- To weaken the Muslims and raise the percentage of Buddhists living among the local population;
- To use the new settlers as tools to spread Buddhist culture;
- To use them as spies for the government;
- To use them as fighters in times of crisis; and
- To control resources and agricultural lands, thereby making the Muslims poorer and unable to resist the government.

2. Education

Although the Malay language used to be the language of instruction in Pattani, the government put a stop to it and imposed the Thai language. They did not only bring in Thai teachers but also changed the curriculum to serve their interests.

The movement ordered the closure of the religious schools.

Those who want to join the government schools must change their Arab or Malay names to Buddhist names.

Those who graduate from the schools in Pattani must master the Thai language otherwise their certificates are useless.

The government intentionally ignores religious education. Moreover, it appoints some of its supporters who are ignorant of Islam to oversee this aspect.

3. Creating Problems

The government did its best to create problems among the religious scholars and between the different *mazahib*.

4. Spreading Vice

Pubs and restaurants were set up, dancing was taught in schools, and prostitution proliferated.

5. Isolation

Muslims were prevented from entering Pattani, and the people of Pattani were isolated from the rest of the world.

6. Jews

The government brought Jewish teachers from Palestine in order to spread hatred against the Arabs.

Other methods include accusing the people in Pattani of communism or of being agents of Indonesia, and propagating the Al-Qadyaniyyah faith—a deviant sect—just to confuse the Muslims and mislead them.

In order to hide its crimes and criminal acts against the Muslims, the government invited the Association of the Islamic World to open a branch in Bangkok.

The Muslims in Pattani are thus faced with the following:

- Heavy pressure from the enemy
- Disregard from other Muslims
- Little resources
- Weapons are only obtainable from the enemy (during attacks)
- Poverty and ignorance

Saudi Arabia, Kuwait, and the Emirates have established some Islamic centres, but much more is still needed from the Muslims.

APPENDIX **6**

Pattani: The Search for Independence*

THE ORIGIN OF THE PROBLEM

According to Mr. Jamal Arafa, Pattani, which lies between Malaysia and Thailand, contains 18 per cent of Thailand's population. For decades, a strong Islamic movement has been calling for the establishment of an Islamic state that includes Yala, Narathiwat, and Pattani provinces, where Muslims form the majority. Constant confrontations between the Thai Buddhist government and the Muslims have never stopped. As a result, the authorities violated Muslim rights. Many international organisations have issued reports about human rights violations and oppression against the Muslims in southern Thailand. In its latest report, the Human Rights Watchdog in New York calls on the Thai government to start investigation regarding the excessive force used (by the government) in the recent events (20 April 2005). Eyewitnesses confirmed that it was possible to solve the issue peacefully, but the government had preferred to use force so it destroyed the mosque.

According to journalist Abdullah al-Pattani, the issue of Pattani is a pure Islamic issue, similar to issues concerning Palestine, the Philippines, the Muslims in Burma, and Chechnya. The Thai government, by attributing the violence to drug traders or the Al-Qaeda organisation, wants to distort the issue. It is an issue of state sovereignty and independence. Pattani used to be an independent state colonised by the Thai government (known in the past as Siam). Pattani Dar As-salam was founded in the middle of the fifteenth century AH and used to be part of Malaya, which includes present Malaysia. However, as a result of an agreement between Britain and Thailand in 1227, the

---

* Taken from www.goalfalaldyn.com, 19 January 2005

country was divided and Pattani came under Thai control. Pattani includes four provinces.

Regarding those who were involved in the recent confrontations with the government, they are a group of young *mujahideen* who want to regain their rights from the Thai colonising government. They are not a group of drug traders as the media has portrayed them.

THE ARGUMENT OF SEPARATION—SIMILARITIES TO THE PHILIPPINE EXPERIENCE

Some political analysts say that separation will harm much of the country. However, the journalist Abdullah Al-Pattani does not agree. He thinks this idea goes against history and fact; he feels that those who say that the region of Pattani prefers separation—similar to Aceh in Indonesia—do not understand the issue as Pattani is not part of Thailand. It used to be an independent state that was colonised by Thailand.

The *Al-Khaleej* newspaper (in Emirates) featured an article entitled 'Will the Philippines Experience Be Copied?' It says:

> The benefit of the recent incidents is that they shed light on the issue after it had been ignored and neglected for a long time. After the Bali incident in Indonesia, where more than 200 tourists (mostly Australian and British) were killed, the world started to pay attention to the problem. In its anxiety to know the bases of Al-Qaeda in Southeast Asia, the world spotted Pattani in addition to southern Philippines as possible locations. It is worth mentioning that the Thai defence minister has denied the presence of Islamic groups that take the country as a base to attack western targets in the region. However, the U.S. did not change its idea that Thailand is one of the Asian countries where money is laundered (by the terrorists as Washington says).
>
> There is a coincidence in the experience of the Muslims in Thailand and in the Philippines as both struggle for separation from the central governments.

The same newspaper confirmed that for decades, the Thai government has been trying to change the demography of the region by replacing the Muslims with Buddhists. In addition, the Thai government has also been doing the following:

- Change the Islamic Malay customs and tradition
- Destroy Islamic Malay historical sites and mosques and replace them with Buddhist temples
- Build idols on top of mountains to show that Pattani belongs to Thailand
- Establish settlements (called *nicom*) similar to the Jewish settlements in the Palestinian occupied lands
- Spread nudist culture
- Impose the use of Thai language in the schools
- Force Muslims to change their Muslim/Malay names
- Ignore religious education and appoint teachers who support the government in religious positions

As a result of the policies of the Thai government, Muslims do not know much about the region. Unfortunately, this ignorance happens at a time when the Buddhist government is practicing all forms of oppression. The tragedy of the Muslims in Pattani is indescribable. The Buddhist government is practicing all kinds of torture such as killing, assassination, and kidnapping. Moreover, it used tanks to crush the people as it did in the village of Kuta, burned Muslims alive in barrels, and raped women.

HOW MUSLIMS OUTSIDE OF THAILAND CAN HELP THE PEOPLE OF PATTANI

A local said: 'We want our brothers the Muslims to pray for us, to ask Allah to give us support and help. We want the Muslim leaders to take up our issue and present it in the international organisations. We want the organisation of the Islamic conference to take care of our issue and give it the needed attention. We want the free world to put pressure on the Thai government for a just solution.

We want the Arab and the Islamic governments to grant our sons scholarships in their universities besides providing job opportunities to our people in their countries.

7

Major Insurgent Groups in Southern Thailand

BARISAN REVOLUSI NASIONAL (BRN), OR THE PATTANI MALAY NATIONAL REVOLUTIONARY FRONT

Barisan Revolusi Nasional (BRN), or the Pattani Malay National Revolutionary Front, was formed with the objective of establishing an Islamic Republic of Pattani, comprising the southern provinces of Pattani, Satun, Yala, Narathiwat, and Songkhla. BRN aimed to achieve this by staging a revolution to overthrow the Thai government. BRN operates in the southern provinces of Thailand, especially in Yala, Pattani, and Narathiwat. Narathiwat is said to be its stronghold. However, BRN's main headquarters is believed to be located in Malaysia. Due to the dual Thai and Malaysian citizenship that many of the BRN members hold, Malaysia has been known to act as a safe haven for the members of the organisation.[1]

History and the Evolution of the Group

In 1956, Indonesian President Sukarno held a conference in Bandung to promote territories under colonial rule to fight for their independence. Spurred on by this manifestation of regional goodwill, BRN was created to fight the Thai government. On 13 March 1960, a secret meeting was held at an Islamic school, known as the Haji Harun School. There, BRN was officially created. Amin Tohmeena, the son of a famous cleric who was allegedly murdered by the Thai government was made President of BRN. (However, some reports suggest that Amin only joined the BRN in 1964.)

Another factor that led to the creation of BRN was that in 1960, Field Marshall Sarit Thannarat decided to put all Muslim schools in the south, known as *pondoks*, under the control of the Thai Ministry of the Interior. He believed that *pondoks* were the rallying point for separatists in the predominantly Muslim south. To protest this move, students and teachers in more than 100 *pondoks* rebelled against what they saw as unwarranted intrusion by the government into the educational affairs of the Muslims. Some schools were shut down. One *pondok* in Narathiwat's Ruso district announced that it would oppose the new policy by taking up arms. Some reports say that this was how the BRN was founded. *Pondoks* have since been seen as a support base for BRN's activities.

When Amin joined the group, he decided to consolidate his rule by cleansing the organisation. Founding members such as Abdul Qayoom, Ahmad Sharriff (known as Mat Bank, a senior bank official) and later Dr. Haji Harun Sulong were sacked from the group.[2]

On 10 October 1968, the first military wing of BRN was formed. It was called Angkatan Bersenjata Revolusi Pattani (ABREP). This military wing shares a similar acronym with the Indonesian army (ABRI). Some reports claim that this signals the close relationship between the two military groupings. ABREP was commissioned by the Supreme Command Council in a remote village of Lubok Bayah in the District of Jeringa, a province of Narathiwat. Pak Yeh was appointed as Commander-in-Chief of ABREP; Pakwa Sof was appointed as Deputy Commander-in-Chief. Second Deputy was Mat Piah and Tok Ki was appointed as Political Commissar to ABREP. Tok Ki was the backbone of the armed forces and played a very important role in training, educating, recruiting, mobilising, leading, and commanding the BRN armed forces.[3]

The history of BRN is plagued with many breakaway factions and divisions within the group, making it difficult to get a clear picture of its organisational composition and operational skills. In early 1970, signs of fractures within the group began to show. In 1970, dissatisfactions with the leadership of BRN led founding member Yusoff Chapakiya to quit from BRN and set up his own group, the National Revolutionary Party of South Thailand (PRNS). In 1972, another founding member—Tengku Jalal Nasir—also quit from BRN and declared his own Pattani National Liberation Front (BNPP). He took Pak Yeh and more than half of the 600 strong ABREP with him. Idris also joined the new formation as BNPP's Commander-in-Chief.

Also in 1972, an urban unit was formed by Cikgu Ding, known as Black 1902. Black 1902 (the year Pattani was absorbed as a Thai territory) was known for urban sabotage. Ding Jerman and Lukman Iskandar, who was also BRN's Secretary of Foreign Affairs and Chairman for BRN's paramilitary outfit—Pattani People's Revolutionary Commando Brigade or PKRRP—for a period of time, were among its leaders. One of its most noted activities was the kidnapping of three Christian missionaries in Saiburi in 1975. Black 1902 was dissolved in 1975 after Ding Jerman joined Tengku Jalal's BNPP.

In April 1974, prior to the dissolution of Black 1902, the Supreme Command Council decided to increase BRN's military offensive against the Thai government. A new Urban Guerrilla Brigade (UGB) was formed. Lukman Iskandar was appointed as its Commander-in-Chief. Other leaders were Kadir Mayor and Masari Savari. Kadir served as Chairman and Masari as Deputy Chairman. Lukman recruited, trained, and commanded more than 600 urban guerrillas from 1974–77.

On 8 February 1977, Lukman was commissioned as Political Commissar to ABREP. Masari took over from Lukman as Commander-in-Chief of UGB. UGB was restructured in 1977, but since then there has been no news about UGB activities or Masari's whereabouts.

Also in 1977, Lukman was appointed by founding member *Ustaz* Karim (alias Abdul Karim Hassan, former Youth Chief of the Islamic Party of Malaysia, or PAS) to lead a constabulary force known as KOGAP. Lukman participated in a conspiracy to overthrow the Malaysian government by unconstitutional means by aligning himself with the Malaysia army. The secret leaked out and the military leaders of the coup in Malaysia were arrested. Nonetheless, the Malaysian government put the entire blame on the BRN. Lukman became the prime suspect. In consequence, the Supreme Council of BRN held a meeting and declared the appointment of Lukman and the creation of KOGAP illegal. *Ustaz* Karim and Lukman were subsequently sacked by the Supreme Command Council. However, Lukman led a rebellion against the Supreme Council and his move was supported by the group's Armed Forces, the Urban Guerrillas and the Constabulary Guards. Three Supreme Council members were shot dead. Amin and another three Council Members fled the country and remained in self-imposed exile in Malaysia.

At the end of 1977, Lukman was arrested by the Malaysian Secret Police under the Internal Security Act (ISA) on allegations of plotting conspiracies in the name of BRN to overthrow a democratically elected Malaysian government by revolution and unconstitutional means. He was jailed for four years without trial.

With the Supreme Command Council effectively destroyed, the ABREP, the Urban Guerrillas and the Constabulary Guards issued a White Paper in 1979, placing the entire BRN under a new formation, the Revolution Command Council. The Revolution Command Council[4] was set up to plan a new strategy and reform the group. *Ustaz* Karim was made President of BRN and Ahmad Subarjo (an Indonesian graduate) was elected Secretary General of BRN. In turn, Lukman was delegated the position of Foreign Secretary of BRN. He was still in Malaysian prison at the time.[5]

In 1984, a newly appointed Commander-in-Chief of ABREP and Lukman's deputy in the Constabulary Guards, led a rebellion against *Ustaz* Karim. Karim dismissed the ABREP Commander and appointed Abu Bakar as the new Commander-in-Chief.

On 25 May 1986, a group of youths from the mainstream BRN joined forces with other youths to form Pasukan Komando Revolusi Rakyat Pattani (Pattani People's Revolutionary Commando Brigade or PKRRP).[6] It was formed reportedly after consultation with veteran leaders of UMNO, the ruling party of Malaysia. PKRRP was an anti-communist organ and pro-Malaysia in its policies. However, other reports say PKRRP's prime objective was to uplift the image of BRN as a respectable and influential organisation. It is led by leaders of the Armed Forces, Urban Guerrillas and Constabulary Guards. The Chairman of PKRRP is known by the codename Colonel A. Yani. Since its formation in 1986, PKRRP was led by Colonel A. Yani. All of his successors subsequently took his codename when they assumed leadership of the PKRRP. Awang Abdullah Kabir, an Indonesian and a graduate from an Indonesian university took over the position from 1986–89. Awang Abdullah (who is also known as Awang Jabat) was replaced by Halim Hasamoh, popularly known as Halim Jabat (another graduate from an Indonesian university). Halim held the post from 1989–92. Lukman Iskandar then took over from 1992–95. Halim Hasamoh was appointed Chairman again from 1995–98. From 1998, Lukman Iskandar took over the position once again.[7] Ahmad Matnor is the Deputy Commander of PKRRP.[8] He is more popularly known as Mat Jabat. He has been BRN's militia chief since the end of 1960s and early 1970s. Mat Jabat is the most destructive and gruesome guerrilla chief of BRN in Pattani history.[9]

PKRRP claims that all BRN factions will be united sooner or later. PKRRP delivered a 22-point demand list, claiming, among other things, autonomy over language, customs, religion, and rule in southern

Thailand. However, other groups blamed PKRRP for violating and betraying the objectives of the original Pattani revolution.

On 28 April 1992, Abu Bakar signed a preliminary peace agreement with the Thai Southern Military Command based on BRN's 22 Points Demand. With this agreement, BRN has since done away with the objective of an independent Pattani state, preferring now to opt for autonomy. According to the 22-point demand list, the Thai government must appoint a Malay Muslim to be governor-general of the Southern Border Provinces of Thailand, to take over the function of the Director of Southern Border Provinces Administrative Centre. The Thai government must also recognise the Malay Language as a second official language in the Southern Border Provinces of Thailand. The Thai government must recognise Islam as the official religion of the Southern Border Provinces of Thailand. A Shariah Court should also be established in the Southern Border Provinces of Thailand, comprising the Lower Shariah Court of District, the Higher Shariah Court of Province, and the Highest Court of Southern Border Provinces. The culture, language, custom, and practice of the Malays must also be preserved in the southern border provinces of Thailand.[10] In parallel with its revised objectives, BRN also wants to be recognised as a legal political party in southern Thailand.[11] The agreement was ratified during General Suchinda's military junta. After the signing, Gen. Suchinda fled the country. An election was held and the Democrat Party of Thailand swept into power. Mr. Chuan Lekpai became Prime Minister of Thailand in 1994. As a result, the agreement was considered void.

Ustaz Karim led another delegation in 1995 to a round table conference with the Privy Council of Thailand and the Southern Military Command known as Region Four Army. Karim delegated his power to Lukman to sign another peace pact with the Thai authorities. It was ratified in the PAS state of Kelantan on 8 April 1995. However, due to the volatile nature of Thai politics in the 1990s, many different governments were successively voted in and out of office. Thus the key points of the peace agreements were not implemented, thereby annulling it in practice.

The year 1995 was also the time when a group of disgruntled BRN members joined their PULO counterparts to form Tantra Jihad Islam (TJI).[12] Thai intelligence sources claim that this organisation is a small loose coalition whose aim is to destabilise the entire southern Thai region through extortion, arson, sabotage, and other acts of violence.

In 1997, *Ustaz* Karim died. BRN took a long time to decide its new leadership and new political strategy, on how to approach its struggle for an independent Pattani state. In 1998, it was agreed that Lukman would become President and Sofian would be the Secretary General of BRN. The post of Deputy Secretary General went to Zagari. The Deputy President of the BRN was an Indonesian graduate known only by the nickname Abang Ding.[13]

On 10 March 1998, 50 members of PULO and BRN surrendered to Thai authorities, in anticipation of the expiration of an amnesty that was offered earlier. Despite the surrender, Thai authorities said that over 100 rebels remained at large.[14]

BRN is also said to have formed another coalition called Bersatu with PULO and New PULO in the late 1990s to early 2000. However, other reports claim that these members who participated in Bersatu were from a breakaway faction of BRN.[15] Hence core BRN members do not consider Bersatu members as part of their organisation.

Yalan Abdulroman is said to be the current chairman of BRN. In August 2002, he reportedly moved from his hiding place in northern Malaysia to Narathiwat in southern Thailand due to the crackdown by Malaysian authorities on southern Thailand separatist groups.[16]

With BRN in the headlines in January 2004, Masae Useng was named a leading member of BRN.[17] However, he is also seen by some other analysts, as well as by the Malaysian authorities, as a member of the Gerakan Mujahideen Islam Pattani (GMIP) as well as PUSAKA. Masae is alleged to have been involved in a series of weapon thefts, including the latest in January 2004 in Narathiwat. Masae's home is in Narathiwat's Joh I Rong sub-district. He has since vacated the premises.

Recent reports claim that BRN has now split into four major factions, due to a conflict of interest. They are: BRN Congress, BRN Coordinate, BRN Asli, and BRN Progressive. However, other reports state that BRN has split into three—BRN Congress, BRN Coordinate, and BRN Uram.

BRN Congress is chaired by Rosa Burako. This faction has mainly been conducting military activities and is thought to be the most active.[18] It has consistently carried out political and military acts of rebellion in the southern provinces. Its main headquarters are located in Malaysia. According to the Bangkok Post, BRN has 3 fighting forces within the BRN Congress.[19] The unit operating in Yala and Narathiwat is led by Masu-ngai Badu. He is also said to have found refuge in Malaysia.[20]

BRN Coordinate is reportedly carrying out political activity in Malaysia. Since Amin Tohmeena was ousted from BRN in the late 1970s, the group is said to exist only in name.[21] However, with the resurgence of violence in 2004, BRN Coordinate has been cited as the vanguard of separatist groups in the south. It is believed to be working with PUSAKA in its plans to take over the southern border provinces and establish an independent Pattani Darussalam. In December 2004, four Islamic school teachers thought to be members of BRN Coordinate were arrested. Waeyusoh Waedeuramae (alias Loh Supeh) was said to be responsible for BRN Coordinate's military affairs and allegedly ordered the 4 January 2004 raid in Narathiwat as well as the torching of 36 southern schools in 1993. Waeyusoh was slated to become defence minister in liberated Pattani. Another teacher—Abdulrohseh Haji Doloh—was responsible for economic affairs, controlling finances sent by overseas donors. He deposited millions of baht in Thamma Witthaya School, where he taught.

Sapaeing Basor, headmaster of Thamma Witthaya, is still at large. He is said to be the leader of the political arm of BRN Coordinate and is slated to become Prime Minister in the liberated Pattani.

BRN Progressive, which was commissioned by the mainstream BRN as its paramilitary wing, has pronounced its stance that it will not allow members from ABREP, Urban Guerrilla Brigade (UGB) and Constabulary Guards (KOGAP) to join any other liberation group with different ideologies, concepts, and principles of Pattani revolution struggle.

BRN Uram was previously headed by the late Hajji Abdul Karim. This faction has emphasised Pattani political and religious work.[22]

BRN's Ideology

BRN is an ethno-nationalist group that seeks to create an independent Pattani state in southern Thailand. It also aims to endow the new Pattani state with an Islamic constitution.

BRN has adopted the phrase 'Progressive and Revolutionary' as its doctrine. This means that it is against all types of imperialism, colonialism, feudalism, racism, capitalism, communism, and bourgeoisie politics. It also aims to uphold Nasosi (Nationalism, Socialism, and Islam).

Structure and Organisation of BRN

Since the BRN is struggling to establish an independent state, its organisational structure mirrors closely the administrative apparatus of the state.

PATANI MALAY NATIONAL REVOLUTIONARY FRONT (BRN)

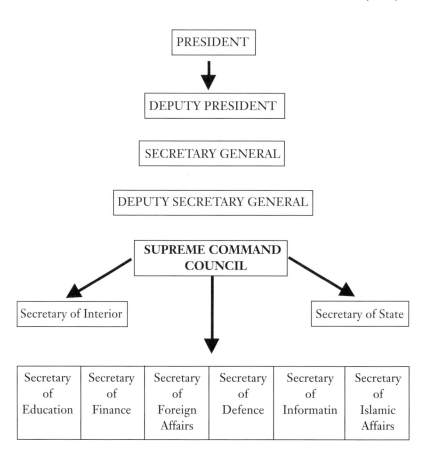

BRN has a well organised military structure with clear lines of command. It also has military training units, and units for logistics, operations, intelligence and recruitment.

Defence Department

SECRETARY OF DEFENCE

Deputy Secretary of Defence

Political Commissar

Commander in Chief***

Armed Forces of Pattani Republic (ABREP*)	Urban Guerrilla Brigade (UGB**)
Commander in Chief***	Chairman
Deputy Commander in Chief	Deputy Chairman
Military Command 1 (Narathiwat)	Recruitment Unit
Military Command 2 (Yala)	Training Unit
Military Command 3	Operation Unit
Logistic, Operation, Training, Intelligence Recruitment	Logistic Unit Intelligence Unit

ABREP

The Commander of each military command controls logistics, operation, training, intelligence and recruitment individually.

After 1977, the armed forces of the BRN were placed directly under the control of Secretary of Defence of the organisation. The post of Political Commissar was made redundant.

The military command of each brigade is divided into smaller units known as regiments. These were led by Cikgu Ding (in Teluk Sumar), Pak Mustakin (in Bukit Budo East) and Tok Gahung (in Bukit Budo West).[23]

UGB

UGB was divided into a number of brigades. These are: Assault Brigade, Combat Brigade, Sabotage Brigade, Commando Brigade, and Destroyer Brigade.

COMMANDERS-IN-CHIEF

All Commanders-in-Chief have the same powers in military action, but they have no powers in politics and organisational matters.

OTHER UNITS

BRN is alleged to have set up a Muslim Commando Unit to conduct non-violent separatism in both rural and urban areas.[24]

BRN also accommodates females in its fold. The group is said to have female guerrillas and even a BRN Women's Wing. It is not known whether the women's wing is political or military in nature.

In terms of military capability, BRN has launched predominantly small attacks. Its main targets are symbols of the Thai government, namely, Thai policemen and government officials. Even with its many military factions and at the peak of its strength in the 1970s, BRN has not carried out many significant large-scale attacks.

It is difficult to give an estimate of the true strength of BRN due to its many factions. What is provided below is a snapshot of the strength of the various divisions within BRN.

Between 1974–6, it is reported that Lukman Iskandar recruited 600 members for the UGB.

By 1981, BRN was able to field a formidable force of more than 1,000 against the Thai government troops. However following the influx of several development projects implemented by the Thai government in the south, combined with a wave of suppressions since 1989, BRN has seen its numbers dwindle. In mid-1987, BRN and PULO were said to number between 350 and 400 fighters combined.[25] In 1998, BRN was reported to have 100 active fighters.[26] In 2000, BRN was estimated to have between 60 to 80 fighters.[27] In 2001, authorities said BRN only had about 60 members left.[28] By July 2002, the group is said to operate with just 30 members.[29]

BRN Strategy, Targets, and Tactics

In its early years, BRN planned to help a group of radical Malaysian generals overthrow the Malaysian government. Once a new Islamic Republic was established, they would march their troops across the border and liberate the whole of southern Thailand. This was the same method used by the Indonesian army when they occupied East Timor in 1975. BRN hoped to apply the same strategy to Pattani.[30]

Since that has failed, BRN has resorted to grass-root militancy, targeting symbols of Thai authority.

The group has also attempted to infiltrate private Islamic schools[31] to spread the separatist cause and to train Muslim youths in militant activities.

As the group's capabilities have diminished somewhat since the 1990s, it has redirected its strength towards conducting surprise, small-scale attacks against the Thai military. It also aims to recruit new members, acquire new weapons, and find new sources of logistical and financial support in order to boost its military capability.[32]

Despite stating its desire to target the Thai military, BRN seems to have shifted its strategy to target civilians. In 1993, BRN bombed a railway station in Hat Yai. Authorities say this showed that the BRN wanted to attack soft targets, where civilians are more vulnerable. The railway station bombing incident also seemed to have a religious overtone. Few Muslims travelled via this train station so the ultimate victims were mainly non-Muslim civilians.[33]

BRN is said to target government officials as well as Thai police and soldiers. From 1993, BRN started targeting Buddhist temples, schools, railway stations, and patrolling troops in the southern Thai jungles. As of 1993, BRN has targeted also non-Muslim civilians.

BRN's preferred modus operandi is abductions, arson, and bombings. The attacks are typically small in scale and not operationally complex. BRN usually leaves a note at the scene of attack. BRN uses small arms such as M-16s. It also uses explosives.

Recruitment and Training Methods of BRN

BRN members are given 'identification cards' which provide them with wide-ranging access rights to places and people on both sides of the Thai-Malay border.[34] This, along with the money offered to recruits who underwent military training, acts as an incentive to lure people from the poverty-stricken parts of Southern Thailand to join the BRN movement.

The group is also said to have resorted to hiring teenagers to stir up trouble at 5,000–10,000 baht a time.[35] These teenagers are however not considered members of BRN.

In 1962, Pattani youths, mainly from BRN military branches had been sent to Indonesia for military training.[36]

Between 1974–6, members of the UGB trained at Cherang Tadung in south Thailand. After Thai authorities found out about the training camp, UGB moved its training grounds to ABREP's camps in Bendang-Yaha areas in the dense jungle of Yala provinces.[37]

According to military intelligence, the southern separatist groups, BRN, PULO and GMIP—forming a coalition under the banner of Bersatu—have all sent volunteers to train in Afghanistan.[38]

In a 1998 report, former Thai PM Chuan Leekpai alleged that Muslim separatists were being trained across the border in Malaysia.[39] Thai Intelligence sources claim there are jungle camps in the Malaysian state of Kelantan where guerrilla training is being carried out.[40]

Thai authorities have also reported that about 10 members of the separatist movement had received training in explosives and sabotage in a Middle East country in the late 1990s or early 2000[41]. It was not specified which group these militants belong to. However, an interview with a BRN member, who later defected, revealed that some BRN members were sent to a secret boot camp in Syria where they received military training on how to assemble and defuse bombs, and also how to stage sabotage operations. In the camp, suicide bombers were also being trained. They were told that suicide bombing was necessary to keep imperialism at bay.[42] The trainees were given a monthly allowance equivalent to about 4,500 baht (US$115). This may be seen as an incentive to encourage the poor civilians in southern Thailand to take up militancy and suicide bombing.

BRN's Financial and Support Networks

BRN receives its funding through criminal activities like extortion. For example, the group would send out letters signed by Poh Ma Su-ngaibatu to petrol stations in Yala province to demand 1.5 million baht from each of them.[43]

ABREP revenues were also collected from ransoms in kidnappings and the imposition of revolution taxes on the Muslim masses and other types of protection funds.

BRN also received money from legitimate businesses. Amin Tohmeena set up a transport company known as Pattani Transport Co. Ltd, and was involved with a group of Indonesian businessmen to incorporate a shipping company into his business. It is believed these companies contributed to the funding of the BRN. In addition, BRN received funds in the form of public donations to Amin's public office.[44]

BRN's source of funds is not limited to southern Thailand. With its official headquarters in Malaysia, one of the neighbouring states such as Kelantan, under Parti Islam Malaysia, allegedly contributes to BRN's funds. In June 2002, counter-terrorist sources said BRN had raised money in Europe and had placed a bounty of 50,000 baht (US$1,200) for every Thai policeman killed in the south. BRN issued leaflets in some rural areas warning people to stay away from police premises or they could be harmed in crossfire incidents.[45]

BRN's support base lies mainly in the *pondoks* or Muslim religious schools.[46] However, some Islamic businessmen and Malaysian political parties provide it with logistical and financial support.

Government Responses to the BRN Threat

With many Pattani separatist groups finding safe haven in Malaysia, the Malaysian authorities have recently started cracking down on such groups. In the late 1970s, Lukman Iskandar was arrested by Malaysian police and detained under the country's Internal Security Act (ISA). He was arrested again under Malaysia's ISA in 1992 and was released in late 1994.[47]

On 13 August 2002, the Thai army announced a new initiative to battle terrorists via official propaganda. A Fourth Army source said

Internal Security Operations Command Region 4's Detachment 2 unit launched its website (www.isoc4-2.mi.th) in late July 2003 to counter the psychological warfare being waged through the Internet by Pattani separatists. The military website aimed to have updated information about the situation in the south as well as to reassure the Muslim population there that they were not being treated as second class citizens.[48] However, the website has since been suspended.

With the new attacks in January 2004, Thai authorities have stepped up their efforts to resolve their problems with the south. Prime Minister Thaksin Shinawatra has said that the government would increase the flow of funds to the region for development purposes. However, he has also called for a probe into the *pondoks* as he believes they are harbouring and breeding militants. This may affect BRN as much of its support comes from the *pondoks*. Thailand has also joined hands with Malaysia to step up patrols along the common border to prevent militants from crossing in and out of the two countries.

BRN Today

BRN's capabilities are as yet unclear since the group seems to have lost its focus. However, they continue to launch regular skirmishes in the south, enough to set Thai authorities on alert. Though the support for Pattani armed groups dwindled to insignificant levels, the attacks in January 2004 show that the Pattani struggle has not been abandoned.

Emerging reports also indicate that BRN (more specifically BRN Coordinate) is working with PUSAKA and that this alliance is now the vanguard for the separatist movement in the south of Thailand. BRN Coordinate provides the military strength and firepower while PUSAKA deals with training and indoctrination. The movement is said to have a 1,000 day plan to take over the three southern provinces of Pattani, Yala, and Narathiwat and establish an independent Pattani Darussalam.

PERTUBUHAN PEMBEBASAN PATANI BERSATU (PATTANI UNITED LIBERATION ORGANISATION, OR PULO)

Pertubuhan Pembebasan Patani Bersatu (Pattani United Liberation Organisation, or PULO) is the largest and most prominent of the various Malay Muslim groups that have operated in southern Thailand since the

1960s. The group feels that the former Pattani state has been illegally incorporated into Thailand and thus wants secession from Thailand for the five southern states of Yala, Narathiwat, Songkhla, Sala, and Pattani. [49] PULO aims to combine the five states into an independent Muslim or Malay state or sultanate with Pattani as the centre, called 'The Patani Malay Republic'.[50] PULO is active in Pattani, Yala, Narathiwat, Songkhla, and Sala and has been known to operate within Bangkok.[51] It is also suspected of maintaining a covert presence over the border in Malaysia, where they are thought to have established operational headquarters.[52]

History and the Evolution of the Group

There are conflicting reports on how PULO was established. According to Peter Chalk,[53] an Islamic scholar named Kabir Abdul Rahman established the organisation in 1968. Kabir was disillusioned with what he regarded as the limited and ineffectual nature of the established Malay opposition in Pattani. He brought together a younger, more militant generation of Thai Muslims, many of whom had been radicalised while studying overseas. However, according to Rob Fanney at *Jane's Terrorism & Insurgency Centre*, PULO was founded by Tungku Bira Kotoniro on 22 March 1968.[54] Tungku Bira Kotoniro was the political leader and has remained chairman of the group ever since. Before founding PULO, Tungku went into exile in 1962 following unrest in southern Thailand. He hails from a well-respected, aristocratic family and has lived in Saudi Arabia and more recently in Syria.

During the 1970s, the leadership was organised in a purely military order, reflecting the primary struggle of that period. At that time, PULO undermined the stability of the region by instigating unrest and civil disturbances in the south of Thailand. It launched its armed struggle against the Thai government on 3 April 1976. But it was not until 1980 that it began to conduct more serious terrorist operations. In June 1980, PULO operatives carried out four bomb attacks in Bangkok, resulting in 47 people being injured. In 1981, the group claimed responsibility for another three bombings in busy shopping areas leaving 50 people injured.[55]

The group suffered a setback in 1984, when the Thai government announced a general amnesty of all PULO members, which many took advantage of since it also offered non-prosecution. Since then, the organisation seemed to have gone underground for a period of time, surfacing to engage in activities for funding and occasional calls for violence against the government.

PULO held its First National Conference (Congress I) from 20–23 June 1988.[56] The PULO Political Committee and the Supreme Council of Struggle (MKP) convened without disturbance. Delegates from all parts of the country attended the conference. Dr. Haji Harun Moleng (Mohammad Bin Mohammad) replaced Bapak Haji Kabir Abdulrahman as the new president. Among the issues discussed were the character of the guerrilla warfare and fighting strategies. PULO decided that more 'hard struggles' were needed and they rejected any compromise with the Thai government. It was decided that urgent changes were needed in political, military and organisational affairs. Delegations were sent abroad on propaganda missions, establishing representative missions abroad in Muslim states and some European countries, and to attend international conferences.

The Thai government responded to PULO activities with an amnesty programme in 1991. The 'Tai Rom Yen' (Cool Shade in the South) programme gave an opportunity to Muslim separatists to surrender in return for a blanket amnesty.[57] Among those that left PULO was Yusouf Longpi, PULO's Secretary-General and field commander.

The group split in 1992, with Hayihadi Mindosali at the helm.[58] Hajji Samaae Thanam was the military commander and regional leader of PULO. Of all the PULO leaders, Samaae Thanam held popular sway. He set up the PULO Army Command Council or MPTP to give support to Tuanku Abdul Kade, the pioneer of the south's insurgent movement in the 1940s. Samaae Thanam was based in Malaysia and was arrested by the Malaysian authorities in February 1998. He was later deported to Thailand.[59]

After the split, PULO held its second National Conference[60] (Congress II) between 22–25 January 1995. The setbacks (for example, the split and the desertions due to amnesty) that it suffered from 1988–94 were discussed. Weaknesses of the group were pointed out: lack of coordination and participation between commands in various regions, lack of exchanges of experiences and lack of confidence in the population. The conference also elected *Ustaz* Haji Hashim Abdulrahman (Baba Abdulrahman Betong) as the new political leader of PULO and Haji Daud Haji Hasan as his commander in charge of the military wing.

In 1995, a PULO splinter Barman National Baru persuaded youths to undergo terrorist training in Syria in exchange for a four-year membership card that guaranteed access to jobs and security in Malaysia.[61]

Although PULO split in 1992, there is evidence that various factions of both the groups undertook joint operations. For example, in the 1990s (exact dates vary), PULO and New PULO joined hands with the BRN, BNPP, and the Mujahadeen Pattani, to form the United Front for the Independence of Pattani, or Bersatu. Bersatu was formed with the idea to unify resources so that there was no need to rely on foreign sources of support.[62]

In mid-1997, Bersatu carried out a series of coordinated attacks (codenamed 'Falling Leaves'[63]) aimed at killing state workers, law enforcement personnel, local government officials, school teachers, and other perceived symbols of Thai Buddhist repression. Between August 1997 and January 1998, no less than 33 separate attacks were carried out as part of this effort, resulting in nine deaths, several dozen injuries, and considerable economic damage. According to Tony Davis, Specialist Asia Correspondent with *Jane's Intelligence Review*, this campaign of violence marked the most serious upsurge of Muslim separatist activity since the early 1980s.[64]

Also, in 1997, PULO underwent reorganisation to improve its structure and policy implementation. It launched many offensives throughout Thailand, particularly between the end of 1997 and the beginning of 1998. This increased activity led to the Thai government to declare war on the so-called 'liberation movements' in the south.

PULO was thrown into disarray in 1998, when some of its leaders were arrested. Tunku Abdulrahman Betong was arrested with three other leading members, including military chief, Samaae Thanam, in Kelantan, Malaysia and extradited to Thailand. They were reportedly told by the Malaysian government to stop their activities against Thailand or face expulsion.[65] Morale plunged and some of its members, who lost faith in the group, gave themselves up to the Thai government.[66]

Military campaigns have since reduced the rebel movement to a shadow of its former self. Only occasional incidents such as bombings in April 2001 suggest the insurgency is not over.[67]

PULO's Ideology

PULO's ideology is based on the Ubangtapekema, an acronym derived from *ugama, bangsa, tanahair*, and *perikemanusiaan* (religion, race/nationalism, homeland, and humanitarianism).[68] Integral to this concept is recognition of the need for a long-term strategy to prepare for the goals of secession. To this end, PULO has placed priority on improving the standard of education among the southern Thai Malay population as well as fostering local political consciousness and national sentiment.

Structure and Organisation of PULO

By its own admission, PULO started as a disorganised group, incapable of launching coordinated attacks. For example, when a region is attacked, PULO forces in other regions fail to launch counter-attacks to distract and disperse government forces.[69] However, after the split in 1992, it set up the PULO Army Command Council or MPTP, headed by Hajji Sama-ae Thanam. It also has an armed wing called the Pattani United Liberation Army (PULA) with some 50 armed fighters.[70] PULA has superior knowledge of the southern Thai terrain, and has support of the locals, who believe in the independence cause.[71] Thus it has carried out many successful militant insurgency attacks against the Thai government. It has claimed responsibility for several bombings and arson attacks against government establishments in the south.[72]

PULO operates under separate military and political commanders although the military command is of greater importance. The leaders of the military command councils set the vision and goals of the organisation and coordinate activities. It has a cellular structure, with members operating in small active service units.[73]

PULO STRATEGY , TARGETS, AND TACTICS

PULO carries out high publicity attacks to garner international support for its cause. This also explains its attempts to establish ties with international militant groups. PULO has close links with Islamic militants in the northern Malaysian state of Kelantan. Bangkok has repeatedly alleged that PULO has benefited from the provision of safe haven in Kelantan and that this support has come with the sanction of PAS, as well as the official indifference of the central government in Kuala Lumpur.[74] There have also been allegations that the radicals in Kelantan have facilitated the trans-shipment of weapons from Cambodia to help in terrorist operations in southern Thailand[75]. Some sources also claim that links exist between PULO and Malaysian group Al Maunah, which has a following in southern Thailand and is believed to include a number of former PULO members.[76]

Thai authorities also believe that PULO has links to other militant groups in Southeast Asia. They have cited the interception of arms shipments from southern Thailand, believed to be heading to Aceh, Indonesia and possibly to Kashmir in 2001 and 2002 as evidence. Reportedly these operations were undertaken with the help of Jemaah Islamiyah and Abu Sayyaf Group. Members of PULO have also met with representatives of the Free Papua Movement (OPM) and the Moro Islamic Liberation Front.[77] Others have also pointed out PULO links with the Free Aceh Movement (GAM).[78]

The possibility of a Pattani/Middle East/South Asia tie-in has been raised in the context of claims that southern separatists currently have a working relationship with radicals trained in Iran, Iraq, and Pakistan. The allegation was first made during investigations into a 1995 bomb blast in Hat Yai. According to Thai security, the blast was a premature explosion of an incendiary device that was actually intended for use in a joint, externally backed PULO–Shi'ite sabotage mission.[79] Since then, repeated accusations have been made by intelligence sources that PULO operatives have facilitated the entry of foreign nationals into Thailand, both for operational and logistical purposes. Allegations have also been made that PULO played an integral role in the foiled 1994 Hizbollah truck bombing of Israel's Bangkok embassy in return for arms and financing. According to Thai security sources, the group assisted in providing logistics such as supplying the truck that military intelligence believed was to have been used in the attack.[80]

Even in its heyday, PULO was never sizable enough to conduct large-scale guerrilla attacks and had to rely on the most basic terrorist tactics. Its traditional forms of attack have been bombing and arson. From the late 1990s onwards, the group has been accused of targeting police and security officials, sometimes in drive-by shootings from motorbikes.[81] The group usually leaves a note or the organisation's emblem at the site, claiming responsibility for the attack.[82]

PULO targets symbols of the Thai government, especially the military. Perceived symbols of Thai cultural dominance have also been periodically targeted, including schools and Buddhist temples.[83] Soft targets, such as shopping areas, railway stations, and infrastructure sites have also been targeted.[84]

PULO mainly uses AK-47, M-16, and HK-33 assault rifles, bullet-proof clothing, 9mm pistols, and bomb-making equipment/materials.[85]

It gets most of its weapons from raids on Thai army and government offices. There are frequent incidents of police stations and other government agencies being overrun and having their weapons and ammunition stolen. For example, in 2001 and 2002, there were repeated cases of men wearing hoods, conducting armed robberies against forestry departments in the national parks. In one such incident in June 2002, four attackers stole weapons and over 1,400 rounds of ammunition from a national park in Than Tho district in Yala.

Weapons are also readily available in the south, which has become a focal point for small arms smuggling from Cambodia and Myanmar. Thai military is also accused of selling weapons to smugglers, who later traffic them to the Philippines, Indonesia, and the Indian subcontinent. These weapons can easily land in the hands of insurgent groups like PULO.

Recruitment and Training Methods of PULO

In the 1970s, at the peak of its popularity, PULO had 1,000 members. Other reports put its strength at 20,000. Thai authorities do not give any official figures about the strength of the organisation. But they have estimated that during the 1960s and 1970s, there were approximately 1,000 armed rebels amongst the main insurgent factions, of which PULO was the largest. By 1980 that figure was down to between 500 to 600, and by the end of the century it had fallen further to under 100. Current estimates of the number of guerrillas operating varies between 20 and 200.[86] However, it is important to note that not all of these insurgents belong to PULO.

To address the decline in membership, PULO has increased its recruitment drive by targeting unemployed young men and drug addicts to conduct terrorist attacks, usually after a minimum of training.[87]

Little is known about PULO training methods. Their training camps are thought to be located within the jungles that skirt the Malaysian-Thai border. It is suspected that some members may have gone to Libya during the 1970s to receive specialised training in bomb-making and assassination techniques.[88] Some reports also state that PULO members received training in Libya and Syria in the 1980s. These members then returned to train others. In recent years, training is seemingly done in Malaysia,[89] often supported by Muslim supporters from Chechnya and Afghanistan, who act as foreign trainers.

176

According to military intelligence gathered in the southern border provinces, PULO, the BRN, and the Mujahideen group under Bersatu have sent volunteers who had combat experience to Afghanistan for training.[90]

PULO's Financial and Support Networks

Funding for the separatist group comes mostly from criminal activity, which flourishes in the southern part of Thailand. PULO runs extortion rackets targeting local businesses particularly in the construction industry. It operates an illegal 'protection' racket. This was confirmed when in 1994, a note bearing the PULO insignia, demanding US$120,000, was intercepted by the police. PULO members are also involved in the smuggling of contraband products, narcotics, weapons, and people.[91]

The organisation also receives funding from outside of Thailand. It privately raises funds in Europe and the Middle East from sympathetic charities. It used to collect funds from Malaysian groups and charities as well, until Kuala Lumpur clamped down on such activities.[92]

In the past, the states of Libya,[93] Syria,[94] and Iran provided funding for the PULO, but these sources are believed to have dried up. PULO is also partly financed by fundamentalists from Pakistan, Kuwait, and Saudi Arabia.[95] The Lebanese Hizbollah[96] is also said to have supplied funds to PULO in exchange for the group's logistical support for Hizbollah operations in Thailand. As a result of its extensive external networking, 'material support from Libya and Syria and ideological support from Malaysia and Saudi Arabia,' PULO 'grew to be one of the most influential and militant secessionist organizations.'[97]

In terms of non-financial support, Muslims, especially Malay Muslims, in the southern parts of Thailand form PULO's support base. However, with the Thai government beginning to show greater sensitivity to the lack of economic and administrative development in the Yala, Narathiwat, and Pattani provinces, this has led to a decrease in support for militant groups such as PULO. Bangkok's provision of 15 million baht to finance occupational training for Malays in the south, including the former militants, has helped to reduce support for PULO among the locals.[98]

However, the risk remains that the historical resentment for the Buddhist Thai government and its discrimination against the Muslims in the south may be exploited insurgents in the future.[99]

Government Responses to the PULO Threat

The Thai government has declared amnesties a number of times in order to lure militants from their separatist ideology. In 1984, the Thai government announced a general amnesty of all PULO members, which many took advantage of in its promise of non-prosecution. The group was severely weakened as a result.

In 1991, the Thai government came up with a 'Tai Rom Yen' (Cool Shade in the South) programme. It was an opportunity for Muslim separatists to surrender in return for a blanket amnesty.[100]

Despite the successes in Thai efforts to clamp down on PULO, the government faced some serious setbacks in 2002. The upsurge in violence was attributed to the changes in security responsibility after the dismantling of Southern Border Provinces Administrative Committee (SBPAC). In April 2002, the Civilian-Police-Military Taskforce 43 (CPM 43), a joint security apparatus which combined Thai police, army, and civil bodies and was charged with security and maintaining law and order in the south was dissolved and the police assumed responsibility. There were allegations that some individuals in the military, angered by the loss of their role and the privileges that went with it, were paying former guerrillas to reactivate and conduct terrorist activities. In July 2002, the government partially reversed their decision and once again gave the military a greater role in intelligence work.[101]

Thailand has long been seeking Malaysian support in neutralising the threat of Islamic militants in the south. The Thai government specifically warned Malaysia that closer economic ties would be at stake if cross-border cooperation against PULO and New PULO was not considerably stepped up. Concerned that this would jeopardise the much touted Malaysia–Indonesia–Thailand Growth Triangle (MITGT), Malaysian Prime Minister Dr. Mahathir Mohamad acceded to the Thai demands. He personally sanctioned joint police raids against Thai secessionists thought to be hiding in northern Malaysia.[102]

The two governments have since cooperated in cutting off the group's escape route into Malaysia.[103] Malaysia and Thailand kept close watch on all movements along their common borders, with police exchanging intelligence with one another on individuals belonging to extremist groups in Thailand.[104]

The joint operations proved rather successful. In 1996, four key separatists were arrested in the Malaysian state of Kelantan. Malaysia has also cracked down on groups and charities providing funding to Thai separatists, as well as moving against members of the PULO residing in Malaysia.

Malaysia has since maintained a fully cooperative border and counterinsurgency stance with Thailand, depriving PULO of important sources of sanctuary and support in Kelantan.

PULO Today

PULO has never posed a sophisticated terrorist or guerrilla threat, although it represents an continual challenge to the general peace and stability in the region. Sources on the ground say that PULO is now focusing on propaganda instead of militant activity. It continues to issue threats and warnings of attacks from its website, although these are taken by security forces to be of little credibility. Despite this, PULO may still provide inspiration to other groups in southern Thailand. For example, in reaction to April 2004, and October 2004 incidents at Krue Se and Tak Bai respectively, in which significant number of Muslims were killed by the security forces, PULO issued statements threatening to widen the conflict beyond the southern provinces. In January 2005, PULO allegedly offered cash rewards for killing of provincial governors and other government officials.

New Pattani United Liberation Organisation (New PULO)

New Pattani United Liberation Organisation (New PULO), like its predecessor, wants secession from Thailand for the five southern states and to combine them into an independent Muslim Malay state or sultanate with Pattani as the centre. However, unlike PULO, it intends to achieve an independent Pattani by way of a focused terror strategy against the Thai authorities. New PULO was not for dramatic attacks but preferred minor attacks, aimed at harassment of the authorities. The idea was to conserve the limited operational resources with the aim of developing legitimacy for a separatist Islamic agenda.[105] The group is active in all the southern provinces, but mostly in Yala and Narathiwat. It is also suspected of maintaining a covert presence in neighbouring Malaysia, where it is thought to have established an operational headquarters.[106]

179

History and the Evolution of the Group

In 1992 PULO split into two factions. Three years after the mother organisation splintered, A-rong Muleng and Hayi Abdul Rohman Bazo established New PULO. Ar-rong Muleng (Muhamad Bin Muhammad) is now in exile in Sweden.[107] Hayi Abdul Rohman Bazo (Haji Buedo), who is Chairman of New PULO, was also the leader of New PULO's political Kadasan wing.[108] According to Thai army intelligence, one of the reasons for the split was that Ar-rong's faction had disapproved of the truce talks being held in 1993 between mainstream PULO and the government, with the purpose of ending the decades-old struggle. The two factions even crossed swords.[109] Another reason for the split was that New PULO preferred to focus on minor attacks that are intended to repeatedly harass and pester police and local government authorities.[110]

In 1995, rifts emerged among the core leaders of the New PULO movement. As a result, Ar-rong decided to remove his group from the movement and to set up a new organisation called 'PULO 88' or the Abu Jihad PULO, while the other group led by Hajji Habeng Abdul Rohman named its armed unit 'Caddan Army.'[111] Other reports suggest that Mazo Tarye heads the Caddan Army.[112]

Although PULO and New PULO split in 1992 due to differences in strategic outlook, there is evidence that various parts of both groups undertook joint operations. In fact, in the 1990s (exact dates vary), PULO and New PULO joined hands with the BRN, BNPP, and the Mujahideen Pattani, to form the United Front for the Independence of Pattani, or Bersatu. Bersatu was formed with the idea to unify resources so that there was no need to rely on foreign sources of support.[113]

However the groups suffered a setback when some leaders were arrested in early 1998 by a joint Thai-Malaysian police force operation code-named operation 'Pitak Tai' (safeguarding the South). Three New PULO leaders were captured on 22 January 1998 in Narathiwat. The three were the founding member Haji Buedo, Supreme Commander of New PULO's operational wing Haji Da-oh Thanam (aka Haji Da-oh Maseng), and Abdulrohman bin Abdul Kadir.[114] The arrests left New PULO's rank and file in a state of confusion. Morale was very low and some of its members, who lost faith in the group, gave themselves up to the Thai government.

Thai authorities believe that both PULO and New PULO have benefited from the provision of safe-haven in the state of Kelantan in

Malaysia and that this support has come with the sanction of the state's ruling Parti Islam Se-Malaysia (PAS), as well as the official indifference of the central Kuala Lumpur government.[115] There have also been allegations that radicals in Kelantan have been facilitating the transshipment of weapons from Cambodia to southern Thailand to carry out terrorist operations there. However, Malaysia has since maintained a fully cooperative border and counterinsurgency stance with Thailand, depriving PULO and New PULO of important sources of sanctuary and support in Kelantan. Strategically, this has represented a major blow to both groups, encouraging many cadres to 'give up the struggle.' In the months following the joint raids, over 900 militants from PULO, New PULO, and various other smaller groups voluntarily joined a government-sponsored 'rehabilitation' program, pledging to become active participants in peaceful national development.[116]

In 2000, the group was dealt another major blow when Sarli Taloh Meeyo, whom some considered one of the New PULO's founders, was killed by security forces in Ra-ngae, Narathiwat. Authorities claim Sarli was responsible for 90 per cent of the terrorist activities in Narathiwat.[117] According to the Bangkok Post, New PULO broke up in 2002, two years after Sarli died in clashes with the Thai army.[118] However, other sources have reported that PULO and New PULO have tried to patch up their differences and to strengthen mutual cooperation. As of 2002, PULO and New PULO leaders have dispatched their armed units to carry out joint military and political operations in some areas of three southern border provinces.[119] According to some reports, Haji Lukman B Lima, PULO's exiled leader, has been instrumental in uniting the two groups.[120]

New PULO's Ideology

New PULO believes that the traditional virtues and 'greatness' of the Kingdom of Patani (Patani Darussalam) should be restored. The group wants the freedom to practice their ethnic Malay customs and culture, speak the Malay language, and to observe their Islamic traditions.

The Structure and Organisation of New PULO

Like its parent organisation, New PULO has a cellular structure with members operating in small Active Service Units.[121] Above the cells in the organisational structure of the group are New PULO's Leadership

Council, the political Kadasan wing, the Armed Force Council and its armed unit, the Caddan Army.[122] The Leadership Council set the vision and goals of the organisation and coordinate its activities. The nature of the relationship between the Armed Force Council and the Caddan Army is unclear.

The Armed Force Council gives the overall direction to New PULO's insurgent activities. It coordinates, directs, and controls the three main separate sabotage wings—each with a specific area of geographic concentration:

- The Sali Ta-loh Bueyor Group, responsible for Narathiwat's Ja-nae and Sri Sakhon districts.
- The Maso Dayeh Group, with responsibility for Yala's Betong district.
- The Ma-ae Tophien Group, with responsibility for all districts throughout Narathiwat and Yala provinces.[123]

The sabotage wings are responsible for training cadres in bomb-making and carrying out sabotage.

New PULO's command headquarters are in Kota Mahligai, Kelantan, Malaysia.[124]

New PULO Strategy, Targets, and Tactics

New PULO is focused on minor attacks that are intended to repeatedly harass and pester police and local government authorities. Choice of this particular modus operandi probably reflects a desire on the part of the New PULO leadership to conserve its limited operational resources. It may also be indicative of an attempt to enhance the perceived legitimacy of the separatist Islamic struggle in the south by minimising the scale of human-directed violence.[125] Furthermore, it also does not have the capability to carry out large-scale insurgent attacks. It generally carries out small-scale attacks like drive-by shootings. The group has also bombed a hotel and a theatre in the Muang Yala district in the 1990s.[126] Another of the tactics often used by New PULO is arson. The group has been blamed for torching more than 30 schools in Narathiwat, Yala, and Pattani in August 1993.[127] New PULO also carries out extortion and kidnappings.

Usually, the movement would leave a note or the organisation's emblem at the sabotage site to claim responsibility. For example, a letter in a plastic bag was found on a nearby tree near the site of an arson attack. The letter claimed that the arson was the work of New PULO. It carried the logo of the Caddan Army and was signed by Mazo Tarye, New PULO's leader.[128]

New PULO uses mostly AK-47 and M-16 assault rifles. It also uses dynamite in its bomb attacks. It mostly gets its weapons by stealing them from police stations and government offices.[129]

Like its parent organisation, New PULO targets mostly symbols of the Thai government, especially military personnel. Perceived symbols of Thai cultural dominance have been periodically attacked, including schools.[130] Soft targets, such as shopping areas, railway stations and infrastructure sites have also been targeted.[131] For example, the Hat Yai rail junction, the commercial and rubber centre of southern Thailand, has been hit by five bombs in 20 years, killing nine people and wounding almost 200. Rich businessmen have also been the target of extortion and kidnapping in order to fund the group's activities.

Recruitment and Training Methods of New PULO

It is difficult to give an estimate of the strength of New PULO as many sources usually provide the combined strength of both the parent organisation (PULO) and its splinter group (New PULO). According to the Thai army, in the 1980s there were about 1,000 armed pro-separatists. The number is about 100 currently, with no more than 20 active members operating along the rugged mountains in the south.[132] However, it is important to note that these figures represent the combined groups in all of Thailand's south and do not reflect New PULO's actual membership.

According to the Thai Interior Ministry, New PULO recruits the unemployed and young drug addicts to carry out many of its more rudimentary sabotage missions. Analysts say that this reflects a desire on the part of the group's leadership to conserve limited operational human resources. In addition, it presumably helps to minimise the possibility of New PULO's security being compromised in the event that a saboteur is captured and made to confess. Thai military intelligence believe that the group is ready to pay up to 500 baht to drug addicts, who agree to carry out basic sabotage attacks such as torching bus depots or bombing bridges.[133] These recruits usually conduct operations after a minimum amount of training.

Very little is known about New PULO's training regime. However, it has been reported that members of the urban sabotage unit undergo courses in bomb-making and carrying out sabotage.[134] New PULO conducts training in jungle camps in the Malaysian state of Kelantan. There have also been reports that the group has received training at Al Qaeda camps in Afghanistan.[135]

New PULO's Financial and Support Networks

New PULO obtains funds by extorting protection fees from wealthy landowners and businessmen in the southern states of Thailand and even Kelantan in Malaysia. The Caddan Army would usually threaten to injure or kill the victim and steal a family's valuables if they failed to pay 'taxes'.[136] New PULO also gets funds through criminal activities such as kidnappings.[137]

In 2003, together with the Mujahideen Islam Pattani, Bersatu, and BRN, New PULO set up a foundation to raise funds for their armed struggle. The groups met in Malaysia to discuss plans to raise funds for separatist activities. Analysts say this joint effort was the result of stoppage of financial support from Muslim countries such as Saudi Arabia, Kuwait, and Pakistan.[138]

Government Responses to the New PULO Threat

The Thai government has worked with its Malaysian counterparts to crack down on groups in the south. In January 1998, the joint operations 'Pitak Tai' netted three New PULO leaders. After the arrests, the New PULO membership went into a state of disarray. In the ensuing confusion, many members lost faith in the group and gave themselves up to the Thai government.

More significantly, several key leaders fled abroad. New PULO founder Ar-rong Muleng[139] went into exile in Sweden and Hadi Muno (Haji Abdul Hadi bin Rozaali), Ar-rong's deputy, fled to Saudi Arabia in early 1998. [140]

Thailand and Malaysia have also cooperated in cutting off the group's route of escape into Malaysia.[141] The two countries have kept close watch on movement along the borders, with police exchanging intelligence with one another on individuals belonging to extremist groups in Thailand.[142]

The Thai military has also aggressively tackled the problems of drugs and unrest by encouraging local people to monitor the movements of suspected terrorists and drug members and to report these to authorities. The clampdown on drugs has also led to a decrease in the number of recruits that New PULO has managed to gather for its acts of sabotage.

New PULO Today

New PULO was once thought to be the strongest armed group in southern Thailand.[143] However, due to the many changes in the group's leadership and membership, not much open source information is available. Despite the arrests and killings of its leaders, New PULO and its parent organisation, PULO, seem to be somewhat resilient. Such persistence can be attributed to the lingering feelings of deprivation and alienation that continue to underscore Malay perceptions in the south. This has provided militant groups with a social context that is passive, or at least not actively opposed, to their activities.

GERAKAN MUJAHIDEEN ISLAM PATTANI (GMIP): PATTANI ISLAMIC MUJAHIDEEN MOVEMENT

Gerakan Mujahideen Islam Pattani (GMIP) or the Pattani Islamic Mujahideen Movement seeks to establish an Islamic state in southern Thailand. It has tasked itself to achieve this objective by the year 2008.[144] However, GMIP is also thought to have wider regional Islamist aspirations. Some of its members are said to support Al Qaeda and its vision of a worldwide Islamic caliphate.[145] GMIP is believed to operate in the Ra-ngae and Rue-Sor districts in Narathiwat as well as the Mayo and Yaring districts in Pattani.[146]

History and the Evolution of the Group

Unlike the other insurgent groups in southern Thailand, GMIP is the organisation most influenced by events in Afghanistan and the global jihad phenomenon. It was established in 1995 by Nasori Saesaeng (alias Awae Keleh) who is GMIP's operational chief, after his return from Afghanistan jihad.[147] While in Afghanistan, Nasori, reportedly befriended Nik Adli Nik Aziz, the son of Nik Aziz Nik Mat, the spiritual leader of

PAS in Malaysia.[148] Nasori has managed to evade the Thai and Malaysian authorities twice. In 2001, Nasori fled from a gun battle with Thai soldiers in Narathiwat's Bacho district.[149] Nasori again managed to escape when in August 2002, Malaysian security forces raided a prestigious hotel in Kuala Lumpur often used by GMIP as a meeting place. Three GMIP members were arrested in that raid.[150] An arrest warrant is out for Nasori for his alleged involvement in the 4 January 2004 raid on the arms depot in Narathiwat.[151]

Another important member of GMIP believed to be involved in the 4 January 2004 incidents is Jaeku Mae.[152] Jaeku is thought to be residing in Trengganu, Malaysia. He has dual Thai-Malaysian citizenship[153] and is believed to have connections in Malaysia as well as in Indonesia.[154] A number of GMIP's organisational leaders are in exile but continue to use propaganda measures rather than resort to armed struggle to achieve their objectives.[155]

GMIP is believed to have close links with the Kumpulan Mujahideen Malaysia (KMM), the Malaysian branch of Jemaah Islamiyah (JI), the regional terrorist network. KMM was founded in 1995 by GMIP founder Nasori's close associate in Afghanistan, Zainol Ismael. According to some analysts, this cross border linkage still persists. In fact, KMM's support to the southern Thai insurgent groups is what as the analysts believe, transformed GMIP and Barisan Revolusi Nasional (BRN) into insurgents with a regional agenda.[156]

GMIP and BRN appear to have a good working relationship. Apart from joining hands with other separatist groups to form Bersatu, it has also collaborated on other ad-hoc projects. Of note is an operation in 2002, which offered cash rewards of 100,000 baht for the murder of police officers or informers. Leaflets bearing the name of both groups were found in Ra-ngae district, which is one of GMIP's strongholds.[157] According to the Thai Internal Security Operations Command, GMIP is a front of BRN.[158]

GMIP Ideology

GMIP allegedly subscribes to the global jihad ideology that is also propagated by Al Qaeda. In late 2001, GMIP leaflets were found scattered in districts of Yala urging jihad or holy war and support for Osama bin Laden in the service of the separatist cause.[159] Apart from Afghan jihad connection, the leaning towards Al Qaeda is thought to stem from members who were educated in the Middle East, particularly Saudi Arabia and Pakistan, as well as at Wahabi institutions in Southeast Asia.[160] The group also allegedly rejects as unIslamic the practices of moderate Malay Muslims.

The group is organised into cells or small units containing five or fewer members.[161]

Strategy, Targets, and Tactics of GMIP

GMIP initially planned to rally Malay Muslim separatists to radicalise the secessionist agenda and to become the leading guerrilla organisation in the country. However, it has thus far failed to realise these goals.

The attacks that the group carries out are largely small scale, the bulk being drive-by shootings and arms raids. GMIP uses locally available weapons such as AK-47s, M-16s, HK-33s, bulletproof clothing, 9mm pistols, and bomb-making equipment/materials. Many of these weapons are stolen, but some are purchased from corrupt members of the security services. There are frequent incidents of police stations and other government agencies being overrun and having their weapons and ammunition stolen.

Recruitment and Training Methods of GMIP

GMIP has an estimated strength of between 30–70 members, of which 30 are thought to form the core of its fighting force.[162] Its members are reportedly hiding in dense jungle between the Thai-Malaysian border. A GMIP training camp is believed to be located near the border in Kuala Berang.[163]

A select number of GMIP members are also said to have received training in Al Qaeda training camps in Afghanistan. Some members have also participated in courses at Taliban funded *madrasahs* in Pakistan.

GMIP's Financial and Support Networks

A considerable amount of funding for GMIP comes from charitable or religious foundations from countries such as Saudi Arabia.[164] GMIP also reportedly owns the Seafood Tomyam restaurant in Kuala Trengganu, Malaysia.[165]

Apart from legitimate sources, GMIP also receives funds from criminal activities such as sabotage and hired killings. The group reportedly has an annual turnover of 10 million baht (US$254,478).[166] As a result of this criminal element, GMIP is often dismissed as little more than a criminal cash cow, possibly raising funds for allied groups operating in other parts of the region.[167] This has some parallels with Abu Shayaf Group (ASG) in the southern Philippines and has led authorities to fear that GMIP could provide Al Qaeda or its associated groups with similar help to that provided by the ASG.[168] This concern is heightened in the light of GMIP's network that was formed during the Afghan jihad.

Government Response to the GMIP Threat

In August 2002, Malaysian security forces arrested three GMIP members from a list of 20 most wanted separatists. The three were arrested in a raid on a prestigious hotel in Kuala Lumpur, often used by GMIP as a meeting place.

GMIP Today

The assessment about the capability of the group is opaque. Some reports say GMIP is the only significant armed Muslim separatist group operating in southern Thailand.[169] However others cite the capture of its members as a loss in the group's operational effectiveness.[170] The group is not believed to enjoy a high level of support from the Malay Muslims in the south, perhaps because of its Wahabi leanings.

BARISAN BERSATU MUJAHIDEEN PATTANI (BERSATU): UNITED FRONT FOR THE INDEPENDENCE OF PATTANI

Barisan Bersatu Mujahideen Pattani, or the United Front for the Independence Of Pattani, known more commonly as Bersatu, was formed with the objective of unifying all Thai separatist groups together for a concerted effort to secede from the kingdom.[171] Thai intelligence also believes that the group wants to act on the international stage by launching more serious attacks to publicise its cause to the world. Bersatu operates mainly in the southern provinces of Yala, Pattani, and Narathiwat.[172] Its members are said to meet often at the house of Seng Yalutong in the Malaysian state of Kedah.[173]

188

History and the Evolution of the Group

On 31 August 1989, the core leaders of all the separatist groups in southern Thailand—Barisan Islam Pembebasan Patani (BIPP, or Islamic Liberation Front of Pattani),[174] Mujahideen Pattani Movement (BNP),[175] BRN Congress, and New PULO—in a joint meeting called 'the gathering of the fighters for Pattani', decided to set up the 'Payong Organisation' to unify all the groups in order to move as one force to secede from the Thai kingdom. Another objective was to streamline multiple channels of funding that the groups in the southern provinces receive from various foreign donors.[176] Members of the Pattani United Liberation Organisation (PULO), and Gerakan Mujahideen Islam Pattani (GMIP) were also reportedly part of this meeting. It was only in 1991 that the organisation came to be known as the United Front for the Independence of Pattani or Bersatu, as it is still called today.[177] (However, other reports state that Bersatu was only formed in 2001.)

Prior to the 1989 meeting, there was little operational coordination among the various separatist groups in southern Thailand. This was partly due to their different ideological outlooks and external affiliations. However, the Thai government's large-scale suppression of these separatist groups weakened many of the groups individually. Some analysts have suggested that the groups banded together under the umbrella of Bersatu to recommence insurgency activities and give Muslim separatism a sustained focus.[178]

However, Bersatu is currently said to be made up of renegade members of the various groups, namely PULO and Barisan Revolusi Nasional (BRN).[179] It no longer functions as an umbrella organisation but as an independent group with its own capabilities. This seems to be likely as Bersatu was named as one of the groups that met in Malaysia in July 2003 to discuss plans for armed struggle, along with the objective of setting up a foundation to seek funds from other Muslim countries for their separatist activities.[180] The group is also named as one behind the string of violence that has plagued southern Thailand since 4 January 2004.[181] One incident that bears mention is the bombing at the provincial headquarters of TOT Corp on 23 March 2004.[182] According to military intelligence, 12 Bersatu rebels, one of them a woman, apparently arrived in Pattani province from Malaysia on 22 March 2004 and split into two groups of six. The group with the woman went to bomb the TOT Corp branch office. A witness said he saw a woman leave a black briefcase with the second bomb inside the Government Savings Bank.[183]

Structure and Organisation of Bersatu

In its original form as an umbrella organisation, Bersatu was an amalgamation of separatist groups, which, while coming together to conduct operations such as Operation Falling Leaves in 1997,[184] also act independently. Bersatu was regarded as an alliance of militant groups.

However, in recent years, Bersatu has been acting independently as a group. Its leader is said to be Samsuding Khan, who is currently residing in Sweden.[185] Mahadey Da-or is Bersatu's Chairman and is said to be in hiding in Narathiwat after crossing back from Malaysia.[186] Dr. Wan Kadir Che Man has also been named as a Bersatu leader. However, he—now living in exile in Malaysia—is thought to be largely a symbolic figure with no real authority in the group.[187]

Bersatu is said to have an armed wing and is thought to have small groups organised geographically to conduct attacks.[188] Lusalan Paluka Peloh is said to be the leader of its armed wing.[189]

Bersatu Strategy, Targets, and Tactics

Bersatu has no permanent base within Thai territory. Instead, its members are on the move all the time. They take care to avoid engaging in armed clashes with Thai government authorities. If a clash occurs, the militants would see to it that they withdraw from the scene promptly. Fighting must not be protracted.

Bersatu has tried to create rifts among the Thai Buddhists and Thai Muslims.[190] It has also tried to disrupt the government's education programme by attacking schools, harming and threatening the life and property of school teachers, coercing parents to stop sending their children to those schools.[191]

The grouping conducts mainly small-scale attacks. It usually conducts ambushes on government security personnel and positions. It also conducts sabotage activities against public facilities in towns or in rural areas. They also conduct guerrilla activities in the jungles.[192]

Bersatu also carries out criminal activities, especially kidnapping and extortion.

Recruitment and Training Methods of Bersatu

Due to military intervention, the number of armed insurgents has dropped from about 1,000 in 1979 to 80 in 1999, and to only 60 in 2000. As of 2001, the group's membership has shrunk to only 30.[193]

Members are said to be Thai and Malaysian nationals and are known to cross the Malaysian-Thai border frequently.[194] Parti Islam SeMalaysia (PAS) in the state of Kelantan, which is geographically close to the southern Thai provinces, is often stated to be a supporter of the separatists' cause. This cross-border connection can also be seen in terms of training.[195] An estimated 60 to 80 members of Bersatu are also said to have trained in the Middle East.[196]

Bersatu Financial and Support Networks

Bersatu has raised funds through extortion and crimes to fund its activities. It has also tried to seek funds from Islamic countries.[197] However, no information is available on which countries these are or whether the efforts of the group have been successful.

Muslims—especially Malay Muslims—in the southern parts of Thailand form Bersatu's support base. However, with the Thai government beginning to show greater sensitivity for the economic and administrative developments in the Yala, Narathiwat, and Pattani provinces, this has led to a decrease in support for militant groups such as Bersatu. However, the risk remains that the historical resentment for the Buddhist Thai government and its discrimination against the Muslims in the south may be exploited by insurgents in the future.[198] The recent attacks on 28 April 2004 in which 108 militants were killed may also cause the public to start backing separatist groups like Bersatu again.

Government Response to the Bersatu Threat

The Thai government has not reacted specifically to Bersatu per se. However, in its amnesty offer to separatist groups in 2004, Bersatu is said to be one of the groups that came forward to lay down their arms and to work with the Thai authorities.

Bersatu Today

Thai authorities feel that Bersatu is no longer a threat as it seemingly degenerated to that of a bandit group, with kidnappings and extortions as their main activities in recent years. However, with the upsurge in violence since 4 January 2004, Bersatu has come under the spotlight again. It has perhaps used this period of relative inactivity to regroup and re-strategise. The latest attacks that have been attributed to Bersatu signal a more violent leaning. While once it used to conduct small-scale attacks such as sabotage, it is now undertaking bombings.

It has also begun to use the Internet to raise its profile. It has posted a statement on the PULO website, praising the dead raiders of 28 April 2004 as 'freedom fighters' and stating that their killing by the army would be paid for 'with sweat and tears'.[199] The statement praised the dead for their bravery and warned foreign tourists not to travel to the southern provinces of Pattani, Narathiwat, Satun, Songkhla, Yala, Phuket, Phangnga, Krabi and Phattalung.

PUSAT PERSATUAN TADIKA NARATHIWAT: THE CENTRE OF TADIKA NARATHIWAT FOUNDATION (PUSAKA)

Pusat Persatuan Tadika Narathiwat or the Centre of Tadika Narathiwat Foundation, commonly known as PUSAKA, is a foundation of tadika, or religious schools. However it is said to be at the forefront for the ideological indoctrination of children up to the age of 12, into the separatist cause. PUSAKSA's has extensive presence in about 56 schools in the province of Narathiwat.[200] It is also said to have factions in Pattani and Yala.

History and the Evolution of the Group

PUSAKA was established in Tanyong Mat, Narathiwat, on 22 September 1994[201] by Thai Rak Thai MP Najmuddin Umar. It was formed as a foundation to teach Islam to Muslim children during weekends. It has a branch in Yi-ngo District, Narathiwat. This branch is slated to be the future headquarters of the group. PUSAKA was established to support Muslim ethics schools, known locally as tadika, helping them draft standard curricula for Muslim ethical teachings and assisting them for spread of Islamic teachings.[202] It also offers free education to orphans, promotes health, Islamic tradition and culture, and engages in public charities.

Born in 1960, Najmuddin was a former student activist from Ramkhamhaeng University, where he studied law in the late 1970s. He formed an association of students from the southern border provinces of Pattani, Narathiwat, Yala, Satun, and Songkhla. The group is known as the Southern Islamic Group of Ramkhamhaeng University. He was famous among members of the group known as PYN—Pattani, Yala, and Narathiwat. Najmuddin is allegedly a staunch advocate of southern Muslim separatism and had reportedly urged his followers to carry out activities which would undermine the credibility of then Deputy Prime Minister Wan Nor Mohamed Normatha.[203] Najmuddin entered politics in 1992 when he was elected as a Member of Thai Parliament. He was chosen as an adviser to Chavalit Yongchaiyudh, who was then interior minister between 1992 and 1995 and also advised Deputy Education Minister Areepin Uttarasin in 1997. He is also a member of the Wadah faction, which is in alliance with the ruling Thai Rak Thai party. Najmuddin is currently an adviser to the Narathiwat Provincial Islamic Committee and an assistant to the secretary of the House sub-committee (Thai Parliament) to study southern incidents.[204]

Najmuddin is now suspected to be one of the masterminds behind the 4 January 2004 attacks on the army camp.[205] According to Anupong Panthachayangkoon, one of the suspects detained in this connection, the group of attackers conducted several meetings at Najmuddin's residence before the attack. The meetings were chaired by Najmuddin who offered high positions to everyone involved if an independent Pattani state were set up.[206] Najmuddin is allegedly the head of PUSAKA in Narathiwat. Fellow TRT MP Areepin Uttarasin is the head of the chapter in Yala, while Pattani Senator Den Tohmena heads the Pattani chapter. The two are also suspected of involvement in the raid.

As a result of these connections, PUSAKA is now being blamed as one of the possible perpetrators behind the 4 January 2004 armoury raid. It is also being held responsible for about 50 per cent of the attacks in southern Thailand since.[207] Security officials claim that PUSAKA was brainwashing children in their schools to rebel against the Thai motherland and to reject Thai nationality. Thai security alleges that under its influence, these schools have radicalised Thai Muslims and have fomented unrest.[208] Thai authorities also believe that PUSAKA was the underground movement that instigated the 28 April 2004 attacks.[209] The movement has been building its ranks for almost a decade by inciting people and training militias at religious schools in the south.

PUSAKA is also under scrutiny for the role Masae Useng plays in the foundation. Masae Useng, a known separatist activist also linked to Barisan Revolusi Nasional (BRN), Gerakan Mujahideen Islam Pattani (GMIP) and Bersatu, is believed to be the Secretary of the foundation. It was during a raid in 2002–3 on Masae's home that Thai authorities found out about the group from some documents.[210] Masae is also believed to be running training camps for PUSAKA and is wanted by Thai security forces in connection with various incidents in the south, including the 4 January 2004 raid.[211]

As part of its responsibilities, PUSAKA visits tadikas, organises training sessions and seminars for tadika teachers and tadika committees who are working under the foundation. It also arranges meetings with other private organisations of Narathiwat, as well as observes tadika activities in Pattani. As such, PUSAKA can be said to have wide-ranging influence in the education sector in Narathiwat, and to a lesser extent, Pattani and Yala. It is highly plausible that PUSAKA may have used its reach to spread separatist ideology among its students and teachers. This concern is heightened as it is said to receive considerable funding. As it is a public institution, PUSAKA receives donations from the community in the south, private and government sectors, as well as the Office of Public Welfare in Narathiwat, Ministry of Welfare and Human Security.[212]

Nothing much is known about the organisational structure of PUSAKA.

PUSAKA's Ideology

It is not very clear what PUSAKA's ideology is. However, as Najmuddin is the founder and is known for his separatist views, it can be deduced that PUSAKA aims to achieve an independent Islamic Pattani state.

Strategy, Targets, and Tactics of PUSAKA

PUSAKA is focused on ideological indoctrination and training. As such, the organisation itself does not carry out attacks. Reportedly PUSAKA has a tactical alliance with BRN Coordinate. The cadres that PUSAKA churns out join BRN Coordinate to carry out operations. The attacks that have been attributed to the BRN Coordinate-PUSAKA alliance are small-scale but persistent, attempting to create an atmosphere of fear in southern Thailand. Large-scale attacks are possibly meant as a show of force to the Thai authorities.

Based on the pattern of attacks in 2004, most of those targeted in attacks conducted by BRN Coordinate-PUSAKA are police and army personnel. However members of the public have also not been spared. Many have become victims of drive-by shootings.

Recruitment and Training Methods of PUSAKA

According to security analyst Panitan Watanayagorn, an estimated 20,000 students have studied in schools under the PUSAKA foundation. Of this number, about 500 to 1,000 radicals have emerged.[213]

PUSAKA is said to provide military training through its schools under the guise of sports[214] and indeed 'sports' figures very highly in its list of activities.[215]

The group is also said to prey on young, unemployed, people who do not have access to education. Some of its recruits are also said to be drug addicts.[216]

PUSAKA's Financial and Support Networks

PUSAKA enjoys the support of some government officials in the south. Deputy Prime Minister Wan Muhamad Nor Matha donated one million baht (US$25,000) while he was Transport Minister and Narathiwat MP Areepen Uttarasin has also donated 100,000 baht (US$2,500) to the foundation.[217]

PUSAKA's support base lies mainly in its network of tadika and tadika alumni.

Government Response to the PUSAKA Threat

Najmuddin Umar is now on trial for allegedly masterminding the 4 January 2004 armoury raid. As for the foundation itself, PUSAKA continues to operate. Thai authorities have not clamped down on its activities as yet.

PUSAKA Today

From the type of attacks for which PUSAKA is being held responsible, it can be said that the group has significant capabilities compared to other separatist groups in southern Thailand. This may be because it has pooled resources with other groups such as BRN Coordinate, and is acting as a tactical alliance for specific missions. Having been recently discovered, very little is known about PUSAKA. It seems to have a ready pool of recruits in the form of students of their schools. Although the separatist ideology in southern Thailand has somewhat waned since the 1980s, PUSAKA has managed to revive it through incitement and indoctrination under the guise of Muslim educational programmes in its schools.

NOTES

1   'Foreign views on Pattani', Patani Hyper Media.
2   Ibid.
3   'National Armed Forces of Patani Republic', *Department of Information of BRN*, 13 March 1983, available at http://www.geocities.com/brn_president/patani.html.
4   'New Political Strategy and Reform', *Institute of Patani Research and Strategic Studies*, available at http://www.geocities.com/brn_president/resinstitu.html.
5   'Split in BRN—Patani Malay National Revolutionary Front', *Institute of Patani Research & Strategic Studies*, available at http://www.geocities.com/brn_president/resinstitu.html.
6   'Brief History: Patani Peoples' Revolutionary Commando Regiment', *Institute of Patani Research and Strategic Studies*, available at http://www.geocities.com/brn_president/resinstitu.html.
7   Ibid.
8   Ibid.
9   Ibid.
10   '22-Point Demand', *PKRRP (Pasukan Komando Revolusi Rakyat Patani) Patani People's Revolutionary Commandos Brigade*, 18 November 1991, available at http://www.geocities.com/brn_president/22d.doc.
11   Lukman Iskandar, 'BRN's letter to General Chavalit Yongchayudh', 19 January 1996, available at http://www.geocities.com/brn_president/chava.doc.
12   'Muslims Chronology', *Institute of Patani Research and Strategic Studies*.
13   'New Political Strategy and Reform', *Institute of Patani Research and Strategic Studies*.
14   'Muslims Chronology', *Institute of Patani Research and Strategic Studies*.
15   'Counter Proposal by Barisan Revolusi Nasional Melayu Patani (BRN) to Privy Council of Thailand Regarding Peace Plan of BRN', *The Office of*

the Secretary General, Patani Malay Revolutionary Front, 17 January 1996, available at http://www.geocities.com/brn_president/22d.doc.

16 'Thai police put on alert against separatist attack', *Xinhua News Agency*, 5 August 2002.

17 'Sketch of 'top rebel' released', *Nation*, 9 January 2004.

18 'Pasukan Komando Revolusi Rakyat Patani (PKRRP)', *Institute of Patani Research and Strategic Studies*, available at http://members.fortunecity.com/pattanicity/amanat.html.

19 Onnucha Hutasingh, '50 bandits operating in South—Informants help members evade arrest', *Bangkok Post*, 14 July 1997.

20 'Thai MP wonders if government determined to remedy untoward incidents in South', *Krungthep Thurakit*, 25 November 2002.

21 'Counter Proposal', *The Office of the Secretary General, Patani Malay Revolutionary Front*.

22 'Primer: Muslim Separatism in Southern Thailand', Virtual Information Center, 23 July 2002, available at http://www.vic-info.org/0a256ae00012d183/626e6035eadbb4cd85256499006b15a6/e42514a843d9a3260a256c05006c2d84?OpenDocument.

23 'National Armed Forces of Patani Republic', *Department of Information of BRN*.

24 'Muslims Chronology', *Institute of Patani Research and Strategic Studies*.

25 'Thailand – Insurgency', allrefer.com, September 1987, available at http://reference.allrefer.com/country-guide-study/thailand/thailand133.html.

26 'Thailand', *Child Soldiers Report 2001*.

27 'Muslim unrest in region raises Thai security tensions', *Asian Political News*, 7 August 2000.

28 Wassana Nanuam, 'Army blames Muslim militants', *Bangkok Post*, 9 April 2001.

29 'All state officials at risk', *Bangkok Post*, 11 July 2002.

30 Lukman Iskandar, 'Deceiving Commander of Region 4 army to sign peace agreement with BRN: Time to speak the truth', *BRN Information Department*, 15 February 2000, available at http://members.fortunecity.com/patani_republic/fourarmy.html.

31 T. Davis, 'Thailand's troubled south', *Jane's Terrorism and Security Monitor*, 1 October 2003.

32 'New Political Strategy and Reform', *Institute of Patani Research and Strategic*.

33 Nanuam, 'Army blames Muslim militants'.

34 'A rebel changes his stripes', *Nation*, 12 May 2003.

35 'Separatist Movement Has Few Supporters', *Bangkok Post*.

36 'New Political Strategy and Reform', *Institute of Patani Research and Strategic*.

37 Iskandar, 'Deceiving Commander'.

38 'Muslim group volunteers from south Thailand reportedly going to Afghanistan', *Matichon*, 30 September 2001.

39 Hamid Papang, 'Thai army launches operation against Muslims', *Muslim Media*, 16–28 February 1998, available at http://www.muslimedia.com/archives/sea98/thai.htm.

40 'Plague of terror ruins Thai economic growth', *Bangkok Post*, 18 January 1998.

41 Nanuam, 'Army blames Muslim militants'.

42 'A rebel changes his stripes', *Nation*.

43 'Teacher arrested, explosives seized', *Bangkok Post*, 4 November 2002.

44 'Den Tohmeena builds his dynasty in Patani', *Institute of Patani Research and Strategic Studies*, 12 December 1989, available at http://www.geocities.com/brn_president/resinstitu.html.

45 'News Summary June 16 to June 22, 2002', *Bangkok Post*, 11 August 2002.

46 Syed Serajul Islam, 'The Islamic Independence Movements in Pattani of Thailand and Mindanao of the Philippines,' *Asian Survey* Vol. 38 (May 1982): 441–56.

47 Iskandar, 'Deceiving Commander'.

48 'Military goes online to combat terrorism', 13 August 2002, *Bangkok Post*.

49 'Exiled PULO leader', *Nation*, 14 May 2003.

50 Hj. Lukman Bin Lima, 'PULO calls for 'self-determination in Patani'', *Pattani United Liberation Organisation*, 29 January 2003, available at http://web.archive.org/web/20030202022511/pulo.org/pulo/calls.htm.

51 Rob Fanney, 'Pattani United Liberation Organisation', *Jane's Terrorism and Insurgency Center*, 31 Oct 2002.

52 Ibid.

53 Peter Chalk, 'Separatism and Southeast Asia', *Studies in Conflict and Terrorism* 24 (2001): 241–69.

54 Fanney, 'Pattani United Liberation Organisation'.

55 Ibid.

56 'The Year of National Reorganisation (1988–1989)', *Pattani United Liberation Organisation*, available at www.pulo.org/reorg.html.

57 'PULO rebel puts down his weapon', *Nation*, 2 April 2002.

58 Fanney, 'Pattani United Liberation Organisation'.

59 Ibid.

60 'The Year of National Reorganisation (1988–1989)', *Pattani United Liberation Organisation*.

61 Rohan Gunaratna, 'Terrorist Trends and Patterns in the Asia-Pacific Region' in Andrew Tan and Kumar Ramakrishna (eds.), *The New Terrorism: Anatomy, Trends and Counter-Strategies*, (Singapore: Eastern Universities Press, 2002), pp. 129–56.

62 'Primer: Muslim Separatism in Southern Thailand', Virtual Information Center.

63 'Operation Falling Leaves chronology of south violence', *Bangkok Post*, 1 February 1998.

64   Peter Chalk, 'Separatism and Southeast Asia'.

65   'Thai Muslim Group Denies Blast', *IslamOnline*, 10 April 2001, available at www.islamonline.net/english/news/2001-04/11/article3.shtml.

66   'Primer: Muslim Separatism in Southern Thailand', Virtual Information Center.

67   'Thailand', *Child Soldiers Report 2001*.

68   Chalk, 'Separatism and Southeast Asia'.

69   'The Year of National Reorganisation (1988–1989)', *Pattani United Liberation Organisation*.

70   'Thailand', *Child Soldiers Report 2001*.

71   'The Year of National Reorganisation (1988–1989)', *Pattani United Liberation Organisation*.

72   Chalk, 'Separatism and Southeast Asia'.

73   Fanney, 'Pattani United Liberation Organisation'.

74   Chalk, 'Separatism and Southeast Asia'.

75   Ibid.

76   Fanney, 'Pattani United Liberation Organisation'.

77   Ibid.

78   Peter Searle, 'Ethno-Religious Conflicts: Rise or Decline? Recent Developments in Southeast Asia', *Contemporary Southeast Asia* vol. 24, no. 1, April 2002.

79   Chalk, 'Separatism and Southeast Asia'.

80   Ibid.

81   Ibid.

82   Par Romain Hayes, 'The Islamic Fundamentalist Threat in Thailand', 1 August 2003, available at http://www.leschroniques-demadamechang.net/textes/textes_monde/textes_asie_sud/r_asie_thaillande_romain_ang.htm.

83   Chalk, 'Separatism and Southeast Asia'.

84   Fanney, 'Pattani United Liberation Organisation'.

85   Ibid.

86   Ibid.

87   'Primer: Muslim Separatism in Southern Thailand', Virtual Information Center.

88   Fanney, 'Pattani United Liberation Organisation'.

89   Hamid Papang, 'Thai army launches operation against Muslims', *Muslim Media*.

90   'Muslim Group Volunteers From South Thailand Reportedly Going to Afghanistan', Matichon.

91   Fanney, 'Pattani United Liberation Organisation'.

92   Ibid.

93   Michael Shari, 'East Asian Tinderbox', *International—Asian Business*, 20 December 1999.

94 'Primer: Muslim Separatism in Southern Thailand', Virtual Information Center.
95 Par Romain Hayes, 'The Islamic Fundamentalist Threat in Thailand'.
96 Chalk, 'Separatism and Southeast Asia'.
97 David Carment, 'Managing Interstate Ethnic Tensions: The Thailand-Malaysia Experience', *Nationalism and Ethnic Politics* vol. 1, no. 4, Winter 1995: p.8
98 Ibid.
99 Fanney, 'Pattani United Liberation Organisation'.
100 'Pulo rebel puts down his weapon', *Nation*.
101 Fanney, 'Pattani United Liberation Organisation'.
102 Chalk, 'Separatism and Southeast Asia'.
103 'Asia Overview', Patterns of Global Terrorism, (United States Department of State, 1998), available at www.fas.org/irp/threat/terror_98/asia.htm.
104 Kazi Mahmood, 'Thailand Perpetuating the Taming of Islam in Patani', *IslamOnline*, 13 March 2002, available at www.islamonline.net/English/Views/2002/03/article9.shtml.
105 Chalk, 'Separatism and Southeast Asia'.
106 Fanney, 'Pattani United Liberation Organisation'.
107 Sersmsuk Kasitipradit, 'Border Separatists Flee Abroad', *Bangkok Post*, 23 February 1998.
108 Chalk, 'Separatism and Southeast Asia'.
109 'Money for nothing', *Bangkok Post*, 19 February 1998.
110 Chalk, 'Separatism and Southeast Asia'.
111 'Primer: Muslim Separatism in Southern Thailand', Virtual Information Center, 23 July 2002.
112 Onnucha Hutasingh and Nauvarat Suksamran, 'Reports list four terrorist groups operating in south', *Bangkok Post*, 13 July 1997.
113 'Primer: Muslim Separatism in Southern Thailand', Virtual Information Center, 23 July 2002.
114 Hamid Papang, 'Thai army launches operation against Muslims', *Muslim Media*.
115 Chalk, 'Separatism and Southeast Asia'.
116 Ibid.
117 'Asia Overview', Patterns of Global Terrorism, (United States Department of State, 2000).
118 Wae-dao Harai, 'New PULO separatist wanted for crimes in south arrested in Bangkok', *Bangkok Post*, 14 June 2002.
119 'Primer: Muslim Separatism in Southern Thailand', Virtual Information Center.
120 Kazi Mahmood, 'Thai regime criticized for 'colonizing' Muslim provinces', *IslamOnline*, 15 May 2003.
121 Ibid.

122 'Primer: Muslim Separatism in Southern Thailand', Virtual Information Center.

123 Chalk, 'Separatism and Southeast Asia'.

124 'Primer: Muslim Separatism in Southern Thailand', Virtual Information Center.

125 Chalk, 'Separatism and Southeast Asia'.

126 Hutasingh and Suksamran, 'Cross-border terrorists extorting money from businesses', *Bangkok Post*, 13 July 1997.

127 'Muslims Chronology', available at http://www.cidcm.umd.edu/inscr/mar/data/thamuslchro.htm.

128 'Thai paper reports school arson in South', *Krungthep Thurakit*, 31 December 1999.

129 Par Romain Hayes, 'The Islamic Fundamentalist Threat in Thailand'.

130 Chalk, 'Separatism and Southeast Asia'.

131 Fanney, 'Pattani United Liberation Organisation'.

132 'Thai army closing in on Muslim separatist group in South', *Nation*, 6 January 2000.

133 Chalk, 'Separatism and Southeast Asia'.

134 'Intelligence agencies warn of possible terrorist attacks in southern Thailand', *Krungthep Thurakit*, 15 November 2002.

135 Stephen Brown, 'Thailand's Rising Terrorism Problem', FrontPageMagazine.com, 17 July 2003.

136 Onnucha Hutasingh and Nauvarat Suksamran, 'Cross-border terrorists extorting money from businesses'.

137 'Alleged Muslim rebels behead kidnap victims', *Phuket Gazette*, 6 June 2001.

138 Brown, 'Thailand's Rising Terrorism Problem'.

139 Chalk, 'Separatism and Southeast Asia'.

140 Kasitipradit, 'Border separatists flee abroad', *Bangkok Post*.

141 'Asia Overview', Patterns of Global Terrorism, (United States Department of State, 1998).

142 Kazi Mahmood, 'Thailand Perpetuating the Taming of Islam in Patani'.

143 'Thailand', *Child Soldiers Report 2001*.

144 Jason Gagliardi, 'Behind the News – Fear and Fervour', *South China Morning Post*, 5 February 2004.

145 Rob Fanney, 'Gerakan Mujahideen Islam Pattani (GMIP – Pattani Islamic Mujahideen Movement)', *Jane's Terrorism & Insurgency Centre*, 31 October 2002.

146 Ibid.

147 'Insurgents face treason charges', *Nation*, 15 January 2004.

148 Ibid.

149 Ibid.

150 Fanney, 'Gerakan Mujahideen Islam Pattani', *Jane's Terrorism & Insurgency Centre*.

151 'Insurgents face treason charges', *Nation*.

152 Ibid.; 'Police claim to have located insurgents', *Nation*, 12 January 2004.

153 Nirmal Ghosh, 'Thai police fired on in new attack', *Straits Times*, 8 January 2004.

154 'Bt1m reward for top suspect', *Nation*, 7 January 2004.

155 Ibid.

156 'Thai Islamic Insurgents', *GlobalSecurity.org*.

157 Fanney, 'Gerakan Mujahideen Islam Pattani'.

158 'ISOC blames separatists for bombs', *Bangkok Post*, 3 July 2002.

159 Anthony Davis, 'Thailand faces up to southern extremist threat', *Jane's Intelligence Review*, 1 October 2003.

160 Fanney, 'Gerakan Mujahideen Islam Pattani'.

161 Ibid.

162 Ibid.; Pares Lohason, 'Malaysia hands over suspected terrorists', *Nation*, 11 January 2004; 'Bt1m reward for top suspect', *Nation*.

163 Tunyasiri, 'Malaysia-based units "running the show"'.

164 Ibid.

165 Tunyasiri, 'Malaysia-based units "running the show"'.

166 Fanney, 'Gerakan Mujahideen Islam Pattani', *Jane's Terrorism & Insurgency Centre*.

167 Ibid.; Lohason and Pathan, 'Two more suspects held on swoop in Pattani village', *Nation*.

168 Fanney, 'Gerakan Mujahideen Islam Pattani'.

169 Ibid.

170 Ibid.

171 'Columnist views activities of Muslim terrorist groups in southern Thailand', *Matichon*, 24 June 2001.

172 'Thailand: Leaders of group blamed for southern weekend bombing named', *Nation*, 11 April 2001.

173 Tunyasiri, 'Malaysia-based units "running the show"'.

174 BIPP is the new name of Barisan Nasional Pembebasan Patani (BNPP, National Liberation Front of Pattani). Formed in 1959, the group is no longer considered to be active.

175 BNP is said to be made up of members who left the BNPP. Established in 1985, its aim was to consolidate the various separatist groups in to one single entity. The group is no longer considered active.

176 'Columnist views activities of Muslim terrorist groups in southern Thailand', *Matichon*.

177 'Primer: Muslim Separatism in Southern Thailand', Virtual Information Center.

178 'Columnist views activities of Muslim terrorist groups in southern Thailand', *Matichon*.

179 Shawn W. Crispin, 'Thailand's War Zone', *Far Eastern Economic Review*, 11 March 2004.

180 'Separatist Groups Raising Funds', *Bangkok Post*, 12 July 2003.

181 Tunyasiri, 'Malaysia-based units "running the show"'.

182 Crispin, 'Thailand's War Zone', *Far Eastern Economic Review*.

183 Muhamad Ayub Pathan and Abdulloh Boonyakaj, 'Bersatu separatists blamed for bombs', *Bangkok Post*, 25 March 2004.

184 'Operation Falling Leaves chronology of South violence', *Bangkok Post*, 1 February 1998.

185 'Police put on alert for separatist attack', *Bangkok Post*, 5 August 2002.

186 Ibid.

187 Don Pathan, 'Separatist wants to return: Bersatu leader Wan Kadir says he will work for peace if allowed to come back', *Nation*, 9 December 2004.

188 'Thailand: Leaders of group blamed for southern weekend bombing named', *Nation*.

189 Ibid.

190 'Army names Bersatu as culprits', *Bangkok Post*, 11 April 2001.

191 Ibid.

192 Ibid.

193 Ibid.

194 Tunyasiri, 'Malaysia-based units "running the show"', *Bangkok Post*.

195 Hamid Papang, 'Thai army launches operation against Muslims', *Muslim Media*.

196 James East, 'New rebel group to blame?', *Straits Times*, 9 April 2001.

197 'Columnist views activities of Muslim terrorist groups in southern Thailand', *Matichon*.

198 Fanney, 'Pattani United Liberation Organisation'.

199 'Don't interfere, warns Thai PM', *Straits Times*, 3 May 2004.

200 Kavi Chongkittavorn, editor of *The Nation*, email interview, 5 March 2004.

201 Intelligence brief.

202 Kavi Chongkittavorn, email interview.

203 Surath Jinakul, 'The plot thickens', *Bangkok Post*, 28 March 2004; 'TRT MPs and senator implicated', *Bangkok Post*.

204 Piyanart Srivalo, Bancha Khaengkhan, 'TRT faction stands by accused MPs', *Nation*, 23 March 2004.

205 'Najmuddin granted Bt3m bail', *Nation*, 4 June 2004.

206 'MP faces treason charge', *Bangkok Post*, 23 March 2004.

207 Chidchanok Rahimmula, 'The Situation in Southern Thailand', Institute of Southeast Asian Studies seminar, 12 April 2004.

208 Surasak Tumcharoen and Sermsuk Kasitipradit, 'MP denies being subversive', *Bangkok Post*, 2 April 2001; 'Thailand fears more attacks as Muslim separatists blamed for violence', channelnewsasia.com, 30 April 2004.

209 'Southern carnage: Kingdom shaken', *Nation*, 29 April 2004.

210 Nirmal Ghosh, 'Shadowy group behind violence', *Straits Times*, 1 May 2004.

211 'TRT MPs 'fund body linked to insurgents', *Nation*.

212 Intelligence brief.

213 'Thailand fears more attacks as Muslim separatists blamed for violence', channelnewsasia.com.

214 Rahimmula, 'The Situation in Southern Thailand', Institute of Southeast Asian Studies seminar.

215 Intelligence brief.

216 Ghosh, 'Shadowy group behind violence', *Straits Times*.

217 Tumcharoen and Kasitipradit, 'MP denies being subversive', *Bangkok Post*.

About the Editors

Rohan Gunaratna is Head, International Centre for Political Violence and Terrorism Research (ICPVTR) at the Institute of Defence and Strategic Studies, Singapore; Senior Fellow, Combating Terrorism Center, United States Military Academy at West Point; and Honorary Fellow, International Policy Institute for Counter-Terrorism, Israel. Gunaratna is the author of the international bestseller, *Inside Al Qaeda: Global Network of Terror* (Columbia University Press, New York, 2002).

Arabinda Acharya is Associate Research Fellow and Manager (Strategic Projects), ICPVTR, Institute of Defence and Strategic Studies, Singapore; and Research Coordinator, Centre for Peace and Development Studies, India. Mr. Acharya has published in *Asian Defence and Diplomacy*, *Georgetown Journal of International Affairs*, *Harvard Asia Quarterly*, *Pacific Affairs*, *Contemporary Southeast Asia*, and *Asia Pacific Review*.

Sabrina Chua was a research analyst at ICPVTR, Institute of Defence and Strategic Studies, Singapore. She led the specialist team that analysed the Al Qaeda collection from Afghanistan. Ms. Chua who headed the ICPVTR project on Southern Thailand, briefed the Thai national Security Council delegation, and was invited to address the Homeland Security Summit in Hawaii in 2004.

Index

Abdul Fatah, 62
Abdul Karim Hassan, 33
Abdul Wahab Data 54, 59
Abdullah Badawi, 109
Abdulrohseh Haji Doloh, 31, 35
administrative measures (counter-
    productive), 12–13
agitprop method, 77
Ahama Bula, 31
Ahmad Matnor (Mat Jabat), 33
Al Qaeda, 8–10, 27, 33. 41, 61–63,
    65–68, 91, 101, 114
Algerian National Liberation
    Front (FLN), 34
Amin Tohmeena, 33
amnesty process, 103
Angkatan Bersenjata Revolusi
    Patani (ABREP), 33, 34
Anglo-Siamese Treaty of 1909, 2
Anwar Ibrahim, 34
Areepin Uttarasin, 44
A-rong Muleng, Dr., 37, 39
ASEAN, 113

Barisan Islam Pembebasan Patani
    (BIPP, Islamic Liberation
    Front of Pattani), 42
Barisan Revolusi Nasional (BRN,
    Pattani Malay National
    Revolutionary Front), 6, 33–
    36, 41–46, 49, 53–56, 96, 103,
    104
Berjihad Di Pattani (The Fight for
    the Liberation of Pattani), 9,
    26, 54, 57–59, 91–92, 100, 109
Bersatu (United Front for the
    Liberation of Pattani), 36, 42–
    44, 103
Boriween Chet Huamuang (Area
    of the Seven Provinces), 2
Buddhism/Buddhist population, 1–
    5, 10–11

catalytic factors, 10–16
Cham Muslims, 2
Chinese Muslims, 2
Chularajamontri, 11, 85
Cikgu Ding, 35
civilian targets, 79, 101
Civilian-Police-Military Task
    Force 43 (CPM 43), 7, 13
communism, 34
corruption, 12, 32, 87
Counter Terrorism Intelligence
    Centre (CTIC), 95
crime/criminal elements, 12, 15,
    32, 95–96
customs and culture, 2–6, 10

Democratic Party, 7, 88
Den Tohmena, 44
development projects, 12
Ding Jerman, 35
distrust, 78
Dusun Nyiur incident, 5

economic deprivation, 14–15
economic development, 7, 11, 49
education, 10–12, 45–53, 64–68,
    84–85, 107–108
Education Act of 1921, 3, 4, 46
education reform, 3, 4
ending the threat, 110–112
entertainment industry, 7
escalation of conflict (potential
    for), 91–97
financial assistance programmes,
    15
foreign policy, 15–16
foreigners targeted, 79
Front Pembela Islam (FPI), 60

General Phibun Songkhram, 4
geographical location, 1, 3–4

Gerakan Mujahideen Islam Pattani
  (GMIP), 27, 33, 40–42, 55, 56
global insurgent links, 59–68, 79,
  91–95, 101–102
Government Lottery Agency, 15
government officials targeted, 79,
  101
government response/strategy, 83–
  90, 110–112
guerilla warfare, 101

Haji Abdul Rohman Bazo, 39
Haji Harun Moleng, Dr.
  (Mohammad Bin Mohammad),
  37
Haji Harun Sulong, Dr., 33
Haji Kabir Abdulrahman, 37
Haji Samae Thanam, 37
Haji Sulong Tohmena, 5
Hambali (Riduan Isamuddin), 15,
  62, 66, 67, 95
Hayihadi Mindosali, 37
history of conflict, 1–7
human rights violations, 78, 90

identity conflicts, 10, 115
ignorance, 13–14
independence of southern
  provinces, 2, 5
Indonesia, 59, 60, 63, 101
Indonesian Muslims, 2
insensitivity, 10, 13–14
integration of southern provinces,
  3
intelligence management/network,
  102–103
Internal Suppression Operations
  Command (ISOC), 13
International Centre for Political
  Violence and Terrorism
  Research, 100
international implications of
  domestic insurgency, 112–114
Islam in Thailand, 2–3
Islam's global identity, 8–1

Islamic Central Committee (ICC),
  14
Islamic Liberation Front of Pattani
  (BIPP), 6
Ismael Lutfi, Dr., 53, 62
Issamul Yameena (alias Isamail
  Jaafar), 59, 109

Jaekumae Kutae, 33, 41
Jemaah Islamiyah (JI), 9–10, 33, 41,
  49, 51, 53, 59, 61–63, 66, 67,
  91, 101
Jemaah Salafiyah (JS), 62–63

Kumpulan Mujahideen Malaysia
  (KMM), 41, 55, 59

language, 3, 10, 12, 46, 67
Lukman B. Lima, 37
Lukman Iskandar, 33–35
Lusalan Paluka Peloh, 43

Mahadey Da-or, 42
Mahamae Maeroh, 56
Maisuri Haji Abdullah, 54
major incidents
  4 January 2004, 22–23, 33,
  40–41, 44, 45, 102
  4 January 2004, anniversary
  of, 31–32
  7 January 2004, 23
  22 January 2004, 23
  24 January 2004, 23
  5 March 2004, 23
  27 March 2004, 24
  30 March 2004, 24
  4 April 2004, 24
  22 April 2004, 24
  28 April 2004, 24–27
  16 May 2004, 27
  29 May 2004, 27
  22 August 2004, 27
  26 August 2004, 27–28
  17 September 2004, 28
  25 October 2004, 28–31

17 February 2005, 96
Malay ethnicity, 1–4
Malaysia, 1, 3, 6–7, 34, 35, 37–38, 51, 59–60, 63, 101, 103, 105, 108–110
managing the threat, 102–110
Masae Useng 33, 41, 44, 53, 55, 56
Masari Savari, 34
militancy and religion, 53–59, 100
military operations, 6
military repression, 10
Monthon Pattani, 2
Muhamad Kanafi Doloh, 31
Mujahid Haji Abdullah, 54
Mujahideen Pattani Movement (BNP), 42
Muslim population, 1, 2

Najmuddin Umar, 43–44
Narathiwat, 1, 6, 9, 22–24, 27, 28, 31, 32, 34, 37, 46
Nasori Saesaeng (alias Awae Kaleh), 40, 56
national assimilation, 10–12
National Association of Muslim Youth (NAMY), 95
national identity, 10
National Revolutionary Party of South Thailand (PRNS), 34
nationalism, 4, 100
nature of insurgency, 7–10
nepotism, 12
New Aspiration Party, 7
New PULO, 6, 36, 37, 39–40, 42, 63, 103
Nong Chik, 2
northern Malay states, 1, 3, 6–7, 105, 108–110

Pak Yeh, 33, 34
Palestinian Liberation Organisation (PLO), 34
Patani Raya, 1
Patronage of Islam Act of 1945, 11
Pattani, 1, 2, 6, 23, 24, 27, 28, 34, 37, 46

Pattani National Liberation Front (BNPP), 6, 34, 35
Pattani People's Revolutionary Commando Brigade (PKRRP), 33
Pattani United Liberation Army (PULA), 38
Pattani United Liberation Organisation (PULO), 6, 9, 30, 33, 36–39, 43, 55, 60, 63, 64, 96, 103
political dynamics, 4–5
politico-religious conflict, 100
politics, participation in, 7
population of Thailand, 1
poverty, 14
Private School Act of 1982, 47
property targets, 80
public support, 105–108
PUSAKA, 32, 33, 43–46, 56, 104

radical educational institutions, 64–68
Ra-ngae, 2
reform, 3, 12
regional implications of domestic insurgency, 112–114
regional neglect, 10
religion and militancy, 53–59, 100
religious schools, 46–53, 64–68, 78, 107–108
Reman, 2
responding to the threat, 100–102
response to threat, government, 83–90, 110–112
reward scheme, 104
Rome Statute of the International Criminal Court, 16
Rosa Burako, 35

Saiburi, 2
Salafi jihadi ideology, 100
Samsuding Khan, 42
Sapaeing Basor, 31, 35
Satun, 34, 37
Second World War, 5

security force personnel targeted,
79, 101
September 11 attacks, 7, 16, 49, 67,
68
Shafi'ee ideology, 58, 100
Shari'ah, 4
Shi'a minority, 1
socio-economic development, 7, 49
Songkhla, 1, 24, 34, 37
South Asian Muslims, 2
Southern Border Provinces, 1
Southern Border Provinces
Administration Committee
(SBPAC), 7, 12–13
Southern Border Provinces
Coordination Centre
(SBPCC), 12
state building, 115
strategies, 77–79, 101
Subay Useng, 56
Sunni, 1
Surin Pitsuwan, 9

tactics, 80–83, 101
targets, 79–80, 101
taxation, 3
Tengku Abdul Jalal, 5
Tengku Abdul Kade, 37
Tengku Abdul Kadir Qamaruddin,
4
Tengku Jalal Nasir, 33–35
terrorism, 7–8, 15–16, 32, 49, 51,
59, 67, 79, 95, 100, 103, 108
Thai Muslims, 2
Thai Provincial Administration Act
of 1897, 2
Thai Rak Thai (TRT), 32, 87, 88,
90
Thai Ratthaniyom (Thai Customs
Decree), 4
Thaksin Shinawatra, Prime
Minister, 12, 15, 77, 83–90,
96, 110
threat, containing the, 104–105
threat, key to ending the, 110–112

threat, key to management of, 102–
110
threat, responding to the, 100–102
tourism/tourists, 7, 14, 79, 80, 104
Tun Mahmud Mahyuddin, 5
Tungku Bira Kotoniro, 36–37

underground separatist movement,
32
unemployment, 14–15
United Mujahideen Front of
Pattani (BBMP), 6
United States, alignment with, 15,
94–95
Urban Guerrilla Brigade (UGB),
35
urban terrorism, 101
Ustaz Abdul Karim, 34, 49
Ustaz Abdullah Akoh, 54
Ustaz Soh (Ismael Yusuf), 54

Waeyusoh Waedeuramae (alias
Loh Supeh), 31, 35
Wahyuddin Muhammad, 6
Wan Kadir Che Man, Dr., 43
Wan Muhamad Nor Matha, 88
weapons, 80–83, 101
West Asian Muslims, 2

Yala, 1, 2, 6, 22–24, 27, 28, 31, 34,
37, 46
Yalan Abdulroman 33
Yaring, 2
Yasser Arafat, 34
Yusof Chapakiya, 33, 34

International Board of Advisors

Other Titles on Regionalism and Regional Security

Terrorism in the Asia-Pacific: Threat and Response
edited by Rohan Gunaratna
ISBN 981-210-246-9

The New Terrorism: Anatomy, Trends and Counter-Strategies
edited by Andrew Tan and Kumar Ramakrishna
ISBN 981-210-210-8

Regionalism and Multilateralism: Essays on Cooperative Security in the Asia-Pacific (2nd ed.)
by Amitav Acharya
ISBN 981-210-267-1

Non-Traditional Security in the Asia Pacific: The Dynamics of Securitisation
by Ralf Emmers
ISBN 981-210-347-3

Studying Non-Traditional Security in Asia: Trends and Issues
Compiled by Ralf Emmers, Mely Caballero-Anthony, and Amitav Acharya
ISBN 981-210-347-3

For information on pricing and availability, please log on to
www.marshallcavendish.com/academic